CRESSMAN LIBRARY

CEDAR CREST COLLEGE

Presented
In memory of

Joan Goldsmith Duncan

by

Class of 1946

THE STORY OF
Musical Instruments

THE STORY OF
Musical Instruments

FROM SHEPHERD'S PIPE TO SYMPHONY

By
HARRY W. SCHWARTZ

ILLUSTRATED

BOOKS FOR LIBRARIES PRESS
FREEPORT, NEW YORK

First Published 1938
Reprinted 1970

STANDARD BOOK NUMBER:
8369-5297-9

LIBRARY OF CONGRESS CATALOG CARD NUMBER:
70-114893

PRINTED IN THE UNITED STATES OF AMERICA

Acknowledgment

GRATEFUL ACKNOWLEDGMENT is made to C. G. Conn Ltd. for the use of most of the photographs and drawings shown in this book, and to Dr Robert Young, physicist of C. G. Conn Ltd., for reading and criticizing the manuscript of the final chapter, "How Music Is Made."

Grateful acknowledgment is made to the following musicians who read in manuscript the respective chapters on their individual instruments: A. Hilsberg, solo violinist, Philadelphia Orchestra; William Kincaid, solo flutist, Philadelphia Orchestra; Thomas J. Byrne, oboist and English horn player, Detroit Symphony Orchestra; Clarence Warmelin, Chicago teacher and lecturer on woodwinds, formerly solo clarinetist, Minneapolis Symphony Orchestra; Lucien Cailliet, solo saxophonist, bass clarinetist and arranger, Philadelphia Orchestra; Harry Glantz, solo trumpeter, Philharmonic-Symphony Society of New York; Simone Mantia, solo trombonist, Metropolitan Opera Orchestra; Max Pottag, French horn, Chicago Symphony Orchestra; Philip Donatelli, principal bass tuba, Philadelphia Orchestra; and William F. Ludwig, former percussionist, Chicago Grand Opera Orchestra and Chicago Symphony Orchestra.

[v]

ACKNOWLEDGMENT

Full responsibility for the contents and treatment of the various chapters is assumed by the author, but these eminent authorities on their instruments have helped make the book more accurate, and they have contributed many valuable suggestions and comments.

H.W.S.

Contents

[*vii*]

CONTENTS

Halftone Illustrations

HALFTONE ILLUSTRATIONS

[x]

Line Cut Illustrations

LINE CUT ILLUSTRATIONS

THE STORY OF
Musical Instruments

CHAPTER I

Recipe for a Symphony

INGREDIENTS AND QUANTITIES

THE GREAT PIPE ORGANS are marvels for variety of tonal coloring. The pipe organ manual has more "stops" to pull and more gadgets to work than the dash of an airplane or the control room of a submarine.

But the orchestra excels even the pipe organ in the variety of beauty of its tonal coloring and in the amazing wealth of its musical effects. The orchestra conductor can "pull stops" on the orchestra that are the envy of the organist and the despair of the organ builder.

In the lower regions he can call out the ominous thunder of the tympani, the sonorous boom of the tuba, the Plutonic mumble of the bassoon, the dark, muffled zoom of the string bass, or the sepulchral moaning of the bass clarinet.

To carry the melody or tell the story of the composition, the conductor can call upon the versatile virtuoso violin, the coloratura-soprano flute, the lyric-soprano oboe, the dramatic-soprano clarinet or the martial trumpet and piccolo.

For middle voices he can choose the tenor trombone or viola, the English horn or alto clarinet, the French horn or cello. To beat a rhythm or set a tempo or punctuate a phrase, the conductor may choose among the many varieties of drums and bells and chimes, or call upon the strings to play pizzicato or the trumpets to play staccato.

The high harmonics of the strings can picture the ethereal realms of heaven, or the brass and the battery can blast the hearing with the echoes of hell. The flutes and oboes can paint a Corot scene of pastoral contentment, the trumpets and trombones can fan our warring spirit to white heat, the French horns can call from Alpine peak to Alpine peak, or the bassoon can perform the antics of the clown and picture the zigzag, uncertain course of the drunkard. The clarinets can dance the swift, sprightly folk dance, the drums and piccolo can beat the cadence of marching armies. Or the slow, measured beat of the tympani and the low, muffled swish of the string bass can pace the funeral march. There is nothing, apparently, beyond the capacity of this greatest of all musical instruments—the symphony orchestra.

The symphony is composed of about a hundred instruments and has a range of about a hundred semitones. Since the sound limits of the human ear are about 125 semitones, the symphony orchestra utilizes about four fifths of the range of human hearing.

The lower threshold of hearing is usually set at sixteen vibrations per second, and while the pipe organ sometimes uses this tone, four octaves below Middle C, the lowest note used in the symphony is the B♭ in the fourth octave below Middle C, sounded by the giant contrabass tuba and having twenty-nine and a fraction vibrations per second.

Composers pretty generally have agreed that the ten semitones in the scale below this B♭ cease to be musical

[2]

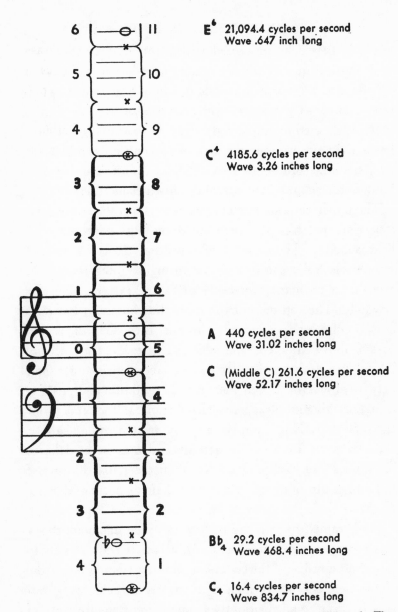

E⁶ 21,094.4 cycles per second
Wave .647 inch long

C⁴ 4185.6 cycles per second
Wave 3.26 inches long

A 440 cycles per second
Wave 31.02 inches long

C (Middle C) 261.6 cycles per second
Wave 52.17 inches long

B♭₄ 29.2 cycles per second
Wave 468.4 inches long

C₄ 16.4 cycles per second
Wave 834.7 inches long

Showing where the musical scale lies within the limits of the audible scale. The musical scale, from B♭₄ (29.2 cycles per second) to C⁴ (4185.6 cycles per second), is shown in heavy lines, while the audible scale below and above this range is shown in thin lines. The vertical numbers to right show the numbers of octaves from the threshold of hearing upward, while the vertical numbers to left show the number of the octaves with reference to the Middle C octave. The open notes in the staff indicate the notes referred to in the notations on the right.

and can better be dispensed with. Not only do they lose their musical quality but they literally fall apart. Instead of sounding as a smooth, continuous note, fewer than twenty-nine vibrations per second tend to become separated into individual, distinct pulsations, just as in moving pictures fewer than twenty-four pictures per second cease to appear as a smooth, continuous movement of events and begin to blink and separate into individual, distinct pictures.

The upper threshold of hearing is about twenty thousand vibrations per second. There are some individuals who can hear sound of higher rates of vibration than others, and women generally can hear sound of higher pitch than men, but this is ordinarily conceded to be the extreme limit for anybody. The top note of the orchestra, however, has only 4185.6 vibrations per second. This note is the C in the fourth octave above Middle C and is delegated to the tiny piccolo. The upper limits of hearing extend about two and a half octaves above this C, but these notes are so thin and piercing that they give no pleasure to the ear and are not scored for the orchestra. This is not to say they are not to be heard in the orchestra, for they do actually exist as high, delicate harmonics and have much to do with the tonal coloring of the music, but our ears do not hear them as notes of definite pitch.

Well-trained human voices have a range of about thirty semitones, or two and a half octaves. Sembrich is said to have had a range of thirty-four semitones, from G below the treble clef to F above high C, or nearly three octaves, but this is exceptional. Curiously enough, most instruments of the orchestra are no more gifted in range than the human voice, most of them having a range of about two and a half octaves. Among such are the oboe, English horn, trumpet, trombone, baritone horn, saxophone and string bass. A few of them, such as the bassoon, clarinets and bass tuba, exceed three octaves, and only two, the violin and cello, can encompass four octaves. The piano comes nearest to equaling the range of the symphony orchestra, having eighty-eight semitones, a few over seven octaves. The harp is runner-up, with a range of about seventy-eight semitones, or over six octaves.

The symphony orchestra was a long time in the making, and its parts were collected from many strange lands. Snake charmers from the Orient contributed the oboe. Ancient Greeks before Homer developed the primitive clarinet. Horns were probably first used in the religious ceremonies of the God-fearing Israelites. Conquering and militaristic Rome brought trumpets to a high point of favor, while fifty generations later this same land took pride in its superb violins. At a late date tubas sprang from Europe, and still later the saxophone and sarrusophone. Africa is famed for its drums and Greece for its pipes of Pan, or flutes; but no one country can claim credit for these two families of instruments, because there is hardly a spot on the globe where these instruments have not flourished, and every primitive people of today makes and uses drums and flutes in some form or other.

Makers of the instruments of the band and orchestra search the world for their materials. The collecting of these materials furnishes enough romance to fill a volume. The mellow clarinet note in today's concert reminds us of great labors and sacrifices of native blacks in the tropical wastes of South Africa. The weird sound from the temple block echoes the woodsman's ax in the depth of the redwood forest of China. The plaintive song from the reedy oboe was made possible by the dry soil and bright sun of the Mediterranean beach in southern France.

Without reeds, we would have no woodwind choir, no clarinets, oboes, English horns, bassoons or saxophones. And if nature had not chosen to throw together in one little spot in southern France a peculiar combination of dry top-soil, a subsoil moistened by the salty seepage from the blue Mediterranean Sea, a unique mixture of organic substances to nourish the roots, and a warm sun from a pleasant sky to bathe the leaves, we would have no reeds. Cane grows in many spots on the globe, but not as it grows in a small area in France along the Mediterranean Sea known as the Var district, near Marseilles. The finest reed cane in the world comes from here, for the soil and climate seem to have con-spired together to produce an ideal material for setting into vibration the column of air in the woodwind instruments. If the climate were warmer and more moist, the cane would grow too fast and the reed would be too porous. If the climate were not so warm and the soil were drier, the cane would grow more slowly and the reed would be too hard. Nor has man been able to add anything to this ideal combination, for the best cane grows wild and in its natural state; cultivated cane is inferior.

Elaborate pains are taken in preparing the cane after it is grown. For three years the cane is carefully cured—one year in the dry and shade, then six months in the sun, with regular periods later on in the sun as the cutting, trimming and sorting process goes on. Finally a small piece of cane about the size of a stick of chewing gum is produced, but there is nothing else in the whole world which can equal it for sounding the characteristic tone of the woodwinds.

If you should suddenly decide one day you were going to make the finest violin bow it is possible to produce, you would have to take a ship to the port of Pernambuco in Brazil. Then you would have to make a hard and long journey to the interior of this great country. There, after diligent search, you would find growing in the hard and rocky ground a tree called the Brazilwood tree. You would then select a small tree, cut away the outside sapwood, and finally come to a small heart, dark red in color. This is the Pernambuco wood known to commerce. It was selected by Tourte, the great French bowmaker of the eighteenth century, as the best material for making violin bows, and nothing finer has ever been discovered. It has just the right weight for balance, the right grain structure for retaining its shape, and the right resiliency for the utmost in bow technique.

Early in the development of the fine violins of Italy, the Amati and Stradivari craftsmen found there was nothing like the giant Norway spruce or Swiss pine for a violin top. These great trees grew up to heaven for a hundred to a hundred and fifty feet, and their grain was even and straight as parallel beams of light. This wood fulfilled the needs for a material of great elasticity but light weight. They didn't know then, but scientists have since found out, that sound travels faster through this wood than any other, attaining a velocity through the grain lengthwise of fifteen thousand feet per second, a velocity nearly equal to that found in steel. They didn't have technical proof of this, but their trained ears told them that this sprucewood gave the best results. They cut the logs through on the quarter and sawed through the center. Then the center edges were glued together. This gave them identical grain structure from the center to both outside edges, the grain being so uniformly even and regular. After three centuries of violin making, nothing has been found which surpasses this wood for violin tops, and so makers today still fell the giant spruce for this part of the violin.

Several tropical woods have been used for making the bodies of the woodwind instruments. The picturesque cocoanut tree was one of them. The best wood for this purpose comes from the West Indies and Central America. It grows best in the sandy soil along the sea, or not far inland. In contrast to Pernambuco wood, only old trees are used. The heart is cut out of the lower portion of the tree trunk. This wood is brown in color, heavy in weight, hard to cut, but can be polished to an almost metallic luster. It is known commercially as cocuswood, and many fine woodwind instruments have been made from it. Some instruments are still made from cocuswood, but it has generally been abandoned, for it contains a resin which causes skin poisoning.

Another wood used for making clarinets, flutes and oboes was boxwood. True boxwood comes from Venezuela, but most of the boxwood used in musical instruments came from the West Indies. It is very tough and has an extremely fine texture, but it has one serious defect—it warps. This defect was not so serious when the key system of musical instruments was limited to a half-dozen single keys, but when several keys were mounted on a single long hinge, slight warping caused the hinge to bind, and boxwood had to be abandoned.

To the rescue came grenadilla wood, known also as Mozambique ebony and as African blackwood. This wood is cut from the arid wastes of Mozambique, South Africa, or the huge island across the channel to the east, known as Madagascar. Great hardships are experienced by the sweating black natives who bring this valuable wood out of the desert lands. Great sand storms come up and bury their camps and even the trees they come to cut and haul to the coast. Such trees grow slowly, and the wood is very close-textured, very heavy, very hard. When first cut it is a beautiful dark purple in color, but becomes black when cured and oiled. When worked in a lathe the wood will almost take the edge off a steel tool, it is so hard, and the fine dust resulting is like pepper in the nostrils. After five to ten years of curing in unheated wood lofts, the grain becomes so fixed, it is nearest to being crackproof of any wood. So far, nothing has been found which quite equals it for making the bodies of the finest woodwinds.

There are many other odd and interesting woods which will be found in every symphony orchestra. Drumsticks will be found made of snakewood from Dutch Guiana, a reddish-brown wood with spots in color from brown to black, similar in markings to that of a snake. The fingerboards, pegs and tailpieces of violins are made from African ebony, brought all the way from the tropical forests of Africa. The bars of xylophones and marimbas and often the castanets are made of rosewood from Brazil or Central America. This wood ranges in color from reddish brown to deep purple or black, with streaks of purple through it, and it gets its name from its fragrance. It is ideal wood for the purpose, since it is hard, dense, takes a high polish and produces a brilliant, resonant tone when struck. Then there is mahogany for drum shells, hickory for drumsticks and drum hoops, walnut for tambourines, maple for violin backs and bassoons, and basswood for cases.

Some people find less music in the orchestra when they learn that the death of from two to three sheep is required before one violin can be equipped with strings. It doesn't seem necessary, but such is the case, and such is the price of great music. So-called "catgut" used on violins is made from the intestines of sheep. The average length of the sheep intestine is twenty-four feet, and it requires from ten to twelve half-intestines to spin a string only four one hundredths of an inch in diameter, since only the fine, soft, submucous membrane is used. A set of four violin strings is eighty-eight inches long on the average, and into a set of four violin strings go the intestines of from two to three sheep.

Even old Dobbin contributes his bit, for what would a violin bow be without horsehair? Makers today use 150 hairs about twenty-eight inches long in a standard bow, although Tourte, who created the violin bow of modern times, used slightly fewer hairs. Then the pig comes in for his share, for tom-tom heads are usually of pigskin. All fine drumheads are of calfskin, the thinner and finest heads coming from the skins of "slunks" or unborn calves. Many different materials are used for mallets of bass drums, tympani, marimbas and bells. Among them are yarn, felt, soft rubber, hard rubber, rawhide, lamb's wool and pyralin.

Copper is the most important metal used in the construction of band and orchestra instruments. The big tympani or kettledrums are drawn from one piece of copper sheet into the half-sphere bowl. Copper is also the principal ingredient of brass used in the bells of brass instruments, about seventy parts of copper being combined with about thirty parts of

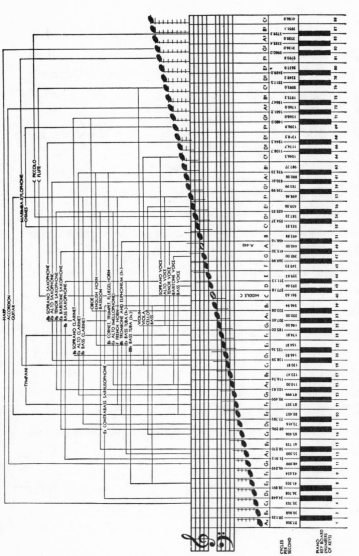

Range Chart for Band and Orchestra Instruments

These are not the extreme ranges, but the practical ranges commonly used. In the hands of skillful players the more than seven octaves of the piano keyboard of eighty-eight notes can be spanned by the instruments of the band and orchestra, a few piccolo players being able to go up to D.

zinc to form brass. Valves, keys, braces and other parts of the brass instruments are made from a brass alloy incorporating in addition small quantities of tin, aluminum, lead or other metals, depending upon what is expected of the part. Metal clarinets and flutes are often made of what is called nickel silver, an alloy of nickel and other metals. Nickel, chromium, silver and gold are used in plating various parts of many instruments used in the band and orchestra.

From the forests, from the foundries, from deep mines and across great seas, from desert wastes and tropical jungles come, in a real and true sense, the great music of the symphony.

If asked to give a recipe for making a symphony orchestra, the historian might start out: Take some oboes from the Orient, some clarinets from Greece and some horns from Palestine. The man of commerce might start out: Take some cane from the Var district of France, some Pernambuco wood from Brazil, and some grenadilla wood from Mozambique, South Africa.

Another and better way would be to say: To form a symphony orchestra of about one hundred pieces, make a mixture of about 40 per cent violins and violas, about 20 per cent cellos and basses, with just a sprinkling of a harp or two. Make another mixture of woodwinds composed of flutes, single reeds and double reeds, up to about 15 per cent. Make an equal quantity of brass mixture, composed of trumpets, trombones, horns and tubas. Pour all three mixtures together and add about 6 per cent tympani, drums, bells and traps.

The recipe for a modern concert band would be something like this: Make a mixture of about 38 per cent clarinets—soprano, alto and bass. Add to it about 10 per cent other woodwinds—oboe, English horn, bassoon, flute. Then make a mixture of about 38 per cent brass, including cornets, trumpets, trombones, horns, baritone horns and bass tubas. Pour these two mixtures together, stirring in at the same

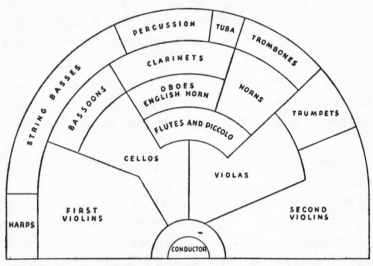

Conventional arrangement of the symphony orchestra. This is often varied to allow the cellos to play on the right of the conductor. The trumpets are also sometimes to the left of the trombones and the tuba to the right of the trombones. Often the harps are placed on the right side of the stage.

time about 8 per cent saxophones. Then add about 6 per cent tympani, drums, bells and traps.

Examination of the instrumentation of the great symphony orchestras of America shows but slight variation from the recipe given above. There may be slight differences within the choirs themselves, but the general balance among the string, woodwind and brass choirs and the percussion section is substantially uniform. Comparison of the instrumentations of the various great symphonies follows:

RECIPE FOR A SYMPHONY

	Philharmonic-Symphony Society of New York	Philadelphia Orchestra	Chicago Symphony Orchestra	Washington National Symphony	Metropolitan Opera Orchestra
First Violins	18	18	14	16	16
Second Violins	18	15	14	13	13
Violas	14	11	10	9	9
Cellos	12	10	10	8	8
Basses	10	10	8	8	8
Flutes and Piccolos	4	4	4	3	4
Oboes and English Horns	4	3	4	2	3
Clarinets	2	3	2	2	2
Bass Clarinet	1	1	1	1	1
Bassoons	3	4	4	3	3
Horns	6	6	5	5	8
Trumpets	4	4	4	3	3
Trombones	4	4	3	4	4
Tubas	1	2	2	1	1
Tympani	2	2	2	1	1
Percussion	5	2	3	4	3
Harps	2	2	1	1	2
Total	110	101	91	84	89

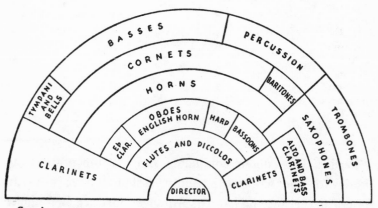

Seating arrangement of the modern concert band. Some arrangements provide for all the woodwinds on the left and the brass on the right, but the tendency is toward this arrangement, sometimes called the symphonic arrangement.

[13]

The instrumentation of bands is not so well formulated, but there is beginning to be greater uniformity among the better bands. Here also there is fairly established balance among the woodwind and brass choirs and the percussion section, even though there is considerable variation within these choirs. Below is a table, showing the instrumentation of several well-known American bands.

	U. S. Navy Band	U. S. Marine Band	U. S. Army Band	The Goldman Band	Joliet (Ill.) H. S. Band
Flutes and Piccolos	3	3	3	4	7
Oboes and English Horns	2	3	3	2	3
Clarinets	26	22	20	21	23
Alto Clarinets	2	1	1	1	3
Bass Clarinets	2	1	1	1	2
Bassoons	3	3	2	2	3
Saxophones	6	7	6		6
Cornets and Trumpets	12	10	11	7	11
Horns	8	7	8	5	9
Euphoniums	4	3	3	2	4
Trombones	6	6	7	6	6
Tubas	6	5	5	4	7
Tympani	1	1	1	1	1
Percussion	3	3	3	2	6
String Basses	1		2	2	
Harp	1	1		1	
Total	86	76	76	61	91

Berlioz, the famous conductor and instrumentation authority of the nineteenth century, should have been an American, because he had the American instinct for "bigger and better." After discussing all the various instruments of the orchestra, in his great work called *Modern Instrumentation and Orchestration*, he closes the book with a suggested instrumentation for a giant orchestra of 467 instrumentalists, which he believed would be capable of great and new artistic achievements. Such an orchestra, he says, would be made up as follows:

120	violins	6	cornets
40	violas	4	alto trombones
45	violoncellos	6	tenor trombones
18	double-basses with 3 strings	2	great bass trombones
15	double-basses with 4 strings	1	ophicleide in C
4	octo-basses	2	ophicleides in B♭
6	large flutes	2	bass tubas
4	third flutes	30	harps
2	octave piccolo flutes	30	pianos
2	piccolo flutes	1	very low organ
6	hautboys (oboes)	8	pairs of kettledrums
6	corni Inglesi (English horns)	6	drums (snare)
5	saxophones	3	long drums
4	bassoons-quinte	4	pairs of cymbals
12	bassoons	6	triangles
4	small clarinets (E♭)	6	sets of bells
8	clarinets	12	pairs of ancient cymbals
3	bass clarinets	2	very low great bells
16	horns	2	gongs
8	trumpets	4	pavilion chinois

467 instrumentalists*

Johann Strauss III once conducted in Vienna what is probably the largest symphony orchestra ever to play under one baton. In this colossal orchestra were one thousand players, or ten orchestras in one. But the laurels for the

*A Treatise on Modern Instrumentation and Orchestration, by Hector Berlioz, translated into English by M. C. Clarke, is the source of this interesting addition. The skeptical reader will have found before referring to this note that the total 467 is not the sum of the figures itemized. The actual total is 465. Reference to the original French by Berlioz reveals the figure 458 as the total, which when added becomes 456! Music in its strictest sense is mathematical, but it does not seem to follow that musicians can add.

[15]

world's largest band ever to play under one baton go to America. This monster band played during the 1933 National High School Band Contest in Evanston, Illinois, held in connection with the Chicago Century of Progress Exposition. Over five thousand bandsmen from over sixty bands took part, and the concert of six selections was broadcast over a national hook-up.

The formation of the band is graphically described by Robert L. Shepherd, editor of *The School Musician,* an eye-and-ear witness:

"From his tall conductor's stand, Mr Bainum now directed the formation of the greatest massed band ever assembled. Using the field amplifier he first brought the color bearers forward. Next the enormous drum section of sixty basses and two hundred and forty snare drums were formed immediately behind the colors in the center of the field. Then, in order, and in relatively fine formation, the first, second, third, fourth and fifth horizontal rows of 'bands, as they were positioned in the stand, marched down and out across the field, falling naturally into their places in the great spotted mass of brilliant color and glistening instruments. It was a thrilling spectacle, a pageantry that would have made a great genius like Richard Wagner fairly weep for the beauty of it. Words seem futile in an attempt to paint the picture. It was a dazzling panorama."

The director passed the beat to the three hundred drums immediately in front of him, and they in turn boomed out the tempo to their fellow bandsmen who surrounded them. In this manner the five thousand musicians played in remarkable unity and with surprising precision. Fourteen hundred clarinets sang together the stirring strains of Sousa's "Stars and Stripes Forever" and five other marches, while seven hundred cornets and trumpets and four hundred trombones chimed in. The harmony was swelled by four hundred French horns, two hundred baritones, and was colored by four hundred saxophones and several hundred miscellaneous woodwinds. Supporting the whole diapason of melody, three hundred and fifty giant bass tubas and sousaphones poured out a flood of sonorous chords. It was a musical spectacle such as the world had never seen before.

CHAPTER II

How the Orchestra Grew

But Opera Blazed the Trail

WE MUST READ three thousand years of recorded history before we learn of the music of the Greeks, and another three thousand years before we learn of the beginnings of opera in Italy, but in the next three *hundred* years the modern orchestra was conceived and developed, with all its new ideas of harmony, instrumentation, orchestration and instruments. These three hundred years are by far the most amazing in the history of music. More progress was made in these three centuries than in the sixty centuries which preceded them.

Although the wonderful Greek mind anticipated most of today's arts and learning, it seems to have been strangely dumb regarding the great possibilities of music. Practically all of the music of the Greeks was encompassed in two octaves or a little more. The central principle of the Greek mind, that moderation should be observed in all things and that extremes should be avoided at all costs, seems to have blinded the Greeks to the possibilities of music in the more than seven octaves used by us today.

The only music the Greeks knew was that used to accompany their poetry, and it was a sickly kind of music, being melody only and lacking both rhythm and harmony. The only accents in the melody were such as occurred in the customary dropping of the voice at the end of a sentence and in the observance of the long and short syllables which marked the meter of the poetry. There was no harmony to enrich the lone melody, for the human race had not yet learned to sing or play instruments together, and even the simple art of singing a fifth or a fourth apart to make an elementary harmony was not learned for more than a thousand years.

It must be said to the credit of the Greeks that they took an intellectual interest in harmony and developed in a scientific way the concepts of the harmonic intervals through the division of the string monochord, a one-string instrument. But this development of the idea of harmony, important as it was, got no farther than scientific principles. This is all the more surprising, since the celebrated Greek genius expressed itself so fully in the other arts of poetry, sculpture, architecture and painting. Music seemed to be the one art in which they could not excel.

The first glimmer of harmony is found in the early Middle Ages, when some musical genius, greater than the Greek musicians, conceived the amazing idea that two voices could sing at the same time a fifth apart. As the voice carrying the melody sang, another voice a fifth below trailed along, always maintaining the same interval. We do not know what prompted this reckless thinking, but it would seem to us a most natural thing to do, since the ordinary soprano and tenor voices have a natural range of about a fifth above the

contraltos and basses. Such harmony seems to us very ele-
mental, but when it was first tried more than a thousand
years ago it must have sounded most unusual and startling.

Thus began the idea of harmony, but the idea of rhythm
was still to come. These early churchmen, chanting their
monotonous music in the churches of the Middle Ages, could
have learned much about rhythm had they consulted the
dark tribes of Africa. Here rhythm had already been brought
to a high state of development, but the religious mind of the
time regarded rhythm as something sensual and therefore
to be avoided.

In the sixteenth century A.D., this type of music reached
its peak with the celebrated musician of the Church, Palestrina. He did not understand harmony as we do, but he
developed to its logical perfection the conception that music
consisted of two or more melodies sung together. He wrote
music which consisted of a number of melodies sung simultaneously, something like the old madrigal, or the "round,"
of which the "Three Blind Mice" is the best known today.
The harmony voices did not simply trail along together,
a set distance of a fifth or fourth or third apart, but each
melody set out independently for itself. So ingenious was
Palestrina that although there were several melodies going
at once, they were so written that they all harmonized together. Such music was like intricate lace, beautifully woven
together with great cunning and skill. But musicians had not
yet learned how to write a melody and surround it and
embellish it with a structure of chords. It was another century before this musical phenomenon was to make its
appearance.

As for musical instruments, the musicians had not learned

to play together. Single instruments had been played for thousands of years. Occasionally some of these had played an octave apart. But the art of playing together as a group was not known until the sixteenth century, and nothing approximating the modern orchestra was known until 1600. Troubadours, minnesingers and meïstersingers twanged their guitars and bowed their fiddles, but these performances were essentially solo in nature. We even read about miscellaneous groups of violins, viols, flutes, oboes, cornettos, fifes and drums playing together for Queen Elizabeth of England in 1561, but we shudder to think what they must have sounded like.

Modern music began shortly after the middle of the sixteenth century with the budding of opera in Florence, Italy, and this was the beginning not only of opera but of the orchestra. A group of musicians in this Italian city became interested in Greek poetry, and in trying to give their version of what it must have sounded like they originated a new kind of music known today as opera. They wrote a dramatic play in poetry, had it recited to music and then called on the musicians of the day to accompany the singing with a miscellaneous group of instruments. The result was not Greek drama or Greek music but a new form of musical expression, out of which the modern opera and the modern orchestra germinated and grew to maturity in the short space of less than three centuries.

These early groups of musicians were not, it is true, much like the modern orchestra. They were a miscellaneous lot of ancient lutes, lyres, viols and wind instruments, led haltingly along by the harpsichord, the grandfather of the piano. They did not play as the instruments play today, but produced chords as a background for the singer. Their performance was much like the performance of the guitar or ukulele today, which is used to "chord" to the melody as it is sung. But this lowly beginning is not to be made sport of, for it was really a remarkable step in music. Here at last was the concept of harmony in music, and it was pregnant with amazing possibilities, as was soon to be revealed.

At first the music for these performances was not written out for each instrument. The group of instrumentalists was very unstable, and the early composers had to take what musicians they could get. Even if they could have had just the instruments they wanted, they were not at all sure what instruments they should use. They finally decided that they would write a sort of shorthand outline of the music and leave the rest to the improvisation of whatever musicians happened to be present. This musical outline was called a figured bass, and it survived for a hundred and fifty years.

Another reason for this indefiniteness of the written score was the lack of understanding of the individual traits and capabilities of the instruments. The musical experience of these composers had been restricted to writing for voices, and in the beginning they looked upon the instruments simply as additional voices. In fact, in many of the musical scores of the time, even those which went beyond the figured bass and provided separate parts for instruments, the score was marked "to be either played or sung." It was the composers' idea that any music could be both sung or played on instruments. When a musician joined the orchestra, he could either chord along with the figured bass or take a written part which was within the range of his instrument. An early historian of music called Praetorius, writing about 1617, says that it was customary for the violins and cornettos to play the music written in the G clef and for the tenor and bass instruments to play the music written in the C, or lower, clef. Beyond this there were few directions or customs to follow.

There is no better way to get an idea of what these early "orchestras" were like than to take a look at some of them. In 1565 two Italians by the name of Striggio and Corteccia collaborated in writing some music to accompany light plays. They called for two harpsichords, four violins, three violas, six or seven lutes and lyres, about the same number of flutes and flageolets, four cornettos and four trombones. Such an "orchestra" must have been mostly top and little bottom, for there was no bass instrumentation except the lower range of the harpsichord. The music, too, must have jumped along rather jerkily, for there were so many plucked instruments. Even the harpsichord, which gave us the idea for the piano, was merely a plucked string instrument, and it was looked upon as the most important instrument in the whole group.

A similar idea was tried out in France by Balthasarini in 1581. He wrote a ballet and conceived the idea of having a little musical accompaniment. For this he wrote a score calling for oboes, flutes, flageolets, cornettos, trombones, violins, viols and lutes. These instruments did not all play at once in one ensemble but in small groups, first the strings, then the woodwinds, and then the brass, the harpsichord playing throughout and furnishing a sort of bass foundation or background. That this seemed like a pretty good idea is seen from the fact that the famous opera composer Lully exactly one hundred years later produced in France the opera "The Triumph of Love," and had the strings, woodwinds and brass play in separate groups.

In 1600 two important musical events occurred in Italy which influenced music ever after. In this year the first opera ever shown in public was performed, and the oratorio was given birth. Jacopo Peri produced his opera "Euridice" and wrote music for a harpsichord, two lutes, a lyre and three flutes. These instruments furnished chord accompaniment while the singers sang or recited poetry. Although the score called for the instruments named, there were no specific parts written for any of the instruments except short passages for the three flutes. The only indication that the other instruments were called for was that the names of the instruments were written at the beginning of the score! Peri was more considerate than most contemporary composers, for usually the composer did no part writing at all, furnishing only the shorthand music of the figured bass part and trusting to luck that the various instrumentalists could make some music from that.

The first oratorio was given to the world by Emilio del Cavaliere and was called "Representation of the Soul and Body." This was a sort of religious musical drama, and a group of instrumentalists was called in to furnish the chord accompaniment. As usual, the harpsichord was one. Others were the lyre, lute, two flutes and two violins, an additional violin being called for to play in unison with the soprano voice throughout. Although these were the principal instruments Cavaliere called for at the beginning of the score, he marked some parts of the music: "To be played by a large number of instruments." This is further evidence of the lack of a definite idea of what an orchestra should consist.

But Cavaliere did set musicians thinking about one important point which was novel for his time. Apparently he was not entirely satisfied to have the instruments play monotonous chords, as they were accustomed to doing. He saw a chance to let the instruments enter a little into the spirit of the drama being sung. His view was that the instruments were not simply there to furnish a chord background for the singing—they could help interpret the plot of the musical drama. Many of the conventional composers of the day must have been a little shocked when he said, "Music should vary according to the sentiments expressed by the singer." Here was attention given to the musical expression of the orchestra, an embodying by the orchestra of the ideas expressed in the oratorio or opera. This was a new idea which had far-reaching effects.

The first group of musicians which deserves the name of orchestra was that called together by Claudio Monteverde in 1608, to furnish music for his opera "Orfeo." He wrote for a string section comprised of two violins, two bass viols, ten tenor viols, two viol da gambas (cellos), a harp and two guitars. The wind instruments consisted of four trombones, two cornettos, a small flute, a clarion, three trumpets with mutes and three organs. Of course, the harpsichord was there —nobody seemed to think in those days that an orchestra was possible without the harpsichord to lead. This was an imposing array of instruments, but they were not handled as are the instruments in today's orchestra. The only music they had was a figured bass part, and the improvising of such a motley group of instruments must have been something amazing to listen to.

But Monteverde learned a lot from this venture, and in 1624 he composed the opera "Tancredi e Clorinda." In this opera for the first time we have a composer writing, not simply music to be "sung or played," but music specifically adapted to the individual nature of the instrument. He amazed both players and audience by having the violinists lay down their bows and strike the string with two fingers, producing pizzicato. He also had them play a note with quickly repeated strokes of the bow, producing tremolo. At first the players refused to perform such nonsense, but after he had persuaded them to try it they were fascinated with the effect, and it is said that when it was played before the special audience of princes and other noblemen of Venice they broke down and cried. At any rate, here for the first time on record is music written for a special musical instrument, music which is impossible to reproduce vocally. Here was the first really instrumental music. Monteverde explained that the vocal style was tender, but that he had called on the instruments to play the "agitated" style. In another place he wrote a descriptive passage which was to be played during a combat by the actors, and the music was so written that it depicted the strife and fighting. Here was "descriptive" music, probably the first of its kind.

During the next hundred years progress was slow and little improvement was made over Monteverde. In fact, most composers did not do as well as Monteverde, either because they did not know about his advanced ideas or because they declined to follow what might have seemed to them a radical course. The greatest advance was made in writing for the string section. The individualism of these instruments seemed to be fairly well understood, and music written for them was true string music. Parts were written for first and second violin, viola and bass, but to these early composers the cello seemed to have no place.

Although the make-up of the string choir was well established, the instruments which made up the brass choir varied. Usually there were trumpets and drums, but the presence of the other brass instruments was uncertain. The composers were familiar with the trumpets from military use, and since the drums always accompanied the trumpets in things military, they thought they should be used together in things musical. The horns and trombones were not so familiar to them, and they were uncertain about their use. Even when they were called into use, their parts were not true brass music, but music which any other instrument having the same range could have played.

And as for the woodwinds, they were in an even worse position. The flutes were common, both the end-blown flute or flageolet and the side-blown flute. Oboes and bassoons were also called for but were as often omitted. The clarinet had not yet been recognized at all, and the music the woodwinds were called upon to play was not individual woodwind music at all; it could just as well have been given to the vocalists.

The harpsichord was looked upon as the most important instrument of them all. Composers felt they could not risk turning the strings, the brass and the woodwinds loose on their own. The harpsichord was needed to hold them all together and to cover up their weaknesses. It must be admitted that the composers' fears had some justification. Not only were the composers of that time ignorant of the resources of these instruments which would have permitted a satisfactory performance without the harpsichord to guide and support them, but the instruments themselves were crude and imperfect compared to those we have today. As the instruments were improved, composers gave them more important work to do, and as they experimented with the resources of the instruments, they learned to take more advantage of what possibilities the instruments possessed. The composers and the instrument makers worked side by side, each encouraging and inspiring the other.

Two great musical figures completely dominate the first half of the eighteenth century—Bach and Handel. The instruments they wrote for were fairly well determined and settled. They usually had a group of well-disciplined strings, and they knew how to write for them and exploit their unique resources. Also, they had whipped into shape a stable brass section, consisting usually of two trumpets and two French horns—but no trombones. The side-blown flute had pretty well won the battle over the end-blown flageolet, and two of these were generally called for. Two oboes and one or two bassoons completed the woodwinds. The clarinets and cellos were still outside the circle of accepted instruments, along with the trombone. The use of the harpsichord was still a crutch which kept these two great composers from venturing too boldly in their writing. And lutes and lyres and other quaint instruments were still admitted into respected ranks.

But, although these three choirs—strings, brass and woodwinds—were becoming stable in the number and kinds of instruments, and although the instruments themselves were written for with due attention given to their individuality, the treatment of the whole was rather different from the harmonic and symphonic writing which developed later. Bach stuck to the polyphonic style of Palestrina and created some great masterpieces in this kind of writing. Handel's music was more like the music we are familiar with today in its harmonic structure and the distribution of the notes of the chord to the various choirs and instruments. Both orchestras had attained solidity and balance but lacked the variety and contrast which later composers used. Bach and Handel had not yet learned the great tonal spectrum of their instruments and used a limited palette. They took more of an intellectual view of their music and worked it out meticulously in form and pattern, especially Bach, but neglected to enrich it with color, contrast and variety of effects.

Haydn is often called the father of the symphony because he weeded out the undesirable instruments and left us with an instrumentation which, except for a few changes, is the orchestra we use today. Gluck, a famous writer of opera, certainly pointed the way, as opera writers have done since the birth of opera in Florence, for he admitted the ostracized trombone, sometimes used piccolo, used the clarinets—although he treated them as if they had been oboes—refused to lean on the harpsichord for support, and filled out the percussion section with bass drum, side drum, cymbal and triangle. It cannot too often be emphasized that not only did the first orchestra enter music through the back door of opera, but as each instrument or instrument effect was added, it usually had to come in the same way.

The writer of opera is a showman as well as a musician. He strives for new effects. When Monteverde taught the string instruments to play pizzicato and tremolo, he was striving for an effect which would heighten the action of the drama. This search for the novel has always characterized the successful opera writer. Naturally, he was always on the alert for new instruments which could produce new colorings and effects. As the plots for operas had to be built up to climaxes, so also did the music. Opera audiences have been taught to want strong contrasts and surprising effects. The early composers of opera saw that the music could assist in the total effect. They studied to make the instruments they had do things they had never done before, and they sought out new instruments which could do things the other instruments could not do. The opera orchestra, therefore, was a sort of training school for the symphony orchestra. No instrument could hope to make its debut in the symphony if it had not previously served an apprenticeship in the opera.

Haydn followed Gluck in his use of instruments in the opera but stuck pretty closely to a more conservative instrumentation for the symphony. He used clarinets in opera but not in the symphony. He and Mozart both used trombones in their opera but refused to give them a place in the symphony. Mozart was willing to try out the basset horn, or alto clarinet, in his "Magic Flute" but did not think it suitable for the symphony. Four horns were used in opera, but in the symphony two were standard. The symphony orchestra of Haydn and Mozart is the so-called classical orchestra consisting of string quartet, two trumpets, two horns, two flutes, two oboes and two bassoons. It lasted until Beethoven, but he let down the bars and included a number of instruments which he thought had served their apprenticeship and which he needed to give musical expression to his more romantic thought.

When Haydn turned over the orchestra to Beethoven he had done a great deal more than catalog the instruments which should be admitted to the symphonic ranks. He also developed to a high point the classical method of orchestrating. To the solidity and balance of the orchestras of Bach and Handel, he added some contrast and variety. He spread his chords over a greater number of instruments and built the chords in a variety of ways, integrating and solidifying the harmonic structure. To his pupil Mozart, though, must go the credit for first using a specific tone coloring. It was this appreciation of tone coloring which prompted Mozart to use clarinets, for he saw that they contributed a contrasting coloring which was new and different from anything in the orchestra up to this time. He taught his teacher Haydn the use of clarinets, and through this schooling from his pupil, Haydn learned in his old age to use, not only the clarinets, but also other woodwinds. He demonstrated how to write individual and characteristic music for the woodwind choir.

The passing of the harpsichord was a great boon to the orchestra. How it managed to hang on for two hundred years is difficult for us to understand. Many of the composers were players of the harpsichord, and they found it convenient to sit at the instrument and direct their compositions by playing along with the orchestra. If a player faltered, the composer could play his part on the harpsichord and set him on his feet again. It was also used as a rhythm instrument, and the composer could beat the tempo by playing chords in measured accents on the harpsichord. But it had to go when music developed beyond the polyphonic style and took on contrast and color, for this instrument lacked these qualities. It was not playable both soft and loud, as is the piano, for notes could not be struck with varying degrees of loudness. The strings were plucked by quills when the keys were struck, and every note had the same monotonous volume. Chords could not be sustained, and the only way the breaks in the musical pattern could be filled in was with cadenzas and other figured embellishments. It lent itself therefore to polyphonic music, in which a continual inter-weaving of melodies occurred. When great and daring harmonic structures were built up in the music, the harpsichord floundered and gradually became more and more outmoded until it passed out, and with it went the old figured bass. A new day in music dawned with their passing.

The first two symphonies of Beethoven were hardly to be distinguished from those of Haydn, but in the third, the "Eroica" of 1805, Beethoven gave expression to a new kind of music. The old classical music had been largely intellectual, and although it was beautiful in its own way, the great Romantic movement of Europe sought expression in music and called for new instrumentation and orchestration. The Romanticist was not satisfied with intellectual pleasures but craved something which stirred the feelings. In the symphony Beethoven satisfied this urge by mixing in a greater wealth of tonal coloring. He welcomed the trombone, the cello, the piccolo, and even the deep-toned contrabassoon, for they contributed a more colorful tonal palette. He wrote in a different style, also. He followed the operatic writer by building up great contrasts and climaxes and introducing a greater variety of treatment.

Beethoven was the first to add the third and the fourth horn in the symphony, and he taught the instruments of the classical orchestra to play music for which they were not thought to be capable. He wrote solos for the string basses which the bass players at first refused to attempt, saying such music was impossible. He sought out new resources in all the instruments and mixed his tonal colors in novel ways. By the time he had completed his great Ninth Symphony he had brought the symphony orchestra to a high level of

performance which in many ways has scarcely been surpassed, if equalled. In solidity, balance, contrast and variety
of effects he wrote the final chapter, but in tonal coloring
there were masters to come who excelled him.

Other great emotional composers followed Beethoven who
enriched symphonic music with their musical ideas and exquisite workmanship. Among these are Schubert, Schumann,
Mendelssohn, and that wizard in orchestration and tonal
color, Berlioz. Although Berlioz himself played no instrument
except the guitar, he understood the instruments of the
orchestra better than the musicians themselves. He was the
first composer who wrote the low pedal notes for trombones.
He knew trombonists were unfamiliar with these notes and
wrote on the manuscript, "These notes are on the trombone
and the players must get them out." He was also the first to
use violin harmonics in full harmony. To achieve a peculiar
muffled clarinet effect, he once specified that the instrument
be put in a leather bag and played. He was constantly striving for new combinations of instruments and often went to
excess in requiring an inordinate number of certain ones.
But if he did not always achieve a musical effect, he un-
erringly achieved the effect he had in mind, for scarcely any
composer, before or since, understood so well the individual
resources of each instrument and the unique tonal color and
effects of which each was capable. His experiments are a
storehouse of experience for composers who followed him,
and many have profited by his pioneering.

But sharing the honors with these great masters were the
instrument makers. In 1832 Boehm brought out his new key
mechanism for the flute, which also became the basic system
for clarinets and contributed improvements to oboes. It is

obvious that composers and musicians could do much more with twenty-three keys than they could do with eight. Boehm's amazing key mechanism made woodwinds chromatic in all keys and made easy passages which before were played with the utmost difficulty; and it made possible many passages which were totally impossible on the old woodwind mechanism with eight keys.

Piston valves were invented in 1815 and rotary valves in 1827. These inventions bridged the wide gaps in the open scale of the simple trumpets and horns and added a great wealth of playing possibilities which the older composers could not entertain. New instruments were now perfected which formerly had lain in disuse because of their limitations, and the tonal coloring was made still more various and brilliant. The English horn was introduced by Rossini in "William Tell" in 1829, and the bass clarinet was included by Meyerbeer in "Les Huguenots" in 1836.

And with the invention by Sax in 1842 of the family of saxhorns, the brass choir for the first time was given a good bass voice—in the brass bass tuba. Composers before Wagner had been handicapped by having too few bass voices. For many years the only wind basses were the bassoons and an occasional bass trombone. The old serpent and ophicleide bellowed and brayed for two centuries, but they were inaccurate in intonation and of poor musical quality. The great success of Wagner in writing for the brass instruments was partly due to the addition of the bass tuba. This rich sonorous voice, added to the new bass clarinet, augmented the bottom of the orchestra and gave it great depth and beauty.

Erard's improvement of the harp and Sax's invention of the family of saxophones further enriched the tonal coloring and gave variety which has enhanced the orchestra. Bells, the xylophone, marimba and other percussion instruments were also used to good advantage in creating musical effects unknown even to Beethoven.

Wagner brought the orchestra to a new peak in musical expression through his consummate mastery of instrumental technique and uncanny feeling for color and effect. Weber and Meyerbeer, two great opera composers, blazed the trail. They were great dramatists and explored the orchestra for dramatic effects. Wagner is especially indebted to Weber, for the latter pointed out a musical realm which Wagner exploited to the utmost. Wagner's skill in handling brass had never been equaled before, and he did many daring things in dividing the strings into many separate parts and creating other beautiful effects which were new in the orchestra.

His harmonic structure was the most complicated and intricate that had ever been constructed. In his "Ring" series he scattered notes over the entire seven octaves, distributing them judiciously to the various choirs, to be sounded together in one great, overwhelming diapason of sound. Fifteen notes are given to the woodwinds, which the flutes, oboes, clarinets and bassoons sound together. To the trumpets, horns, trombones and tubas of the brass choir he gives seventeen notes, making a total of thirty-two notes in the harmony played by the woodwinds and brass alone. Add to this the multiple division of the strings, equal to that of the brass and woodwinds, and we have an absolutely overpowering effect of wonderful beauty.

After Wagner it might be thought that there remained nothing further to try. But, although composer, musician and instrument maker had traveled a long way since Monteverde, Bach and Handel, new adventures in music have been made recently. This advance has been made in developing exquisite tone color. Ever since Liszt, Chopin and the other tone poets, composers have been absorbed in creating new color schemes. Their maxim was beauty for beauty's sake, and they have created some amazing compositions. Of these composers, Debussy and Richard Strauss are typical. They go in for tone poems and descriptive music. The perfection of musical instruments in the twentieth century and the use of newer instruments such as the saxophones have given them greater musical resources for carrying out their ideas. They have also called in some unusual instruments for their specific purposes. Strauss, for instance, has revived the heckelphone, the baritone voice of the oboe family; he has also written for alto and bass flutes, E♭ and D cornets, alto, tenor and baritone tubas, and even the sarrusophone, a sort of brass bassoon.

Such, in broad outline, has been the development of the orchestra. Much of its course has been determined by accident, and speculative "ifs" mark every step. If the Italians of Florence had not experimented with Greek drama combined with music, we might never have had anything like the orchestra, and we might still be in the era of the troubadours and minnesingers. If the writers of opera had not been such prospectors for the gold of musical effects, we might still be twanging lutes and lyres and blowing our lungs out on serpents and ophicleides. If the romantic urge had not taken hold of music, we might still be spinning out the intellectual intricacies of Bach, Handel and Haydn. If inventive genius of the instrument makers had not produced the ring key of the Boehm system flute, the piston and rotary valves of Blumel—to say nothing of needle springs and hinges mounted on posts—we might still be playing the music of Beethoven and his predecessors and be unaware of the beauties of Wagner, Debussy and Strauss.

The gripping story of how each instrument worked out its own destiny and won a place for itself in the great symphony orchestra and concert band of today is told in the following chapters.

CHAPTER III

The Violin Family

ARISTOCRATS OF THE ORCHESTRA

NOW THAT THE VIOLIN has "made good" in the symphony orchestra, many countries and peoples claim it as a "native son." Although the true ancestry of the violin will probably never be determined to the satisfaction of all, there seem to be about three chief contenders: Arabia, Wales and Greece.

Little did the Moors realize, when they invaded Spain in 711 A.D., that they would precipitate a fight about the ancestry of the violin that would reverberate down the centuries of history for over a thousand years. One of the musical instruments which these fierce fighters brought with them was the Arabian rebab, a small stringed instrument played by plucking the strings. Shortly after arriving in Europe the rebab became a favorite of the troubadours of Spain, France and Italy. This is the famous troubadour fiddle, celebrated in story and song of the Middle Ages.

Unquestionably the rebab was a plucked instrument when it arrived in Europe, for the ancient peoples of the Eastern world never did develop the art of sounding an instrument by bowing. This is a fact, in spite of the widely accepted fable that Nero fiddled while Rome burned. Nero may have plucked a lyre, but he never bowed a fiddle. It wasn't long after the rebab was taken up by the troubadours, however, until certain innovators began playing it with a bow, and it is generally conceded that bowing the fiddle became common toward the latter part of the eighth century.

Venantius Fortunatus, the poet, started a lot of argument when he wrote, back in 617 A.D., an ode in which he referred to the "chrotta Brittanna." Many think he was referring to the Welsh crwth, a sort of primitive lute. No doubt this instrument was at first plucked, but as far back as we are able definitely to trace its history it was played with a bow. Therefore many look upon the crwth as the father of the modern violin, and others who will not grant the complete title admit that the crwth is the first instrument ever played with a bow. Even this honor should be enough to make the Welsh crwth immortal.

There is another school which will have neither of these instruments. These critics point out that while we find the Welsh crwth and the Arabian rebab both played with a bow in the eighth century, neither has a sound chest like that of the violin, and that this feature and not bowing is the distinguishing mark of the violin. They go on to say that the violin has ribs between the back and sound board, as distinguished from the lute, which has a sound board glued directly to an arched back without the intervening ribs. Both the rebab and the crwth are lutes, they say, and regardless of when they were first bowed, neither of them can qualify as the ancestor of the violin, for bowing has nothing to do with earmarking the violin lineage.

Judged on this basis, the Greek kithara is the first violin, for it is the first instrument we know of which used a sound chest constructed with sound board and back separated by ribs. It is admitted that this instrument was not bowed by the ancient Greeks, but after all this point is nonessential. The important fact is that in the Greek kithara we find the first sound chest of the violin construction. Besides, there is philological evidence. It is easy to see the resemblance between the words kithara and guitar, the latter being a name often used by the troubadours in referring to their fiddles.

All of this speculation is very interesting, but those who require more solid ground for a take-off on the history of the violin will prefer to start with the troubadour fiddle. From this point there is only one hurdle before the violin is reached, and this is the viol family. The viols descended directly from the troubadour fiddle, and the violins in turn descended from the viols. The latter two families are quite similar, differing principally in the fact that the violins do not have such deep ribs, have swelled or curved backs instead of flat, and have a much better tone. One characteristic of the viols has survived to this day in the bass of the violin family, for some string basses are still found with flat instead of swelled backs.

The first true violin was made by Caspar Tieffenbrücker, born of German parents in the Alps mountains of Italian Tyrol about 1467, or twenty-five years before Columbus discovered America. His instruments are said to have been heavily inlaid and ornately decorated and must have excelled in appearance more than in musical quality. By 1520 a number of violin makers, building on the work of Tieffenbrücker, had gravitated to Brescia, a town in Lombardy less than fifty miles from the Tyrol border, and had founded what was soon to be known as the Brescian School. This group of craftsmen flourished for one hundred years and boasted such men as Gasparo da Salo, Maggini, Kerlino, Zanetto, Cortesi and Peregrino.

The finest of all violins were produced about forty miles from Brescia, at Cremona. This little town on the banks of the Po River began attracting attention because of its fine violins about 1550. Illustrious names were those of Andrea Amati, his son Geronimo, and Geronimo's son, Niccolo, three generations of great craftsmen who brought the Amati violins to such a high stage of development. One of Niccolo's most talented pupils was a young man named Antonio Stradivarius, born in the midst of the violin-making industry of Cremona about 1645. He studied under Niccolo until he was about twenty years old, when he left the Amati tutorship and began making violins after his own ideas. For the next fifteen years, however, his violins still strongly resembled the Amati models. Gradually he progressed to the so-called "Long Strads," and by 1700 he had pretty definitely formulated the ideas and methods which resulted in the famous Stradivarius violins. The violins made between 1700 and 1730 were his greatest; from 1730 until he died in 1737 he made few violins, and these were of varying quality. It is no wonder, for by 1730 Stradivarius was about eighty-five years old, and a number of the violins which he commenced were finished by his son and by his pupils.

Other great names associated with the Cremona School, besides the Amati and the Stradivarius families, were the Guadagnini, Ruggeri, Guarnerius, Bergonzi and Storioni families. Carlo Bergonzi was a famous pupil of Antonio Stradivarius who undoubtedly finished some of the late

Stradivarius violins started by the master. Of the Guarnerius family, Joseph was the most famous, having made a fine violin used after his death by the greatest of all violin virtuosos, Niccolo Paganini. The middle of the eighteenth century had hardly passed when the glory of the Cremonese School began to fade, marking two hundred years of great achievement, the golden age of the violin. No other one group of violin craftsmen has ever equaled the famous makers of Cremona, but it is not true that the art of violin making died with them, for there have been many wonderful instruments made since then, and they are still being made today.

Many of these old violins are now worth thousands of dollars. Some of them have been sold for as high as $50,000 and others have brought $15,000, $25,000 or $40,000. But just because an old violin has lain in the attic for generations, or has been handed down from father to son, is no sign it is a valuable Stradivarius, Guarnerius or Guadagnini. There are many "phony" Stradivarius violins circulating around, and it takes an expert to tell whether they are genuine or not. If all the so-called Stradivarius violins were gathered together their number would be so great that it would have required a score of Antonio Stradivariuses to make them, even though they all lived to be ninety, as did the great master. Experts say that Stradivarius made about 950 violins during his whole lifetime, besides about one hundred and fifty violas and cellos. There are today authentic records of about 425 genuine Stradivarius violins, besides seven or eight violas. There no doubt are others still in existence, but the chance of finding one is slight.

Labels mean little to the experts; their trained eyes and ears look for more dependable information, such as tone quality, varnish, workmanship, and many little telltale clues which only the experts see at all. There are many copies of famous violins made—copies made to the smallest details. The shape and position of the *ff* holes, the size and shape of the upper, middle and lower bouts and their size relative to each other, the length of body from base of button to tail pin and length of button to notch of *ff* holes, the depth of ribs at all points, the curve of back and top—all these measurements have been meticulously duplicated to small fractions of an inch, and yet violin authorities can tell they are only copies and not originals. The only safe way to avoid swindles in buying genuine old-master violins is to consult a reliable authority.

There is a great deal of hokum surrounding the violin, especially the violin of the great masters. It is popularly believed that what made the old violins good was a collection of trade secrets which died when these great old craftsmen died, just as the art of making stained glass died with the thirteenth-century Gothic cathedral builders. There is much talk about varnish, as if it were some sort of magic bath which could transform an ordinary violin into a great masterpiece. Since no one today is able to make a varnish which will perform this magic trick, several ingenious stories have arisen which lay the blame for our alleged inability to make violins equal to those of the old masters, to our lack of the proper varnish. One story has it that the resin used by the old masters to make their magic varnish came from a certain balsam fir tree of northern Italy. Owing to the great demand for the resin from this tree, it was tapped excessively and the species finally became extinct. For about two hundred years this tree has ceased to exist; for about two hundred years there have been no violins made which equal those of the masters: therefore it is evident that it was the varnish which was the secret of great violin making!

Another easy explanation is the method of curing the wood. It is claimed that the process of drying and seasoning the wood was the secret of the old masters and that we do not know today how this was accomplished. Closely allied with this story is the fable about the age of the finished violin. Certain magic has been attached to age, as if an ordinary violin could be made a masterpiece if only it could attain a ripe old age. If this were true, any old cigar-box violin or cornstalk fiddle could hope to be a tolerably good musical instrument after two or three centuries. Much speculating has also been done about the shape of the violin and its various parts, particularly the curvature of the back and top, the shape and position of the *ff* holes, the relative sizes of the upper and lower bouts, and so on.

Most authorities on the violin now agree that the achievements of the old masters were due, not to any magic formulae or trade secrets, but to more prosaic reasons. These craftsmen were born into the violin-making art. They grew up with it. They thought of nothing else. To be a great violin maker was the ambition of every boy in the village. This singleness of purpose is at the basis of all great achievements in art and craftsmanship. Apprentices were given long and exacting training. Journeymen labored years before they were graduated into masters of the craft. All their work was done with infinite care, unflagging patience, consummate skill and an inspired desire to achieve great things. Among these craftsmen there grew up a distinct *esprit de corps* similar to the religious fervor which was the driving force behind the conception and erection of the great cathedrals in the thirteenth century, and similar to the artistic standards and devotion to a craft which characterize the wood-carving Passion Players of Oberammergau. There was just one end in life for the Cremonese workman, and that was to make each violin a masterpiece and to make each successive instrument a bit better than the former one.

That these old masters reached a high stage in the development of this instrument is attested by the fact that their violins never have been surpassed, if ever quite equaled. Many experiments have been made during the past two hundred years without contributing a single important improvement. Violins have been made of all kinds of wood, seasoned and treated in all kinds of ways. Many materials other than wood have been used, but without success. A modern invention is the aluminum violin, but it is generally conceded that this type of instrument reproduces too many of the higher harmonics and is of too brilliant tone. The shape has been varied in many ways, and the dimensions have been changed, but it seems that the old masters must have been over all this ground before, for always these innovations are found to be no better than and usually not as good as the standards set up over two centuries ago.

With slight variations, the best violins made today are duplicates of those made by the masters. Seventy parts are used, the most important being the straight-grained spruce top and the curly maple back. The spruce top is always of two pieces, sawed on the quarter from the same log, so the grain matches on each side of the center where the two pieces are glued together. The back is usually made of two pieces in the same manner, although some fine violins are of one-piece back. The proper thickness and curvature of the top and back require shrewd judgment, and it is here that the masters excelled. Wood varies in density, resiliency and grain structure, and these old makers attained their marvelous results by patient shaving of the wood here and there and by indefatigable trial and error in testing results. After the top and back are shaped, the *ff* holes are cut in the top, an operation of great importance. The maple sides are then shaped by a heating process. The linings and six inside blocks are cut from spruce, and the fingerboard, pegs, tailpiece and saddle are fashioned from ebony. All parts are fitted together with fine accuracy and glued. A light oil varnish is used for finishing, heavy varnishes having been found to destroy the mellowness of tone desired.

Contemporary with Antonio Stradivarius were such great violinists as Corelli and Tartini; but Stradivarius was dead nearly fifty years when the greatest of all violinists was born —Niccolo Paganini. Although unquestionably endowed with amazing ability, Paganini could not have achieved his great technique had it not been for François Tourte, the great French "Stradivarius of the bow." The masters of Cremona had brought the violin to a high stage of development, but they seemed to have neglected the bow. No doubt Corelli and Tartini would have developed greater technique and would have composed more brilliant solos and concertos for the violin could they have availed themselves of the improvements in the violin bow made by Tourte after they were dead.

Ten years after Stradivarius laid down his tools and glue-pot and was buried in Cremona with fitting honors, François Tourte was born in Paris. He early became interested in improving the violin bow. His first specimens were made from staves of sugar casks, but he experimented with many kinds of wood and finally decided Pernambuco wood was best suited to his requirements. How well founded this conclusion was is attested by the fact that no other material has been found which quite equals this red, rare wood from Brazil. Before he was thirty, Tourte was famous as a maker of fine violin bows. The bow before Tourte was short, heavy and clumsy; he made it light, flexible and resilient. He worked out a delicate balance and graceful shape and fixed its length at a fraction over twenty-nine inches. He also invented the movable nut for loosening and tightening the hair. The hair itself was carefully selected and placed in the bow, and a few less than 150 hairs were found to give the best results.

Violins at the beginning of the seventeenth century were of two types: the viola da gamba, played by holding between the knees, and the viola da braccia, played by holding against the shoulder. Of each of these two types there were several sizes, but during the process of development a number of these dropped out and the well-known members of today's violin family survived. The treble viola da braccia became the violin, while the alto viola da braccia became the viola. The tenor viola da gamba survived the selective process and became the violoncello, or cello. Our present-day double-bass has had quite a struggle for its place in the orchestra, having been almost nosed out by the ancient bass viol, with the deep ribs and flat back. This obsolete instrument survived until well into the eighteenth century, and some of its characteristics are still seen in a certain type of flat-back double-bass found in the modern orchestra occasionally.

Members of the violin family had been used for centuries

by the troubadours and minnesingers of Europe as accompaniment for their songs, but the first record we have of the use of the violin in the orchestra is in 1565, when Striggio and Corteccia scored for a group of instruments used to play between the acts of early Italian opera and to accompany light plays and ballets. In this odd assortment of instruments we find four violins and three violas, besides six lyres and lutes and some flutes, cornets, trombones and other miscellaneous instruments of the day. In France sixteen years later we find Balthasarini scoring for a primitive-type orchestra used to play accompaniment for his "Ballet Comique de la Reine," first performed in Paris in 1581. In this collection of instruments, which hardly deserves the name of orchestra, he used ten violins, a viola da gamba, and some lutes, besides an assortment of woodwinds and brass.

It was the custom in Florence during the notorious reign of the house of Medici to stage big celebrations when a member of the reigning house was wed. Italian opera during this period was having growing pains, and some kind of operatic performance was usually a part of the festivities. In 1600 when Marie de' Medici was married to Henry IV, King of France and Navarre, Peri and Rinuccini staged the celebrated "Euridice," in honor of the event. This is the first opera of which we have the entire score, and the instruments used in the orchestra are an interesting lot. The only member of the violin family found in this so-called orchestra was the viola da gamba, but there were a number of near-violins, such as the lute, the theorbo (large lute) and the lyre. Add to these a harpsichord and three flutes and try to imagine such an orchestra playing chords together as a sort of musical background to dramatic recital of how Orpheus tried in vain to waft his dead wife Euridice back from Hades on the wings of song, and you get a rough idea of the orchestra of the time and the kind of company the violin kept in those days.

The violin family had a little more prominent part in the birth of the oratorio. In 1600 Emilio del Cavaliere produced in Rome his celebrated first oratorio, bearing the prodigious name of "La Rappresentazione dell' Anima e Corpo." The violin used was called upon by Cavaliere to play in unison with the soprano voice. The viola da gamba, the only other member of the violin family found in this famous cast, joined in with a double-lyre, a harpsichord, a bass lute and a couple of flutes.

The term orchestra is used very loosely when we apply it to such motley groups of instruments as the foregoing examples. In 1608, however, Monteverde, an Italian opera composer, wrote an orchestra score for his opera "Orfeo," which called into service a rather presentable group of instruments. Among them were "two little French violins," two viola da gambas, ten tenor viols, two bass viols, besides two large guitars and a number of brass and woodwind instruments. This group is really the first which deserves the name of orchestra, and to Monteverde is usually given the honor of having founded the orchestra.

Monteverde seemed to have a particularly good understanding of the possibilities of the violin family, and in 1624, in his opera "Tancredi e Clorinda," performed in Venice before the Italian nobility, he made the violins do tricks which overwhelmed his audience. It was at this time that he introduced pizzicato and tremolo effects.

Following Monteverde, composers and conductors gradually learned more about the use of the violin family. The story of this development is an interesting one of trial and error. Many experiments were tried and abandoned, but others became standard practice from then until today. As was true of all instruments, the violins were looked upon in the beginning as voices, to be used simply for singing, just as human voices. Gradually, however, the violins, along with the other instruments, were regarded as new vehicles of musical thought and were boldly experimented with in order to exploit their full possibilities. They became the famous "string quartet," consisting of first violin, second violin, viola and contrabass. With the recognition of the place of the cello in this string choir, the violin family finally became the famous "string quintet" of the orchestra, consisting of the soprano first violin, the mezzo-soprano second violin, the alto viola, the tenor cello and the bass contrabass.

Two important composers of Naples contributed much to this development. Scarlatti at first had cellos and violas play in unison with the bass, but occasionally wrote an independent part for the viola. He soon saw the beauty of distributing parts to various members of the string choir, and he began writing parts for violin, viola and bass. That this style of writing is highly satisfactory is shown by the fact that it is used frequently by all composers since Scarlatti. Later he diversified his writing still more by distributing four notes of a chord to the strings, giving the treble part to the first violin, the alto part to the second violin, the tenor part to the viola, and the bass part to the bass. Stradella, a fellow countryman and contemporary of Scarlatti, often wrote parts for two solo violins and a solo cello, these lead voices being accompanied by violins, violas and basses which filled

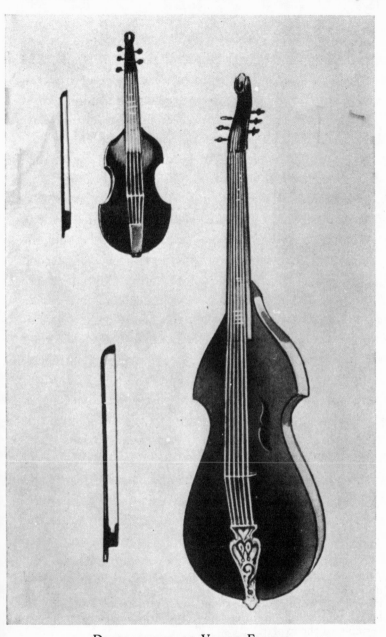

DEVELOPMENT OF VIOLIN FAMILY

(*Above*): Viola da braccia—viol held against shoulder—from which the violin descended. Note short, heavy bow. (*Below*): Viola da gamba—viol held between the knees—from which cello descended. Note heavy, clumsy bow.

STRADIVARIUS VIOLIN, FRONT AND BACK

Although all violins look alike to most people, there are individual differences in size and shape of upper and lower bouts (convexly curved parts of body), the shape, size and location of the *ff* holes, length and width of entire body, and other features readily discernible to the expert.

in the harmonies. This style of writing appealed to Bach and Handel and was used in their compositions known as the "concerti grossi."

About this same time the great French opera composer Lully was using as the foundation of his orchestra a body of strings. Violins played the upper parts, while violas played the middle and lower parts, trumpets, flutes, and oboes being used for creating greater volume of tone. In Venice about this time Legrenzi wrote for a rather peculiar orchestra consisting of nineteen violins, two violas, two viola da gambas, four large lutes, two cornets, three trombones and a bassoon. The lack of string basses and of woodwinds was a serious defect of this instrumentation, and this type of scoring gradually died out after Legrenzi.

Two great musical figures completely dominate the first half of the eighteenth century: Johann Sebastian Bach and Georg Friedrich Handel. Bach was most at home on the organ, and the bulk of his compositions was for this instrument, but he cannot be accused of neglecting any of the instruments of the day. He was a most inquisitive man, and he tried about everything which offered any chance of producing music. We find him writing for violins, violas, cellos, double-basses, violino piccolo (a small violin tuned a minor third above the violin), viola d'amore (a tenor viol with seven gut and seven steel strings vibrating together), viola da gamba and lute, besides a flock of woodwinds and brasses. Bach apparently didn't think even these instruments of the day were all that were needed, for he was the inventor of the violoncello piccolo, a small cello.

Bach's use of the string instruments follows the practice of his predecessors. His first "Brandenburg Concerto," composed in 1721, follows the practice established by Scarlatti of writing the score around the string quartet, this main body of strings being aided by the double-bass and the violino piccolo, besides horns, oboes and harpsichord. He also followed the lead of Stradella by featuring several solo instruments and supporting them with a full harmony choir of strings and other instruments. That he knew the resources of the violin as a solo instrument is shown in a number of compositions, notably in his "Chaconne," and more popularly in his "Air for G String," originally written as a movement in the Suite No. 3 in D Major. Contemporaries of Bach were Corelli and Tartini, and while it is not known how well acquainted he was with these great violin virtuosos, we do know he was a warm admirer of Vivaldi. No composer could have written that tremendous violin composition "Chaconne" if he had not been thoroughly and intimately acquainted with the resources and potentialities of the instrument.

Handel often adopts the ordinary arrangement of first and second violins, violas and basses, using oboes and bassoons to contrast with the strings, the oboes doubling violin parts, the bassoons playing with the basses. In his "concerti grossi" he followed the practice of Stradella, or rather of Corelli, who perfected and made classical this kind of scoring for the orchestra and from whom Handel is supposed to have learned it during his sojourn in Rome in 1708. Handel is credited by some with being the first to bring out the unique beauties of the cello, and he did many bold and effective things with the viola.

Besides learning how to distribute the notes of various chords among the capable members of the violin family, composers and conductors learned new refinements in the actual playing and handling of the strings. Johann Karl Stamitz, the Bohemian violinist and conductor, became director of the famous orchestra for the Elector of Mannheim in 1745, and he devoted himself to the task of drilling and disciplining the string players to a point of perfection unknown before his time. He taught the strings to bow in unison and to play with precision and refinement. He drilled them in phrasing and in playing as a great body of strings, either piano or forte. He showed his contemporaries how to produce a quality of tone from many violins which sounded nothing like an equal number of violins playing together in the ordinary way: he produced a distinct ensemble tone which was a revelation. His orchestra became the best in all of Europe. The famous composers and conductors of the day, such as Mozart, listened to this great body of strings and went away amazed and deeply influenced.

When one calls the roll of the instruments of the orchestra before Haydn, one is somewhat surprised to find so many queer and unusual names. After Haydn, though, we are always among old friends. We no longer encounter lutes, lyres, theorbos, viola da gambas, viola d'amores, violino piccolos and cembalos. It was Haydn, as has been stated, who with almost uncanny insight selected the instruments worthy of inclusion in the orchestra and threw the others into the discard, from which not a single one has been able to stage a comeback into the respected ranks of the orchestral instruments. In his first symphony in 1759 he does not include the cello among the strings, but in his famous Symphony in D, written in 1795, we find the cello in its rightful place.

The cello's place was not secure until some time after Haydn, however. Even Beethoven did not always use it, for it is missing from his First Symphony, written in 1803. Two years later, though, we find Beethoven has added the cello in his great "Eroica" symphony. The contrabass was first brought into prominence by Beethoven in his Fourth Symphony, at the end of the last movement. This passage contains some of the most difficult playing ever written for the string bass. At first it provoked much criticism as being beyond the resources of the instrument, but Beethoven as usual had satisfied himself about what the contrabass was capable of. Other composers followed his lead, and before long such scoring was taken for granted and was played by the musicians without protest.

Other composers than Monteverde have contributed additional effects on the violin. Gluck in his "Armide" was the first composer to call for the use of the violin mute. Weber enriched the tapestry of violin playing by dividing the first violins so part of them played one strain while the rest played a counter strain. This practice was followed by composers after Weber, and Wagner takes the laurels in dividing the strings, in the second act of "Tristan and Isolde," where he has written fifteen separate parts for the violins. To Philidor goes the distinction of first writing harmonics for the violin when he included this effect in his opera "Tom Jones," written in 1765. Berlioz was the first composer to attempt writing a full harmony in harmonics, and the effect is a heavenly revelation. Paganini, a contemporary of Berlioz, entered into the competition and reached the ultimate in something or other by producing harmonics as high as the twelfth series, by using fine, light strings. Although not much of a contribution musically, this is quite a feat, as can be realized when we consider that Koenig, famous acoustician of Paris, was able to reach only six series above this, by the use of fine-spun wire.

Without the violin family we could not have the symphony orchestra. This is not to say we could not have a great musical organization without the strings, for that is exactly what we have in the modern wind band. The wind band, however, is distinctly different from the symphony orchestra and always will be. It is not far from the truth to say that the strings *are* the symphony orchestra, so important has been their part in its glorious development and so characteristic of its performance and color have they become.

Besides sheer agility, the violin has a wealth of technique and effects which have made it the valuable instrument it is. In addition to tremolo and pizzicato, violinists learned to mute the violin by putting a small clip on the bridge, and music was marked "con sordino." Novel and useful effects were developed by bowing the strings with the wood part of the bow instead of with the hair, and music was marked "col legno." Bright, crisp effects were discovered by playing close to the bridge, and music was marked "sul ponticello." Two notes can be played together, and broken chords of four notes can be sounded, besides characteristic passages in which the notes alternate between the adjacent strings. Some of the most beautiful effects in music and colorings which cannot be duplicated on any other instrument are the delicate harmonics, produced by lightly touching the bowed strings at certain spots. Notes can be played "portamento" and "glissando" or can be separated by "staccato" or even bouncing bow, called "spiccato." Most of these effects are possible on the viola, but as the size of the instrument increases, some of these effects become too difficult or entirely impossible on the cello and string bass.

Since the strings are such an extremely versatile family, it is no wonder they have become the great nucleus around which the entire orchestra has been built.

CHAPTER IV

The Flute

A STORY OF GREAT INVENTIONS

THE FLUTE is the oldest wind instrument known, and its development is a story of great inventions, as thrilling as the discovery of steam power or radio. The fundamental principle of the flute was probably discovered thousands of years ago by some Neanderthal or Cro-Magnon man, when he noticed that the soft wind blowing across the top of a broken reed made a pleasant sound. This was an observation requiring intelligence of the highest type in primitive man and takes its place alongside of his awareness of numbers and of time.

No doubt centuries passed before our remote ancestors rose to an intellectual stature which enabled them to comprehend that low notes came from long reeds and high notes from short reeds, and to combine these reeds of varying length like the pipes in a pipe organ to make the well-known syrinx or pipes of Pan. As far back as we can go in history we find the syrinx. The Egyptians played this ancient flute long before they wrote history. In their mythology the invention of the syrinx is credited to Osiris, the great god of the underworld. Thus do they prove the existence of the syrinx before recorded history.

Plato was acquainted with the pipes of Pan, and in one of his best-known dialogues, "The Republic," he has Socrates engage Glauco, a musician, in conversation about these primitive flutes. It is evident Socrates does not think well of the pipes, saying they are bad for the morals of the people. He amplifies this statement by saying no woman can listen to the Lydian pipes and remain virtuous, and he finally concludes they should be banned from his ideal state. Most people who have heard these primitive pipes played seem to think Socrates was unduly alarmed. Some people, though, conjecture there may have been something to what Socrates said, for three hundred years later the notorious Cleopatra strode spectacularly across the pages of history—and Cleopatra's father was a flute player! This is shown by his name, Ptolemy Auletes, which means: Ptolemy, the flute player.

Hundreds of years after the syrinx was invented another great musical discovery was made, quite by accident. All primitive peoples are fond of ornament, and a favorite way of ornamenting wood articles is by burning designs on them. It is only natural that the pipes which made up the syrinx should be decorated in this manner. These designs were often a series of spots, placed according to the fancy of the primitive artist. One day, we can imagine, a man sat dreaming in the sun and lazily burning spots on his syrinx. Through carelessness or through curiosity, he burned the holes completely through the walls of the tube. When he tried to blow the pipe he found its pitch changed. He also found that by covering the holes with his fingers he could still blow the original note for which the tube was intended, and that as he uncovered each lower hole the pitch ascended step by step. Here was a miraculous discovery and one which had far-reaching effects on the history of music.

Although the syrinx survived for centuries, it was finally supplanted by this new type of flute. The single-tube flute with the holes in its side was more compact, easier to carry, easier to make and easier to blow. The notes in the scale were accidents, governed at first by designs which seemed attractive and later by a spacing of holes which seemed to fit the fingers most conveniently. The design on the tubes or the convenient placing of the finger holes was of primary concern, and what sounds came out of the holes just happened. Inspection of many of these primitive flutes shows that some of them have holes equidistant apart, while others have holes in two groups. Sometimes there are two holes to a group, sometimes three or four. Often there is a hole on the back side for the thumb, showing definite interest in the musical purpose of the flute as distinguished from the merely ornamental.

It is more than a coincidence that there are eight notes in our scale and eight fingers on our hands. The scale that could be played was composed of those notes coming from the eight holes which could be covered conveniently by the fingers. If man had been created with only two fingers or with eleven, the chances are our scale now would be composed of a different number of notes. If man's fingers had been thicker or longer, the chances are our scale now would have different intervals. As it turned out, our ancestors became used to those notes which could be sounded by covering and uncovering eight holes spaced so the fingers could reach them conveniently.

Some authorities go still further and show the reason why there is a semitone between the third and fourth and between the seventh and eighth tones in the major diatonic scale. This theory has resulted from the inspection of scores of primitive flutes. When the two hands are placed along the flute, the eight fingers covering the eight holes, the fourth finger of the right hand covers the hole from which the lowest note is emitted. As each lowest finger is raised, an ascending scale is sounded. The intervals are alike except those between notes one and two and between notes five and six. It will be observed that both of these short intervals lie under the third and fourth fingers, and it is believed that these intervals were made short in order to accommodate the short fourth finger. The first consideration was comfort for the short fourth finger, but after this scale was played for thousands of years, it became familiar and was judged sweet to the ear. In order to prove how at home we have become with the conventional scale having the two half-steps, we need only try a scale composed entirely of whole steps. These whole-step scales sound strange and weird. We expect the half-steps to occur in their accustomed places, and when they do not appear, we immediately feel that something has gone wrong. Not one person in a hundred can sing an octave of whole steps without the aid of the piano or some other musical instrument. Involuntarily and in spite of ourselves, we drop into the established mode of the diatonic scale, with the two half-steps.

Of course, in ascending our major diatonic scale, the half-steps do not appear between one and two and between five and six, but between three and four and between seven and eight. Here again we are under the influence of musical custom. If we go to the piano and start our scale on "mi" instead of "do" and play up the scale eight white notes, we get the scale which was built into the primitive flutes. Many people believe this is the primitive scale from which all others in use today were derived. Still other scales were developed by starting them on other notes in the primitive scale. The Greeks recognized seven of these scales and called them Lydian, Phrygian, Dorian, etc., after the peoples who were supposed to have originated them. In this classification, the Dorian scale is the one which was built into the primitive flutes. We have adopted the Phrygian, which happens to begin on "do," and we have become so familiar with the scale beginning with "do" that what was probably our first scale sounds odd to us, as do all other scales beginning on the other notes in the scale.

The flute with holes in its side is found among all primitive peoples in all parts of the globe. Next to the drum, the flute is the most common musical instrument of which we know. It is made of every conceivable material capable of forming a tube through which holes can be pierced. It is made of cane, wood, pottery, stone, metal, leather, bones. The Surinam Indians of Guiana, South America, have the gruesome custom of making flutes from the shinbones of their slain enemies. The shinbone, or tibia, of animals has always been a favorite material for making flutes. In fact, the Latin name for "flute" is "tibia."

Many strange uses are made of the flute by various peoples. The ancients used to use the flute to encourage and inspire their armies, and the fife, together with the drum, is still used for this purpose. The Carib Indian of South America has the quaint custom of warning his household of his approach home. This is not only a beautiful idea but it has, as usual in such matters, a very definite utilitarian value. When the man approaches home in the dusk or dark, playing a familiar tune, he is spared being mistaken for a hostile warrior and is welcomed into the domicile. The North American Indian used the flute as a trysting instrument and for calling to his sweetheart. The African Kaffir uses the flute for calling his cattle.

Ancient peoples were fond of the flute. It played a prominent part in the lives of the Egyptians, Hebrews and Greeks. The latter developed flute playing to a fine art, as they did other arts. Great flute-playing contests were held as a part of the athletic games, and there was keen rivalry for the flute-playing honors as well as for the athletic. In Europe flute playing became popular in the eleventh century, and it increased in popularity until, in the sixteenth century, it became the vogue even for kings to devote themselves to the art. When the notorious Henry VIII died in 1547 he left a collection of flutes consisting of seventy-six end-blown flutes, seventy-two side-blown flutes and six fifes.

The fourteenth century marked the parting of the ways of flutes blown in two different manners. Some flutes were blown across the end and were called flageolets, beak flutes and recorders, or English flutes. Other flutes were blown from the side and were called transverse, or German, flutes. After the fourteenth century, the end-blown flute gave way in Europe to the side-blown flute, and today this is the type flute with which we are familiar. The only survivor of the end-blown flute is the flageolet, or tin whistle, which schoolboys buy for a dime. In England, however, the end-blown flute found greater favor than on the Continent and is often called the English flute for this reason. Samuel Pepys in his diary has made this flute immortal by his repeated references to it and by his praise of its musical qualities. After 1700, though, even in England it had to step aside in favor of the superior transverse, or German, flute. Bach and Handel wrote for both types of flutes, but by the time of Haydn the flageolet was no longer found in the orchestra.

In spite of Pepys' praise of the English flute, or recorder, it had serious defects which eventually spelled its doom. In principle, the recorder was constructed like the common tin whistle or the spring variety of whistle which small boys make by slipping the bark from a small sapling when the sap begins to run. The mouthpiece constructed on this principle is fixed and cannot be controlled as can the reed on a clarinet, the lips of the trumpet player, or the air stream employed in blowing the transverse flute. For this reason, the only method of obtaining the higher notes on the instrument was by blowing with more force. When this was done, of course the loudness increased, too. It was therefore impossible to play the upper notes softly or the lower notes loudly. If the lower notes were played loudly the instrument would "overblow" and the higher notes would sound. Conversely, if the upper notes were played softly, they would fade out and the lower notes only would sound. Since it was necessary to play the complete range of the instrument both loudly and softly, as the music required, the recorder had serious limitations. As musical appreciation increased, the defects became more and more evident, until the recorder is now only an interesting antique or a plaything for children.

When Striggio and Corteccia made their daring experiment

in 1565 with their crude orchestra to be used as accompaniment for light plays and embryonic opera, they naturally called upon the popular flute to take part. Along with a few string instruments and several brass instruments, six flutes and flageolets of various sizes were used by these two Italian pioneers in orchestra. The flute also took part in another venture in orchestra building, when, sixteen years later, Balthasarini gave his first performance in France of his "Ballet Comique de la Reine." Three flutes were scored for in 1600 by Jacopo Peri in his odd assortment of instruments used to supply chord accompaniment to singing and dramatic reciting in his famous "Euridice" opera. Also in the same year Emilio del Cavaliere showed his appreciation of the flute by giving it a place as the only wind instrument among his otherwise string orchestra, which played in his oratorio "La Rappresentazione dell' Anima e Corpo," the first oratorio ever produced. His "orchestra" was a sort of ensemble consisting of a harpsichord, a double-guitar, a viola da gamba, a violin which doubled the soprano voice, and two flutes.

The "Founder of the Orchestra," Claudio Monteverde, seemed to have a poor opinion of the flute, for in his "Orfeo" opera orchestra—the first orchestra really worthy of the name—he used only one flute. It seems likely that even this one flute was not a full-grown flute, for it is designated as an "octave flute," and it is likely that the instrument is similar to our piccolo. Later Bach wrote for the piccolo, and Handel used it in the aria of "Acis and Galatea" for piccolo obbligato.

When the flute began to take its place in the first orchestras it was by no means the great instrument it is today. It was a plain wood tube with finger holes only. The wood was usually yellow boxwood, sometimes cocuswood or grenadilla. The better flute was ornamented with rings of ivory at the joints and the edge of the bell. It had no keys, and its musical possibilities were accordingly limited. Considerable improvement had been made in the tone quality and the intonation over the first crude flutes fashioned by our primitive ancestors, but it was substantially the same instrument invented quite by accident back in the Stone Age. With the awakening in music which was taking place in the sixteenth and seventeenth centuries came an interest in improving the musical resources of the instruments; and about 1677 came the third great invention in the story of the flute —the invention of a key! This invention played a prominent part in the creation of the modern orchestra.

Nobody knows who invented the first key for the flute, but he undoubtedly had an ingenious and resourceful mind. At some indefinite time keys seem to have appeared for the first time on bagpipes, but this fact hardly minimizes the achievement of the man who first used the key on the flute. Before this great invention the conventional flute had six holes from which could be coaxed a more or less satisfactory diatonic scale. The lowest note was D above Middle C, played with all holes covered, the note coming from the end of the tube. As each lowest hole was uncovered, the notes E, F, G, A, B and C were sounded. The second octave could be played in a similar manner by overblowing. To obtain the half-steps needed for the chromatic scale, two practices were resorted to, neither of which had much to recommend it. If a hole were only partially covered by the finger so it leaked air, the resulting note would be about a half-step lower than the note which would be sounded when the hole was completely covered. Another practice was to leave an open hole between covered holes. For instance, if the three top holes were covered, G would sound; and if the four top holes were covered, F would sound. But if the three top holes were covered, the fourth left open, and the fifth covered, something resembling F♯ would sound. This practice was known as fork fingering.

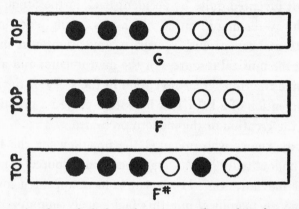

Illustrating how fork fingering was used to play the semitones on flutes and other woodwinds before keys were invented. When the top three holes were covered, G was sounded. When the top four holes were covered, F, a whole tone below, was sounded. But when the top three holes were covered, the fourth hole left open and the fifth covered, F♯, a semitone below G, was sounded.

By these two practices it was possible to obtain the half-steps necessary to play the chromatic scale, but these notes were weak, "fuzzy," of poor quality and decidedly capricious. Flute players of the day prided themselves, though, on the perfections of the flute. They really thought it was nearly perfect. This is difficult for us to believe, just as it is always difficult to believe those things which are strange and unfamiliar. After a musical standard has been accepted, it is difficult to understand how any other could be tolerated,

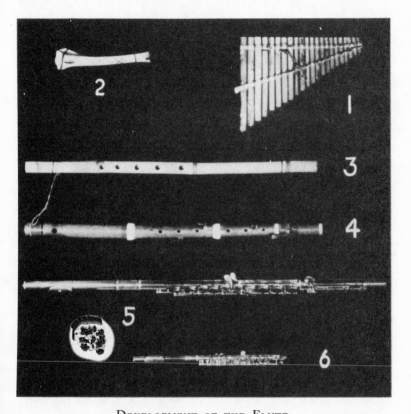

DEVELOPMENT OF THE FLUTE
(1) Egyptian pipes of Pan used five thousand years ago. (2) Ancient bone flute made from the shinbone of the deer. (3) Chinese cane flute. (4) Boxwood flute with four keys, used about 1750. (5) Modern Boehm-system flute. (6) Modern Boehm-system piccolo.

just as the old Phrygian scale seems to us the only sensible scale, even though the Dorian at one time was accepted as perfect by primitive musicians.

It was a flute of this kind which called out the famous remark by Cherubini. An orchestra conductor who had only one flute sighed for more and remarked to Cherubini, "What is worse than one flute in an orchestra!" The great composer quickly remarked, "Two flutes." No two were alike, and the disharmony of two flutes must have justified Cherubini's caustic remark.

Not only did the flute players before the invention of the key accept this crippled and decrepit scale, but they made a great virtue of its very faults. Much depended upon the player. Almost any note might come out of any hole. The player must favor the note one way or the other to make it fit into any scale. This very uncertainty and lack of dependability of the notes focused the flute player's attention on playing the notes sharp or flat to make them in tune. The result was that they began to talk of enharmonic differences! In a time when it was difficult to play a simple diatonic scale in tune and when it was next to impossible to play a chromatic scale, these flute players became obsessed with the idea that C♯ should be sounded sharper than D♭, that B♭ had fewer vibrations than A♯!

When flute players had such odd ideas about the perfections of the flute, it is a wonder that the first key was accepted at all. Apparently, though, the D♯ was more difficult to obtain than other semitones, and the D♯ key was an improvement which was readily grasped. There had been only one good way to play D♯, and that was by partially covering the E hole. According to William Kincaid, first flutist of the Philadelphia Orchestra, it was also possible to play D♯ on the old flute by fingering E♮ and stopping the end of the flute against the knee, but this produced a D♯ of poor quality. It was impossible to play it by fork fingering, for D was played with all holes covered, and the tone came out the end of the tube. For fork fingering it would have been necessary to close all holes above E, leave E open, and close the D hole immediately below it. This was impossible, since there was no D hole. The only way left was to compromise the E hole. This had to be done with the third and weak finger of the right hand, and since this finger is the least agile on the hand, the playing of D♯ always presented a problem.

With a real flash of genius, some unheralded inventor conceived the idea that if he bored a hole between the E hole and the end of the tube, he could obtain a semitone between E and D. After he had bored the hole he found difficulty in covering it. The fourth finger of the right hand was short and did a poor job of covering and uncovering it. Finally the inventor adopted the key idea. With a hinge as a fulcrum, a pad for covering the hole at one end and a spatule at the other, within easy reach of the little finger, he could open and close the hole with greater ease. A spring was placed under the spatule end of the key which raised this end in the air and depressed the other end, thereby keeping the hole covered. When the player wished to open the hole to sound D♯ he covered the E hole and all other holes above and pushed down on the spatule; when he wished to close the hole to obtain D♮, he released pressure on the spatule.

As is always true in instances of this kind, we who are

familiar with an invention or discovery cannot comprehend the originality of mind which first conceived it. The key on the flute seems to all of us most obvious and nothing to get excited about; but when it is realized that thousands of musicians for thousands of years did not hit upon this idea, the greatness of the achievement begins to dawn upon us. For the same reason it is difficult for us to comprehend why the Ancients, who invented mathematics, geometry and astronomy, and brought to a high stage of perfection the arts of poetry, painting and sculpturing, never discovered the art of sounding a string instrument by bowing. The strange fact remains that they did not.

In all our thinking, whether about music or anything else, we are hedged about by the great, black unknown; and usually when original minds pierce the unknown, it is because of some new urge which focuses men's attention on certain sectors.

For a hundred years before the first flute key was invented, there had existed in Italy particularly, but also in France and Germany, a great and new interest in music. Many experiments had been conducted with opera and oratorio and with instrumental music to go with them. The idea of making music a part of drama—not an accessory, but an integral part—was a new idea. Men were intrigued with the experiments. The effects found favor with the people. Attention was focused in this direction. Whereas for centuries no great pressure had been brought to bear upon musicians and the makers of musical instruments for something new and novel of this kind, now there began a great and intensive movement which has finally grown into what we know as the classical music of the masters. Bach and Handel were the first great fruits of this movement in composers. The superb violins of the Italian master craftsmen were the first great fruits of this movement in musical instruments. The invention of the first flute key by an unknown genius was another important fruition of this great musical urge.

Strange as it may seem, it required of the fertile mind of man a half-century more to invent the second key. The supposed perfection of the flute of the time kept anyone from thinking there could be any further improvements. Now that the player could make D♯ it was assumed that the millennium of the flute had arrived.

The greatest flute virtuoso of the day was Johann Joachim Quantz, who is famous as the flute instructor of Frederick the Great of Prussia and later as court musician during Frederick's reign. Imbued with the musical thought that enharmonic differences should be recognized, Quantz finally came to believe that there was a slight shortcoming in the flute which he had been taught to believe was perfection itself. Year after year this conviction grew upon him, until he finally decided something should be done about it. He conceived the idea of a second key, a key which would correct the final error in this almost perfect flute.

And what was this error or shortcoming, and how did Quantz overcome it? It is a little difficult to take Quantz and his invention seriously, but it seemed a very serious matter to Quantz. Accustomed to playing sharps and flats with due recognition of their enharmonic differences, Quantz could not accept for E♭ the note which came out when the D♯ key was used. This is a classical example of straining at a gnat and swallowing a camel. That Quantz would pick out this difference between E♭ and D♯ as a serious fault—the only surviving fault—on a flute which was so obviously out of tune throughout, is an absurdity which is hard for us to understand. Quantz could not rest until he had corrected this fault, so in 1726 he invented another key, for playing E♭. This was placed alongside the D♯ key, with the hole made slightly larger and located a slight distance below that of the D♯ key!

Few players appreciated this invention; it was not used outside of Germany, and but very little within Germany. Quantz never seemed to suspect the real reason, but thought it presented too great difficulties for the player. In one of his instructions for the flute he goes to considerable trouble to show that this key was really not so difficult to play as it might seem!

If Quantz's inventive genius went unrewarded, his ability as a player was widely acknowledged. It was Quantz who first convinced Scarlatti, the composer, that the flute was a musical instrument of merit. Someone asked Scarlatti to listen to a flute. He replied that he detested wind instruments because they were never in tune. After some persuasion he finally consented, much against his better judgment. The player happened to be Quantz, and Scarlatti had to admit the instrument could be played with artistry. He thought so well of the flute—or rather of Quantz, the flute player—that he afterward wrote two solos for Quantz.

Two years after Quantz invented the E♭ key he became instructor to Frederick, heir to the throne of Prussia. Frederick was only eight years old when he began to take lessons from Quantz, and he was an apt and talented pupil. The old Prussian king became alarmed when he saw his son becoming an addict to flute playing. He considered it effeminate and told Frederick and Quantz it would have to stop. Frederick, though, was such a lover of the flute that he could not give it up. He continued his lessons with Quantz on the sly, and on several occasions the flute lesson nearly became disastrous for both. Once the old king came upon them by surprise, but Frederick saved the day by hiding his tutor and his flute in a closet by the fireplace, used for storing wood. When Frederick finally became king the loyalty and help of Quantz were rewarded. He was made royal court musician at a liberal salary, and when he became old he was pensioned. Frederick became an accomplished player and composer on the flute. He played for court audiences and often selected difficult concertos which he played with the court orchestra. Although a great monarch, he always was conscientious in his playing and wished to be judged by his playing alone and not because he was king. He was very nervous when appearing in these concerts, and he would spend the time before he was to play practising difficult parts. The only person he would allow to criticize him, however, was Quantz, his old and trusted tutor. Once a member of the orchestra had the temerity to offer a criticism, and the next day he lost his position.

Although the E♭ key did not long survive, Quantz made another improvement which we find on flutes today. This is the movable cork in the head joint which makes it easier to tune the flute. Another inventor or inventors found that the small blowhole on eighteenth-century flutes could be improved by changing the shape and size. After considerable experimenting it was determined that the tone could be produced easier and could be controlled better if the hole were oval instead of round and also if it were made larger.

At various times after this the hole was changed, one time to square, but the conclusion of these earlier inventors has been substantiated by the fact that the finest flutes today still have the large oval blowhole. The hole on many modern flutes is more rectangular than oval, the shape being rectangular with the inside corners rounded.

The bore of the early flute was also changed about this time from cylindrical to slightly conical; that is, the flute near the blowhole was about an eighth of an inch larger in diameter than it was at the open end. The conical bore was supposed to improve the intonation and response of certain notes, but it also weakened the notes in the lower part of the scale. Finger holes were reduced in size, and flutes were made in as many as four joints. Credit for the conical bore and small finger holes is sometimes given to Jacques Hotteterre, the French instrument maker, but it is more likely that Johann Christoph Denner, celebrated instrument maker of Nuremberg, was responsible.

Forgetting the ludicrous E♭ key, the next keys added to the flute were G♯, B♭ and F♮. These three keys were found on flutes by the middle of the century, and C♮ was added about 1780. Some flute players who had considered the flute as perfect without keys began to say that the adding of many keys spoiled the tone and intonation. Among these, of course, was Quantz. Wendling, the successor of Quantz, also talked against keys, being particularly hostile to the low C♯ and C♮. So strong was the influence of these men that some of these keys were abandoned temporarily. Pietro Grassi Florio, first flute of the Italian Opera Orchestra, thought well of these latter keys and revived them. He valued them so much he hung a little curtain over the foot joint

[*73*]

to conceal the keys so other flute players would not discover how he had increased the resources of his instrument.

Quantz, the first great flute player, was born in 1697. One hundred years later was born a musical and mechanical genius who was destined to transform the flute into one of the most nearly perfect of all wind instruments—Theobald Boehm. When Boehm was a boy he began his study of the flute, using a four-key model patterned after one made by Karl August Gresner, famous instrument maker of Dresden. It had six holes and four closed-type keys for playing D♯, G♯, B♭ and F♮. Before Boehm was twenty-one he had mastered the eight-key flute and had become flutist in the Royal Bavarian Court Orchestra. Later he distinguished himself as soloist in Paris and London. During all this time he was intensely interested in the construction of flutes and did a lot of experimenting with tuning and the key mechanism.

Manufacturers seemed to have decided that the way to improve the flute was merely to add keys. Finally a model was produced with seventeen holes, eleven keys and four special levers. But even the eight-key flute was difficult enough to make work, and this complicated mechanism must have been impossible. The keys were crudely made, and many were hinged on a wire run through a hump of wood on the body of the instrument and slotted through the center for the key. Being unable to get flutes made according to his wishes, Boehm finally set up his own factory in 1828 and began building flutes as he felt they should be built. Boehm was by trade a goldsmith, and his knowledge of this craft came in handy for him. He developed a key mechanism hinged on small axles pivoted between metal posts screwed into the wood. This was a much more positive mechanism and gave the smoothest, fastest action known at that time.

Boehm also did a lot of work on the intonation, response and tone quality of the flute. The notes in the scale were dreadfully out of tune, and only a very skillful musician could play a scale with good intonation. Many notes were of poor quality, being dead, "fuzzy," colorless. Some notes were difficult to play, and only a powerful man with a well-trained embouchure (shaping of lips, tongue, etc., for playing) could bring them out. Other notes boomed out with little effort. Running up the scale of the flute of those days was just like running up a flight of stairs whose steps are all of assorted sizes. First would be a low step, then a high one; next a wide step, then a narrow one. To make any speed up a flight of steps such as this, one would have to be an acrobat. It required much of the dexterity of an acrobat to play a flute in Boehm's day. This problem occupied Boehm during every minute he could spare from his concert work, but he did not accomplish a great deal.

Then, during one of his trips to London, Boehm chanced to hear the great English flutist Nicholson. This experience changed Boehm's entire views about the flute and started him on the line of work which completely revolutionized this instrument. Boehm was especially amazed at the big and powerful tone Nicholson was able to produce. When he examined Nicholson's flute, he found the holes were very large, some of them too large for Boehm's fingers to cover. The irregular spacing and size of the holes offended Boehm's innate feeling for symmetry and orderliness. He immediately decided that he could get nowhere trying to patch up the old eight-key flute. Such a flute had too many serious faults. He saw he would have to discard entirely the flute as constructed then and start from scratch. The new flute must have holes all the same size, and they must be placed scientifically along the tube according to the exact divisions of the scale.

With this objective in mind he set to work. He first made a flute without any holes in it other than the blowhole. Then he carefully cut off the end little by little until he had cut it to a length which gave him the first note in the scale. Measuring very accurately the distance from the embouchure (blowhole) to the end of the tube, he determined where the hole should be for this note. Having found this measurement, he incorporated it in a second flute. After hours and hours of such tedious work he finally produced a flute with fourteen holes, all of the same size and spaced along the tube for accurate intonation. Here was the most nearly accurately built chromatic scale that had ever been constructed for the flute. So far, so good.

But Boehm immediately faced a problem that would have crushed a less bold or less resourceful inventor. He sat down and counted his fingers. He knew without counting that he had only ten. In actual playing only nine fingers were available, for the thumb of the right hand had to support the flute. The problem boiled down to this stubborn question: How can I cover fourteen holes with nine fingers? Nobody had ever done it before. It seemed to have no solution. To Boehm it must have seemed as if he would need some mathematician who could work out a new kind of arithmetic, for as long as two plus two makes four there was no way of covering fourteen holes with nine fingers. To continue thinking there was a way of cheating at numbers to make this possible was likely to drive a man crazy.

One flute inventor of Boehm's time actually did go crazy over this problem. Captain Gordon of the Swiss Guards of Charles X was a flute player. Equipped with an ingenious mind but with little mechanical skill, he started improvements on the flute in 1826. Four years later, in the revolution of 1830, Charles lost his throne. During one of the battles in the streets of Paris, Captain Gordon's men became seized with panic and in this disorganized condition were massacred. Such a terrible experience is said to have affected his mind. Having lost his position in the army, Gordon turned his mind to the flute. Such a knotty problem was not a mental task suitable to a man whose mind had been so upset. After many discouraging attempts to develop his ideas of a new flute, he completely lost his mental faculties and is said to have died in an insane asylum. Ever since Gordon's death there has raged a controversy over whether Gordon or Boehm was the inventor of the modern flute. Some of their ideas and developments were similar, and many claimed that Boehm used some of the unfortunate Gordon's ideas, but nobody has been able to deny the great contribution Boehm made to flute building.

Boehm faced the unanswerable question of how nine fingers could cover fourteen holes and finally found the answer! His answer was the famous ring key. This key was like other keys, with a pad at one end for covering the hole and a spatule at the other end which the finger touched, thereby operating the key. It was different, though, in that the spatule was really a ring. This ring was situated so that when the finger pressed it down, the ring encircled a hole;

and at the same time that the pad covered a hole, the finger on the ring key also covered a hole—the hole encircled by the ring. With this ingenious device one finger could cover two holes, and the unanswerable problem in arithmetic had been solved.

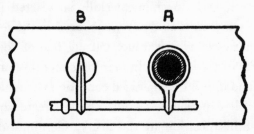

How Boehm was enabled to open and close fourteen holes with nine fingers, by the use of the ring key. Ring key A and pad key B are mounted on the same axle and are sprung open. When the hole A is closed with the finger, the ring is also pushed down. As the axle turns, the pad key B also closes the hole B. In this way two or more holes can be closed with one finger.

Since it was not always desirable, when closing the lower hole, to close the hole encircled by the ring, Boehm made the mechanism so the lower hole could be closed without closing the one above. This was accomplished by attaching an arm to the ring key which articulated with the key below. When the ring key was pressed down, the arm swung down onto the key below and closed it. The lower key, however, could be closed without disturbing the ring key above. This ring-key principle revolutionized the entire family of woodwind instruments and is at the basis of practically all the key mechanism of our modern instruments. Boehm did not invent the ring key and never claimed to be the inventor, but he unquestionably established its worth by incorporating it with other useful ideas on his flute. Reverend Frederick

Nolan of Ireland invented and patented the ring key in 1808, but it lay buried for the most part in the patent office until Boehm put it to this ingenious use on his new flute.

To an acoustically correct chromatic scale and ingenious ring keys, Boehm contributed still another feature—open keys. The first D♯ key had been a closed key; that is, it was sprung closed with a spring and was opened by pressing down on the spatule end of the key. All the other keys which were added after the D♯ key were closed. It is true that in 1800 Johann Tromlitz, a flutist of Leipzig, had made and invented an open key, but it was Boehm who first developed the idea successfully. The open key works in a manner exactly opposite from that of the closed key. It is mounted so it is poised above the hole and the pad covers the hole only when the spatule is depressed by the finger. Boehm chose open keys because he saw they could be worked faster and with greater ease than closed keys, for in order to spring a closed key shut tight enough so the hole could not leak, a stiff spring must be used. To open the hole the finger must overcome the action of the stiff spring. The open key, on the other hand, requires a spring stiff enough only to keep it from dropping over the hole, and it takes little strength of the finger to overcome such a light spring and depress the key. Light action meant speed and ease of operation, and that was what Boehm was striving for.

When Boehm had completed his new flute in 1832 he played it in concert and amazed his hearers with his perform-ance. Boehm was not a stunt player like Nicholson but ex-celled rather in musicianship, interpretation, phrasing. But his new flute gave him greater technical display as well as more finished performance. It was more nearly accurate in intonation and had a positive, light and fast mechanism. Best of all, it was playable in any signature. Boehm could modulate all over the scale with amazing ease, and his hearers could hardly believe their ears.

He took his flute to Paris and to London. During one visit to Paris he took his flute to show it to the great composer and conductor Rossini. When he arrived at Rossini's quarters, Rossini was shaving, and Boehm was invited to wait in an adjoining room. While Boehm was waiting, he took out his flute and began practising scales, arpeggios, skips and trills in various keys. Finally he came to the key of D♭, in which key it was practically impossible to play on the old eight-key flute, the flute with which Rossini was familiar and whose resources and limitations he understood. Without hesitation Boehm launched into difficult arpeggios and trills in this key. Soon Rossini came rushing out into the room, one side of his face shaved, the other covered with lather, and a razor in one hand. He confronted Boehm with the incredulous remark, "You can't play a flute in that key."

Boehm replied quietly, "But I'm playing it."

"I don't care if you are," Rossini maintained. "It is absolutely impossible."

This little anecdote illustrates the general astonishment at the new Boehm flute. Although some great flute players of the day changed to the new fingering system, many opposed it as newfangled. They criticized it on various points, one of them being that the lower and higher notes were of poor quality. This was a just criticism and one which was not remedied until Boehm produced his 1847 flute with a cylindrical bore. But soon after bringing out his first new flute, Boehm became interested in various other activities, among them being the development of a new type of blast furnace for smelting iron ore, and during all this time the flute remained unchanged.

In 1847 Boehm came out with an even more radical flute. He had taken up the study of acoustics and had applied some of the laws of sound to the practical building of the flute. He established as most efficient that tube which is thirty times as long as its diameter. He also found that the defective notes in the extreme top and bottom of the scale could be improved by making the bore cylindrical rather than conical. His new flute was therefore cylindrical, except for the head joint, which was shaped somewhat like a parabola or truncated cone. In the development of this flute Boehm made over three hundred experiments, mostly with metal tubes. He found that the larger the hole, the more nearly the center of the hole approximated the cut-off of a plain tube. By making the holes large he was able to build a scale even more nearly acoustically perfect. Large holes also improved response and gave greater volume of tone. He finally finished by making the holes so large they could not be covered by the fingers. To overcome this trouble, he adopted covered keys, sometimes known as plateau keys. Boehm's experiments with the metal tube led him to use metal for this flute, the first metal flute ever made.

Boehm outdid himself on the second new flute. It was superior to anything that had ever been built, having fifteen holes and twenty-three keys. But it is often overlooked that three important inventions of another man greatly helped Boehm in making this flute as good as it was. Between the time of Boehm's first and second new flutes, August Buffet, Jr, instrument maker of Paris, had invented the needle spring to replace the conventional flat spring, the clutch to replace the articulating arm on Boehm's ring key, and the sleeve to permit keys with reverse action being mounted on the same shaft. These ingenious inventions speeded up the action of the mechanism, made it more compact and efficient and made practical certain other inventions which without them would have been impractical. Next to Boehm, Buffet probably did more than any other man to make our wood-wind instruments what they are today.

Although our modern flutes are built with the open-key system, catalogs on these instruments carry a phrase which is more or less confusing. Sometimes flutes may be had with "closed G#" or with "open G#," but in America most flutes are "closed G#." The introduction of the closed G# key has an interesting history. Coche, prominent flute player of Paris, objected to Boehm's open G#, because when the little finger of the left hand is pressing the key down to close it it is difficult to lift the third finger. In making high E on the open system, for instance, the little finger is down, and the first and second as well. To play this note it was necessary to raise the third finger, a slow and difficult action. Coche reasoned that if this key were of the closed type, the little finger would not have to be down and the third finger could be lifted more easily. In spite of Boehm's opposition to this suggestion, the closed G# has become universal in France and America. The only place Boehm's open G# key is popular is in England and Germany.

In 1851, at the Industrial Exhibition of All Nations, held in London, the Boehm flute carried off all the honors. Its fame spread all over the world. An American flute made by Pfaff of Philadelphia was entered in this exhibit, but it had little chance against the product of the master Boehm. The Boehm flute was first made in America by Laribee, but many were imported from England and France. Two of Boehm's own pupils came to America—Wehner and Heindl —and helped popularize the Boehm system here. Among the more noted American flutists was the poet Sidney Lanier. He prophesied a great future for the flute when he said that the twenty first violins of the symphony orchestra would soon be counterbalanced by twenty flutes. Today the flute duties of the symphony orchestra are handled by one or two and sometimes three flutists.

Few important changes have been made in the flute since Boehm finished his 1847 flute; it is substantially the same in all respects. We are directly indebted to Boehm for our system of fingering, the cylindrical bore, the metal tube, and are indirectly indebted to him in numerous other ways for his good judgment in selecting and his skill in perfecting the suggestions of other inventors.

Almost all our flutes today are made of metal. At first there was much criticism of the metal flute on the score that it was inferior in tonal quality to the flute made of cocus- or grenadilla wood. Boehm himself seemed a little doubtful on this point but finally straddled the issue by saying much depended on the individual player. When the first metal flutes were used in Wagner's Bayreuth orchestra, the old master spied them and ordered them out. He said, "Those are not flutes—they are cannons." It is doubtful if Wagner could have known the difference from their tone quality alone. Numerous blindfold tests have been made with metal and wood flutes, to the complete confusion of everybody, showing that few people can tell the difference from the sound alone, although it has been proved by delicate recording devices that there is some difference.

Alto and bass flutes have been made but have had no wide use. Boehm made himself a bass flute in G, and he declared when he was an old man, after playing this flute for many years, that it was his favorite instrument. The alto flute is used in many modern scores with good effect, especially in the works of Stravinsky and Ravel. The little octave flute, generally called the piccolo, is really a small edition of the Boehm flute, having the same key mechanism and being made of metal. Strangely enough, however, the best piccolos are conical in bore instead of cylindrical, like the flute.

Since Cavaliere's oratorios in 1600, the flute has been one of the important instruments in orchestra. In the scores of this composer, the two flutes were the only wind instruments used, all other instruments being strings. The classical composers since Cavaliere's time limited the number of flutes to two, until Haydn called for an extra one. Later, Wagner and Verdi made the use of three flutes common, and symphonic bands often have as many as five flutes.

The flute is called the coloratura soprano of the woodwinds, to distinguish it from the other woodwind sopranos: the oboe, or lyric soprano, and the clarinet, or dramatic soprano. The flute gets this name from its unusual abilities to execute highly embellishing and ornamenting passages.

Most of the early composers, and some of the more modern, use the flute to double the violins. It is also used to give color to the ensemble of woodwinds. Much music has been written for the flute, not only that of a harmonic nature, but concertos and other solo parts. The flute is especially brilliant as a solo instrument.

THE FLUTE

In its lower register, the flute is soft and melancholy; in the middle register it is peculiarly sweet and clear, the voice taking on a liquid quality; while in the upper register it is brilliant and hard. Its range of two octaves and part of another, and the shades of color in the three registers, make it a valuable instrument.

The piccolo is used for such effects as whistling of the wind, to imitate the shrill voice of the fife in military music, and for certain satanic portrayals which have won for it the title of "imp of the orchestra." Its voice is generally too high and shrill for extensive use, but it is indispensable for certain purposes.

Besides being one of the sweetest instruments in the band or orchestra, the flute is the most agile of the wind instruments, being surpassed only by the violin in technical capabilities. Staccato or legato playing, double and triple tonguing, trills, arpeggios, runs, skips—it seems there is nothing the flute cannot do and do with great velocity. This great ability is due both to the fact that the acoustics of the flute are almost perfectly worked out and also that the key mechanism is exceptionally close to the body, extremely light in action and lightning fast in response.

CHAPTER V

The Double-Reeds

THE EXPATRIATED ORIENTALS

THERE IS A PECULIAR NOTE of sadness and mystery in the voices of the oboe, English horn and bassoon which suggests the far Eastern lands from which they were brought nearly a thousand years ago. Although they have been used in Europe for eight or ten centuries, they have preserved their oriental character and suggest an expatriated people who will not forget and who still yearn for the homeland.

When the Crusaders streamed down through Constantinople, Venice and Genoa to Palestine and the holy city of Jerusalem, they found the double-reed instruments used by the Saracens in their worship, in social and military activities and in the small details of daily life. These instruments were almost as characteristic of the Turks and Arabs as the turban, the scimitar and the Moslem prayers. The thin, nasal music of these oriental woodwinds hung in the air like the perfume in the Sultan's harem, like the call to prayer sounded from the towers of the mosques. This music fascinated the rough and hearty Crusaders, and they brought the double-reed

[*86*]

instruments back with them to Europe, along with the silken robes, water pipes, jewels and other accessories of the leisurely life of the more cultured Orientals.

But when the Crusaders discovered the primitive shawms with their double-reed mouthpieces, these instruments were already thousands of years old. As far back as we can go in Egyptian history and even beyond into Egyptian mythology, we find the double-reed shawm. Actual specimens of these little instruments have been found in the ancient Egyptian tombs of the Fourth Dynasty, or about 3700 B.C. They were made of a piece of cane with some finger holes in the side and a double-reed mouthpiece on the end. Except for the mouthpiece, they were much like ancient cane flutes, but the mouthpiece was the part which distinguished them from all other instruments and which was responsible for their characteristic tonal coloring. This mouthpiece was for all the world like a soda straw which has become collapsed at one end. By forcing a thin stream of air between the two sides of the mouthpiece, the player could produce a reedy, nasal sound which we have come to associate with the oboe.

The making of this little mouthpiece was a great discovery which has figured in music for over sixty centuries. In all the sounds of nature there is nothing quite like it. It has a character all its own. String instruments, brass instruments, percussion instruments and other woodwind instruments are as different from the double-reed instruments as night is different from day. These two thin pieces of reed which are made to vibrate together produce a strange mixture of musical coloring which has not quite been duplicated in any other way. The weird, mysterious, plaintive sound of the shawm has come down to us unchanged and unmodified through

[*87*]

the centuries, and its secret is wrapped up in the tiny mouth-piece made of the two thin lips of cane.

Nobody of course knows just how the double-reed mouth-piece was discovered, for its inception is shrouded in the unwritten story of the centuries before history, but the soda-straw illustration is probably as good and as accurate a way to explain its discovery as any. Everyone knows how a soda straw will collapse at the end when it becomes soaked with water by holding it in the mouth. This is probably just how the first shawm mouthpiece was discovered. Some ancient Egyptian boy was probably chewing on a piece of cane as he tilled the black soil along the Nile or herded his sheep in the plains. Gradually the reed became soft at the end and col-lapsed. When the boy attempted to open up the tube by forcing air through it, the lips of the cane tube were made to vibrate and the characteristic reed sound was produced. The sound was sweet to the ear, and this little noisemaker was used for amusement. Gradually it became more and more popular as its nature became better known and as through improvement it became easier to blow. In time it became a real musical instrument.

This is all speculation, but it is a fairly accurate descrip-tion of how the shawm mouthpieces were made for centuries. A piece of reed was soaked in water until it became soft, after which the end was flattened. This end was then scraped and made thin, leaving two lips of reed with a fine slit between them. This was essentially the double-reed mouthpiece, and no doubt at first only one note could be sounded on it. Possibly various lengths of cane were used and were left as a part of the mouthpiece to serve as a handle by which to hold the instrument. At some time or other the rest of the cane tube was decorated and ornamented with colored dyes or by burning. One eventful day holes were burned clear through the sides of the tube, as related in the story of the flute, and a full-fledged shawm was created, capable of sounding several notes, all of the same oboe character.

Certain sounds seem to appeal to certain peoples, depending upon their national character. The African tribesman seems to have a peculiar liking for the deep boom, boom, boom of the drum. The Romans seemed to like best the shrill martial blast of the trumpet. The Chinese love the tinkling sound of cymbals and the plucking of thin wire strings. The Turks and Arabs seemed to like best the nasal twang of the shawm. They developed a wide variety of cymbals and gongs, flutes and trumpets, string and reed instruments, but the double-reed shawm was by considerable odds the favorite of them all.

For thousands of years the oriental fakir used the shawm to charm snakes in the streets of the cities along the Nile and along the Tigris and Euphrates rivers, ancient cradles of civilization. In the harems of Baghdad and in the temples of Cairo the weird music of the Orient was intoned on the double-reeds. Shepherd boys herding their sheep on the hills of Palestine whiled away the hours by playing the shepherd's pipe with the double-beating reed mouthpiece. As Arabs squatted in their white tents and as camel caravans crossed the deserts, the thin, nasal whine of the primitive oboe was constantly heard. Even as the snake of the fakir became captivated by the strains of the shawm and moved from side to side in lazy rhythm, so the whole Orient seemed to be held in the magic spell of this little musical instrument made from a piece of cane.

The Crusaders who came to Jerusalem to oust the infidel and worship in this holy place also fell under the spell of the infidel's music and carried the shawms back with them to Europe. There may have been double-reed instruments in Europe before this, but there is little evidence to support the theory. Possibly the Phoenicians, who were supposed to have landed on European shores hundreds of years before the time of the Crusades, brought shawms with them in their strange boats, but there are no records of it. In any event, the use of the shawm to any extent in Europe can definitely be traced to these adventurers of the Middle Ages who conquered the Saracens, only to be conquered in turn by the Saracens' favorite musical instrument.

It was not long, after the first Crusaders returned to Europe, until the shawms spread through France and Germany. Instead of the dark-skinned, black-eyed shepherd boy of the Nile, the shawm was played by the flaxen-haired, blue-eyed shepherd boy of Europe. Instead of being blown by the snake charmer, watchmen who made the rounds of the towns during the reign of Henry III in the thirteenth century used shawms called "waeghts" for signaling. Soon the shawms in Europe graduated from instruments of the fields, hills and market place and were adopted in musical organizations. In the fourteenth century Edward III used three shawms in his royal band. In France in 1588 shawms and drums took the place of the older fifes and drums, and this custom spread soon to Germany and finally to England.

The shawms were made in various sizes, and they were known under various names. Sometimes the larger shawms were called bombards, and the smaller were called bom-

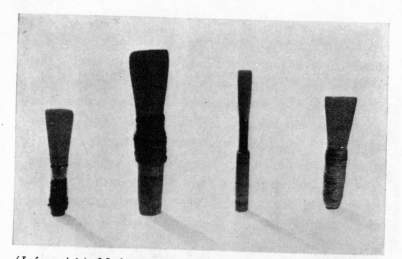

(*Left to right*): Modern bassoon reed, old-type bassoon reed, modern oboe reed, old-type oboe reed. Note that the old-type reeds for both bassoon and oboe were considerably wider and larger. The tone produced was louder and coarser than the tone produced by the smaller, narrower reeds of today.

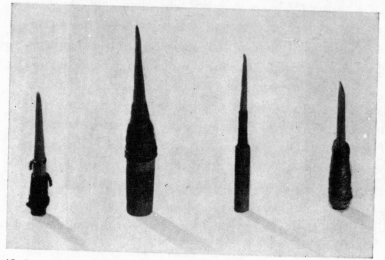

(*Left to right*): Modern bassoon reed, old-type bassoon reed, modern oboe reed, old-type oboe reed. This view shows how the two pieces of cane meet at the tip, permitting a thin stream of air to flow between them. Note also that the modern reeds are held together by wire, whereas the old-type reeds used waxed string.

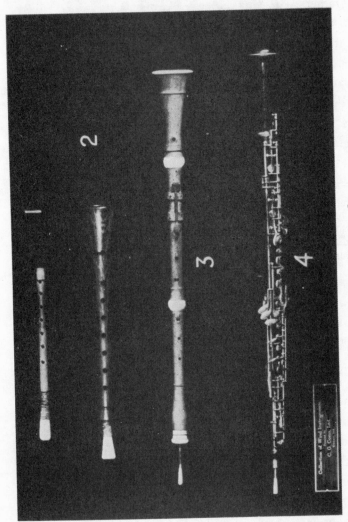

Development of the Oboe

(1) Egyptian shawm found in Egyptian tomb 3700 B.C. (2) Russian oboe, called the zourna. (3) Boxwood oboe in D, used in Florence, Italy, in the seventeenth century. (4) Modern Conservatory-system oboe in C.

bardinos, or little bombards. In Germany the popular name
was pommers. In Shakespeare's time they were called
hoboys, or hoeboys; and later they were called hautboys,
which literally means "high wood," so called because they
were made of wood and their voices were pitched high. This
is the name which has evolved into the present English word
oboe. Besides the soprano hautboys, there were larger
shawms of various sizes, which eventually developed into
the English horn, bassoon and double bassoon. Praetorius, who
wrote a treatise on musical instruments in Europe in 1619,
describes seven different sizes of shawms in use at that time.
European soil seemed favorable to the shawms in more
ways than one. Besides attaining wide popularity all over
Europe, they multiplied in variety. Instead of trying to bring
the few sizes of shawms to greater musical efficiency, instrument makers tried for years to see how many different kinds
and sizes of shawms they could invent. At various times there
were as many as a dozen varieties being played in Europe,
but as the orchestra began to take definite shape, these
various shawms one by one dropped into oblivion. The
soprano shawm in C has survived in the present-day oboe.

Another soprano of the family, called the oboe d'amour,
pitched in A, a third below, struggled along for several years
but could not quite make the grade. Bach was a great admirer
of this instrument and wrote some beautiful music for it, but
after Bach died it was left without a champion, and it was
buried with the great master. Several composers since Bach
have attempted to revive the oboe d'amour, notably Richard
Strauss in his "Symphonia Domestica" in 1903, but all of
these attempts have failed. This seems a pity, for the instrument possessed a sweet, wistful voice.

Thomas J. Byrne, oboist with the Detroit Symphony, regrets the discontinuance of the oboe d'amour and believes it should be used in the scores of such composers as Bach and Strauss. It is used effectively in the Detroit Symphony, and other orchestras using the oboe d'amour are those of Philadelphia, Cleveland, Cincinnati and Chicago. An outstanding solo passage for this instrument is found in the original score of Ravel's "Bolero," but the music is often arranged for English horn where the oboe d'amour is not available.

There were two altos in the family which fought each other for years for a place in the orchestra. These were the oboe da caccia and the cor anglais, better known today as the English horn. Both were built in F and were quite similar in most respects. The oboe da caccia was in the field first. Its first recognition was obtained through Bach, in his "Passion Music," composed in 1723. There seemed to be at this time other altos similar to the oboe da caccia, such as the tenoroon in F and the bassoon quinte in F, but there is considerable controversy about just exactly what they were like. They may have been in the contest along with the oboe da caccia, but the extent to which they were similar is not at all definitely known. Bach's choice of the oboe da caccia over the other two would seem to indicate the superiority of the former, and for several years this instrument seemed to have the alto position in the family fairly well clinched. But in 1760 an instrument maker in Bergamo named Ferlandis invented the English horn, and the oboe da caccia, which had easily vanquished the tenoroon and the bassoon quinte, found itself faced with a more formidable contender.

Haydn, Mozart and Beethoven followed the example of Bach in the use of the oboe da caccia instead of the English horn, and with such champions as these it is a wonder that the oboe da caccia did not win over the English horn by an easy margin. After Bach died Gluck made the acquaintance of the English horn and found a liking for it, as he used it in a number of his operas. Apparently, though, there was some doubt in Gluck's mind as to whether or not the English horn deserved a place in the orchestra, for in his Vienna score of "Alceste," published in 1767, he included the English horn, but in his Paris score of the same opera, published nine years later, the instrument was dropped. It was not a question in Gluck's mind about the relative merits of the oboe da caccia and the English horn, but rather about the need of either of these two alto voices of the double-reeds. Later composers, such as Schubert, Schumann and Mendelssohn, wavered between the oboe da caccia and the English horn, using sometimes one and sometimes the other. The question was not settled until in the second quarter of the nineteenth century. Although the German composers seemed loath to accept the English horn over the oboe da caccia, the French and Italian composers, such as Meyerbeer, Rossini and Berlioz, quickly recognized the superiority of the English horn and admitted it to the ranks of the orchestra. The turning point seemed to be when Rossini gave the English horn a good part in his "William Tell" opera score in 1829, and when Meyerbeer called for it in his score of "Robert le Diable" in 1831. Today all double-reed alto parts are played by the English horn, and the oboe da caccia is known only as an interesting antique.

It is entirely possible that this battle of a century was as much a matter of names as of relative merit, and possibly the English horn as we know it was actually used when it is referred to as the oboe da caccia. Possibly the state of affairs between these two alto oboes was similar to that which exists today between the two brass sopranos, the cornet and trumpet. Trumpet parts in the orchestra are often played by the cornet, and cornet parts in the band are often played by the trumpet. At least we do know that the English horn has been the most unfortunate of all instruments in the matter of names. How it ever managed to come down to posterity with the name of English horn is still considerable of a mystery. As has been pointed out many times, it is neither English in origin nor horn in nature. Some authorities say it took its name from the fact that it resembled in tone quality an old English instrument called the hornpipe. The instrument is also known by the name "cor anglais," which is French for "English horn." Some say this name was given to distinguish it from the French horn, which was called merely "cor" by the French; one instrument was looked upon as a horn of English descent, while the other was looked upon as a horn of French descent. The point is not justified, for the "cor anglais" is not a horn at all. In its early form, the English horn was bent on an angle so the player could reach the lower keys. This fact has led to another explanation of "cor anglais," this explanation arising from the resemblance in the French language of the words angle and English; persons holding to this explanation think of the name as meaning angle horn and not English horn. But all of this controversy is really unimportant in the final analysis, for regardless of what name it goes by, it will sound just as sad and melancholy.

The middle voices of the double-reed family seemed to have had the greatest difficulty justifying their existence, and they finally failed entirely. There are some early instances of the use of a baritone oboe in C, an octave below the soprano oboe, and Richard Strauss tried over a hundred years later to revive this instrument but without success. In its revived state it was called a heckelphone, after the famous instrument maker Heckel, whom Strauss induced to build it. There was also another early baritone sometimes called the bassoon quinte in E♭. This instrument seemed to be pitched a whole tone below the oboe da caccia. It was often classified as a small bassoon rather than a large oboe, for it is described sometimes as a bassoon raised in pitch. Haydn scored for such an instrument in his "Stabat Mater." This instrument managed to survive until the time of Berlioz and seems to be the instrument Berlioz had in mind when he referred to the bassoon quinte in his *Modern Instrumentation and Orchestration*, published in 1848. He reported at this time that it was not a common instrument but was found only occasionally. He added, however, that it should be used more than it was, because it had more power than the English horn in its lower range and would be beneficial in the military band. Apparently this bit of advice went unheeded, for little is heard of the bassoon quinte after Berlioz.

The bassoon in C, which plays two octaves below the oboe in C, won an accepted place in the orchestra about the same time as the oboe. There seemed from the first a need for such a bass voice, and there were no other important contenders. Although Afranio, a Catholic priest of Ferrara, is often said to be the inventor of the bassoon, all he actually did was to give the bassoon its modern shape by doubling the tube back upon itself, his invention being used first on a form of bagpipe. It is this shape, resembling somewhat a bundle of sticks or fagots, which gave to the bassoon the name "fagott" in German and "fagotto" in Italian. In 1550, Schnitzer of Nuremberg, a celebrated instrument maker of his day, is reported to have made some exceptionally fine bassoons, and from this time on down to the present the bassoon in C has held the bass position in the double-reed family. The double bassoon in C, an octave below the bassoon, was created later, and even as early as Bach and Handel its place in the orchestra was accepted.

After this long sifting process of three or four hundred years, four double-reeds have been found to be all that are needed in the orchestra and band: the soprano oboe in C; the alto English horn in F, a fifth below; the bass bassoon in C, two octaves below the oboe; and the contrabass bassoon in C, an octave below the bassoon. Out of all the shawms which were brought by the Crusaders from the Orient across the Mediterranean Sea and overland through Constantinople, and out of all the offshoots from the shawms as implanted in Europe, only these four have found a place in the orchestra and band of the present time. It has been a case of the survival of the fittest: the useful instruments have won for themselves musical immortality, while those less useful have dropped into oblivion.

Confining our attention to these four survivors and forgetting the civil war among the double-reeds for a place in the orchestra, it is interesting to trace the development of the modern double-reed choir from their first entrance into the orchestra until the present day. It seems that the oboe first attained a place of importance in music in the military and open-air bands. Both the English and the French bands seem to have adopted them in the fifteenth and sixteenth centuries, and although Lully was one of the first composers to use the oboe in the orchestra, he used the oboe extensively in the military band before he decided he could use it in the orchestra. The oboes of the time were not the sweet-toned instruments with which we are familiar, and no doubt composers were more than justified in their doubts about admitting them to the orchestra. They have been described as coarse and raucous in tone. The reed used was wider and thicker than that used today, and the sound produced was rough and strident. No more reliable testimony to this fact need be cited than that it was an almost universal practice to muffle the oboe by stuffing the bell full of wool cotton. The oboe was not common in the orchestra until some time after the middle of the seventeenth century. For about a hundred years following this, however, oboes were very popular, being used more than flutes and rivaling the trumpets in favor.

There is some dispute about who was the first composer who saw enough musical possibilities in the shawm to admit it to the orchestra. The honors seem to go to Balthasarini, for he used oboes in his "Ballet Comique de la Reine," performed in Paris in 1581. Ninety years later Cambert used both the oboe and the bassoon in the orchestra for his pastoral play "Pomone," and about the same time, or before, Lully was using both the oboe and the bassoon freely in his opera scores. Besides these two Frenchmen, there were two Italians, Scarlatti and Legrenzi, who about the same time had found the oboe and bassoon useful in their opera orchestras for giving greater volume and for very simple color effects. The former considered the oboe the principal wind instrument, and he used the bassoon to strengthen the string basses, but it was seldom heard alone.

Bach was the first composer to use all three voices of the double-reeds—the soprano oboe, the alto English horn and the bass bassoon. This he did in his "Passion Music," composed in 1723. It must be admitted, though, that his English horn was an early form of double-reed known to Bach as the oboe da caccia, the English horn not having been invented until 1760, by Ferlandis of Bergamo, as pointed out above. Bach wrote some beautiful music for the double-reeds and especially for the oboe. In his second "Brandenburg Concerto" the oboe holds a place in the quartet equal to that taken by the violin, flute and trumpet. It is amazing, especially in the second movement, how much music can be obtained from the three weakest voices in the orchestra—the oboe, flute and violin.

Handel, Bach's great contemporary, was not content to use two oboes and one or two bassoons, as did Bach and as was customary; he was particularly fond of oboes and used them as freely as he did violins. In fact Handel often marked parts in his scores to be played "either by violins or oboes." Sometimes he had oboes doubling violins. It is difficult to imagine the effect as pleasing, unless the oboes he used were very weak. Bassoons were also used in greater numbers than they are today. Because Handel seemed to love the oboe and bassoon so much, it was entirely fitting that when the hundredth anniversary of his birth was observed in 1785, the commemoration orchestra used twenty-six oboes, twenty-six bassoons and a double-bassoon against forty-eight first violins and forty-seven second violins. The use of the double-bassoon was appropriate also, for Handel was the first to introduce this instrument to the orchestra, in some anthems he wrote especially for the coronation of King George II of

DERIVATIVES OF THE OBOE

(1) English horn in F, invented in 1760 by Ferlandis of Bergamo.
(2) The bassoon whose characteristic shape was invented by
Afranio of Ferrara in 1540. (3) Contrabass sarrusophone in E♭,
invented in 1856 by the French bandmaster Sarrus.

England, in 1727. Handel was not alone in his use of a high proportion of double-reeds, for the Electorate Orchestra of Dresden in 1750 was comprised of five oboes and five bassoons against six other woodwinds and twenty-five string instruments. The extravagant use of the oboe did not last, however, and the use of two oboes and two bassoons came to be general.

Joseph Haydn used two oboes in his First Symphony in 1795, and in his Symphony in D, written in London in the same year, he used two oboes and two bassoons, as well as a double-bassoon. Two of Mozart's three greatest symphonies —the Eb Major, the G Minor, and the "Jupiter," all written in 1788—use two oboes, and all three use two bassoons. Beethoven used substantially the same orchestra as that of Mozart. Although later composers made some changes in the orchestra, the use of the oboe and bassoon remained practically the same. Mozart and Beethoven, for some unknown reason, did not use the English horn in the symphony orchestra, and its more common use after their time is one important gain made by the double-reeds.

When clarinets were introduced to the orchestra, some composers seemed to look upon them as a new kind of woodwind which would take the place of the oboes. When clarinets were used, oboes were usually dropped. An example of this form of writing is seen in Mozart's early Symphony in Eb. Sometimes clarinets were used to reinforce the oboes, but the prestige of the long-established oboe is seen in the fact that when both forms of woodwinds were played together, the oboe always had the more prominent part. After 1800 the natures of these two woodwinds were better understood, and composers came to take the view held today, that they were both needed in the orchestra because of their different natures and different tonal colorings.

Nobody seems to know for sure when the first key was added to the oboe, or by whom. After keys were added to the flute with such success in the beginning of the eighteenth century, makers of the oboe seemed to take their cues and added keys to the oboe. The two-keyed oboe was standard practically throughout the eighteenth century, although it is claimed Hofman of Rastenburg added keys for G# and Bb in 1727, and there are some reports of a low C# key. The conventional two-keyed oboe had keys for playing low C and D#, while additional chromatic notes could be obtained by an ingenious arrangement of double holes. These holes were very small and were placed close together. When both holes were covered, the diatonic note of the scale would sound; but when only one hole was covered, the chromatic note of the scale, a half-tone higher, would sound. Before the close of the century Delusse of Paris had concerned himself with the bore of the oboe and had changed it, improving the accuracy of the notes in its scale and the ease of its response. In 1800 five-key oboes were not uncommon, and after this keys were added rapidly, as in the case of the flute, makers seeming to think that if a few keys helped the instrument, a lot would make it nearly perfect. Before 1850 some oboes had as many as fourteen keys, including the octave key. At first the oboe descended to C only, but later the range was lowered to B♮ and sometimes to Bb. Berlioz mentions the oboe in Bb, in his famous treatise on instrumentation published in 1848, and in Mendelssohn's "Midsummer Night's Dream," composed in 1832, the score calls for an oboe which descends to Bb.

Barrett, a well-known oboe player of the day, and Triebert, oboist and woodwind maker of Paris, collaborated in developing the modern oboe mechanism. Although their work was done at the same time during which the Boehm flute was being developed, the key mechanism Barrett and Triebert produced was original and different. Incidentally, a genuine Boehm-system oboe was constructed about 1850, but it was a complete failure. Some have held that the systems are the same because the oboe system uses some Boehm ring keys, but the key system created by Barrett and Triebert is developed along different lines from that of the Boehm flute system. Their system is characterized by a great many alternate fingerings of various notes—in some cases as many as three or four—which feature makes a number of otherwise awkward intervals much easier to play. They also introduced the double automatic octave key and in other less important points brought the oboe to a high state of development. In the latter part of the nineteenth century the wide, heavy reed which had always been found on the shawms gave way to the thinner, narrower reed, changing the tone from a rather coarse quality to a thinner but more pleasing quality. The Germans still use a wider reed than the French, but it is narrower than the reed found on the old shawms.

The key system used almost universally today is the Conservatory system, so called because of its connection with the Paris Conservatory. Important improvements were made to the Barrett and Triebert mechanism by Gillet, who was considered the greatest oboist of all times. He was professor at the Paris Conservatory for many years, and his great ability on the oboe called for changes in the mechanism to facilitate his playing. During his regime the oboe was brought to a high state of perfection, and few important changes have since been made to the oboe he was instrumental in developing.

As is true of all the woodwinds, the bassoon was used for centuries with finger holes only. Some of these holes were plugged shut with pegs and were opened or left plugged shut, depending upon the key of the music. When makers started adding keys to the other woodwind instruments about 1700, the bassoon was not excepted. By the middle of the eighteenth century the bassoon commonly had four keys—low B♭, D, F and G♯. All of these were down on the lower part of the instrument and were used for getting some chromatic intervals in the bottom of the scale. Before the close of the century, four more keys were added, making eight, only one of these being on the upper or "wing" joint, while three were on the boot joint, three on the butt or long joint, and one— the octave key—was on the bocal or mouthpipe. Karl Almenräder, of Cologne, famous player and maker of bas‧ soons during the first half of the nineteenth century, retuned various holes, added certain notes in the top of the scale and improved the response and quality of tone. Triebert, who helped develop the oboe key system, also worked on the bassoon, as did Triebert's brother. By the middle of the century it was possible to play a chromatic scale from low B♭ upward three and a half octaves to F. The key mechanism consisted of from twelve to sixteen keys, and there were six finger holes and two thumb holes besides, not operated by keys. Today the modern bassoon has from twenty to twenty-two regular keys, besides several miscellaneous special trill keys.

Afranio of Ferrara gave to the bassoon its bundle-of-sticks appearance by doubling it back once upon itself, and this shape has survived for four hundred years. The first double-bassoons were made like the bassoon, but when doubled back on itself only once, the instrument was very long and awkward to handle. Therefore, most double-bassoons are doubled back twice; that is, instead of there being only two sticks in the bundle, as in the bassoon, there are four sticks in the bundle. Occasionally a double-bassoon of the old type is used in the orchestra, and it is odd to see the long bell of the instrument sticking up high above the player like a giant bedpost.

Practically all the important composers since Bach and Handel have given a place of importance to the oboe and bassoon. They call upon the oboe usually to intone passages expressing contentment, and wherever a pastoral or oriental theme is introduced it is almost invariably given to the oboe. The oboe is adapted to extremely legato playing but can also play staccato. Some of the more modern composers have called upon the oboe to play rapid arpeggios and octave skips, and some gifted oboe players have written for themselves brilliant solos in which the oboe is blithe and gay. The majority of composers, however, are content to write for the oboe only slow cantabile and sustained-note passages.

The oboe cannot be played for a long period at one time, because such a tiny amount of air can be forced between the thin lips of the double-reed that playing the oboe is like holding the breath. The composer recognizes this and is careful to allow a few bars of rest in the music every so often so the oboist can get his breath. Bach sometimes failed to observe this restriction and wrote solo passages for the oboe which are almost impossible to play. Schumann, who understood the piano much better than he ever understood the instruments of the orchestra, completely forgot the plight of the poor oboe player, and in the second of his three romances for the oboe he wrote a passage of eighty-four bars without a rest!

Mr Byrne of the Detroit Symphony believes, however, that too much emphasis is placed on the breathing difficulties in playing the oboe. Modern instruments and training in correct breathing have eliminated much of this trouble, so that the oboist today can rival the clarinetist and flutist in playing extended passages. Oboists take a tip from the oriental snake charmer who can play the "Musette," a short double-reed instrument of primitive design, for long periods at a time. The secret of his ability is that he breathes through his nose while playing, and the modern oboist does likewise.

In the orchestra the oboist often is the highest-paid player of them all. One reason for this is that good oboe players are scarce, but another reason is that the oboist has an extremely hard job. His instrument is one of the most delicate and sensitive, both in the key mechanism and in the response of the vibrating column of air. The bore of the instrument is considerably smaller than a lead pencil up near the mouthpiece, and consequently attack and control of the tone are difficult. The many alternate fingerings for various notes result in a mechanism which is finely and delicately articulated and likely to go out of adjustment at the slightest rough handling.

Nor do the oboist's troubles end with the mechanism: the making of the reed is not only an important part of playing the oboe but a task which requires considerable skill. It is possible to buy finished reeds for the oboe, but a great many oboists choose to make their own. They start with the seasoned cane and patiently cut, shape and shave the cane until it has just the right thickness and taper. Then they tie it to a small piece of metal pipe which fits over the mouthpipe, or bocal, of the oboe. The two pieces of cane must have just the thickness and shape required and must be matched for resiliency so they will work together properly in producing the capricious tone of the oboe.

There is a rather widespread superstition that playing the oboe will make the performer go crazy. Although there is no basis in fact for this belief, it seems a wonder sometimes that so many difficulties with which the oboist is faced do not sometimes drive him out of his mind.

The pitch of the oboe is more difficult to change than that of the brass instruments, with their tuning slides, or the string instruments, whose strings can be tautened or loosened. For this reason Handel established the practice of having the orchestra tune with the oboe. Since it was so difficult to change the pitch of the oboe, it was easier to have all the other instruments tune to it. This custom has survived until today. If Handel had had clarinets in his orchestra, he might have elected them to set the pitch for the other instruments, for they are also difficult to put in pitch.

The oboe is a small instrument, and its tone seems small in comparison with that of a trumpet or trombone, but it has such a peculiar timbre that two oboes can hold their own in a great orchestra. Even in the wind band, two or three oboes will stand out definitely above the great power of the brass and the other woodwinds.

In the orchestra one of the oboists usually doubles on the English horn. This instrument is in general respects just like the oboe except that it is about 50 per cent larger. In the band one of the oboists also doubles on the English horn, and when the band marches, all the oboists double on drums or saxophones or some other instrument. The reason the oboist cannot play in the marching band is that the embouchure, or control of the reeds by the lips, is so delicate it cannot be done while walking.

The bassoon is even more peculiar than the oboe and English horn. The very names which refer to the various parts are ludicrous. The mouthpipe is called the bocal, as on the oboe, while the first joint is called the wing joint, the end opposite from the mouthpipe is called the boot, and the next joint is called the butt. The inside of the boot is lined with rubber, so the bassoon can be said to wear a rubber boot—on the inside! To assist the player in holding the instrument, it is equipped with a "crutch" for the thumb. Several of the holes controlled by the fingers are bored, not straight into the body of the instrument, but on a slant. This may seem peculiar, but it is done to bring the top of the hole nearer the finger. The bottom of the hole determines the pitch of the note, and the top of the hole is placed near the finger for convenience. Even then, the fingers of smaller hands must be spread uncomfortably to reach some of the holes.

The composers Beethoven and Mendelssohn seemed to understand the bassoon best. This instrument was a favorite with Beethoven, and he wrote some beautiful passages for it. Consciously or unconsciously, though, both of these great composers cast it in such roles that ever since it has been known as the "clown" of the orchestra. Beethoven in his "Pastoral" symphony used it to depict the gyrations of an inebriated musician in the village band, and Mendelssohn wrote a march for two bassoons which describes the antics of two clowns. Other composers have obtained laughable and grotesque effects by compelling the large and clumsy bassoon to do little dances and capers which would be more becoming to the smaller oboe or flute.

This is not to imply that the bassoon does not have its serious and impressive moments. When playing music fitted to its nature, it is truly a great and beautiful instrument. In its lower register it is solemn and grave and foreboding, as in the fourth movement of Berlioz' "Symphonie Fantastique." In its middle register it is weird and sepulchral in character, as in the Meyerbeer's "Robert le Diable," where is described the resurrection of the nuns. Its highest notes are dramatic, penetrating and not unlike a "human cry of agony." Its range of three and a half octaves is unusual for a wind instrument, and within this wide range is such a variety of colorings that the bassoon has come to be a most valuable instrument.

Some compositions use the bassoon only as a harmony instrument, but even in such passages the instrument adds touches of color which would be greatly missed. It must have been a passage of this kind around which an amusing anecdote about Hans von Bülow centers. It is related that the famous conductor was rehearsing his orchestra when he noted some visitors in the auditorium, much to his annoyance. Rather than order them out, he used a little piece of strategy. He turned to the orchestra and said, "Gentlemen, we'll now rehearse the bassoons." He then began solemnly to direct thirty-two measures of rests, after which the bassoons gave a couple of grunts and lapsed into silence. Von Bülow continued to beat out sixty-four more measures of rests with the same precision as if the whole orchestra had been playing. When he came to the end he looked around—but his uninvited guests had long ago slunk out!

Although the bassoon is quite an old instrument, its key mechanism is surprisingly undeveloped. Apparently players will put up with crude and clumsy keys on the bassoon which they will not tolerate on other woodwinds. There can hardly be said to be a key system on the bassoon; it is a sort of miscellaneous collection of keys of one kind and another. The French system for the bassoon is less developed than the German, or Heckel, system, and the latter system is becoming almost universal in the United States. Berlioz dropped a hint about the bassoon which unfortunately has not been acted upon. After seeing what the Boehm system had done for the flute and clarinet, and to a less degree for the oboe, he wrote that, of all instruments, the bassoon would benefit most by adopting the Boehm ring-key system. Frederic Triebert, brother of the oboe maker, actually constructed some bassoons after the Boehm system, but they were not successful. Possibly someday another courageous manufacturer will try it again.

The early oboes, bassoons and English horns were mostly made of yellow boxwood and had a few brass keys. As more and more keys were added, the key hinges became longer and longer. This development spelled the doom of boxwood, for while it is hard and close-grained, it has the one weakness of warping. When short, single keys were all that were used on the body, it did not matter if the body warped a little. But when the hinges became long, a slight warping caused the long hinges to bind and stop working. Sometimes cocuswood was substituted, but grenadilla wood finally became the most universally used and is the best material for fine oboes and English horns today. Occasionally these instruments are made of ebonite, or vulcanized rubber. So far, no one has been successful in making an oboe or English horn out of metal. German bassoons are usually made of curly maple, stained a beautiful, rich red, while French bassoons are usually made of rosewood. English bassoons are made of both woods. The keys are no longer brass on any of these instruments but nickel silver or silver-plated.

Berlioz laments the fact that the bassoon quinte was not more used in the military bands, because he says it had more power than the English horn, whose place in the band it could have taken to good advantage. This same form of reasoning must have prompted Sarrus, a French bandmaster, to invent the sarrusophone in 1856. This instrument is made of metal but shows its family resemblance to the oboe, English horn and bassoons by its double-reed mouthpiece. It has a shape similar to that of the bassoon, but its fingering system is a sort of cross between that of the saxophone and the French-system bassoon. An instrument more nearly approximating a metal bassoon was made by Stehle of Vienna in 1835. This was a contrabassoon made of brass, which was later improved by Cerveny of Königgrätz and Mabillon of Brussels. Sarrus, however, is credited with this family of brass double-reeds because he was first to produce the complete family.

In inventing the sarrusophone, Sarrus evidently hoped to combine the characteristic double-reed tonal quality with the greater power of the brass, but while he did succeed in producing an instrument with greater power, it is generally conceded that he was not able to preserve the beautiful quality of tone of the wood double-reeds. Originally there were six members of the sarrusophone family: the soprano in B♭, the alto in E♭, the tenor in B♭, the baritone in E♭, the bass in B♭, and the contrabass in E♭, giving a combined tonal compass of over five octaves. Although several members of this family are still used in parts of Europe, the only one found to any great extent in America is the contrabass in E♭. This instrument is used chiefly in the concert band as a substitute for the bassoon, especially in open-air concerts, and is gradually growing in popularity.

CHAPTER VI

The Single-Reeds

THE UGLY DUCKLINGS

UNLIKE THE FLUTE AND OBOE, the clarinet cannot trace its ancestry back to the beginning of civilization. Apparently the genius of Mesopotamia and Egypt was not sufficient to create the ancient chalumeau, father of the clarinet, and it remained for the greater genius of the Greeks to bring it forth. It is true that the natives of the Nile today play the primitive chalumeau, and this type of instrument is also found in Palestine and other spots in the East, but these instances no doubt show a spreading of Greek culture to these spots rather than the existence of the chalumeau in ancient times. After the chalumeau appeared in Greece, we find it in Persia and India. Chalumeaux also were found in the British Isles at an early date among the inhabitants of Cornwall, Wales and Ireland, this little instrument being called the pibcorn, or pipehorn.

The chalumeau apparently was never a popular instrument, and the clarinet into which it developed was one of the latecomers into the orchestra. The late discovery of the single-reed and its slow development into a great musical instrument were due to two main reasons. In the first place, the making of the single-reed is rather more complicated than the making of the flute blowhole or the double-reed of the oboe. The primitive chalumeau mouthpiece is made from a short length of cane cut at the septum so one end is closed. Back about two inches from the closed end a deep gash is cut, and a sliver of cane is partially split away from the body of the tube. The septum keeps this sliver from splitting away entirely from the body, and at the place where the split stops the sliver is thinned. This produces a little tongue of reed attached to the cane tube by a piece of thinned and resilient cane and constitutes the mouthpiece of the chalumeau. If the description of its making seems complicated, the actual job of making the mouthpiece is just as complicated as it sounds and requires considerable skill.

This mouthpiece is inserted in one end of a longer tube of cane, open at both ends and pierced by finger holes along its length. The instrument is played by putting the mouthpiece inside the mouth until the lips close over the short length of tube beyond the sliver. This swallowing act is one of the peculiar parts of playing the chalumeau, noted with particular interest by those who see the natives of Eastern countries playing these primitive instruments for the first time. The mouthpiece is thus enclosed in the oral cavity, which acts as a sort of wind box whose only outlet is through the slit in the side of the cane tube, out through the open end into the body of the instrument. If working just right, the sliver of cane vibrates as the air escapes, and produces the chalumeau sound.

This sliver of cane really opens and shuts as the air escapes, and therefore transmits pulsations of air into the body of the

instrument. The sliver of cane is sprung away from the body
when the cut is made, and the thinning process enables the
tongue of cane to move back and forth more easily. When
pressure of air is increased in the mouth, the sliver of cane is
forced down against the body of the tube, shutting off the
flow of air; but the resilience of the cane overcomes the air
pressure and causes the sliver to pull away from the body
and to open up the hole. This fluttering of the reed goes on
very rapidly and creates the air pulsations which strike the
ear and are translated by the brain into sound. The pitch of
the note is governed by the rate of these vibrations, which in
turn is governed by the size of the sliver of cane, the thickness
of the thinned part, and the size and length of the tube which
constitutes the body of the instrument.

The second reason for the delayed appearance of the
chalumeau in the orchestra is that it has acoustical principles
which are different from all other wind instruments. When
a single-beating reed produces vibrations in a cylindrical
body, we have what the science of sound calls a "closed"
pipe. All other instruments, such as the flute, oboe, trumpet,
etc., are of the "open" pipe variety. Why this is so will be
explained in the closing chapter of this book. Here it is
needful to know only enough to understand why the clarinet
was slow in developing. On all open-pipe instruments it is
easy to obtain two octaves of diatonic scale. It is done simply
and in the following manner: all the holes are covered to
sound the lowest, or fundamental, note, and as each lowest
hole is uncovered, the diatonic scale is played in ascending
order, as described more in detail in the story of the flute.
The scale thus ascends: C, D, E, F, G, A and B—all played
with about the same blowing pressure. When the player is

ready to play top C, all the holes are again covered, and by increasing the blowing pressure and lip pressure the instrument is "overblown" to the octave C. Then, by uncovering each lowest hole and continuing to overblow, the D, E, F, etc., of the higher octave can be played. This is easy to do and accounts for the wide popularity of open-pipe instruments.

Now the chalumeau cannot be played in this way, because it cannot be "overblown" at the octave. No doubt this greatly puzzled all primitive musicians and prevented them from using the chalumeau as freely as they did the flute and shawm. They would start in and uncover each lowest hole in turn and play up to B. Here they would try to overblow to the octave, but it would not come. The only way for them to continue playing on up in the higher octave was to open holes nearer the mouthpiece. But there were only eight fingers, and that was not enough to carry the scale on up. This short and incomplete scale no doubt was in a large measure the cause of the disrepute in which the chalumeau was held for so many years and accounts for the long delay in its acceptance in the orchestra.

Chalumeaux were found in Europe in the thirteenth, fourteenth and fifteenth centuries, but they did not attain any popularity until the sixteenth century. Even then they did not have the popularity of the flute and shawm. The early composers didn't seem to know anything about them, or else they were not interested in them as musical instruments. There is a great deal of confusion on this question, due to the lack of definite terms for various instruments. The terms shawm, flute and chalumeau were used carelessly to refer indiscriminately to one or all of these different instruments,

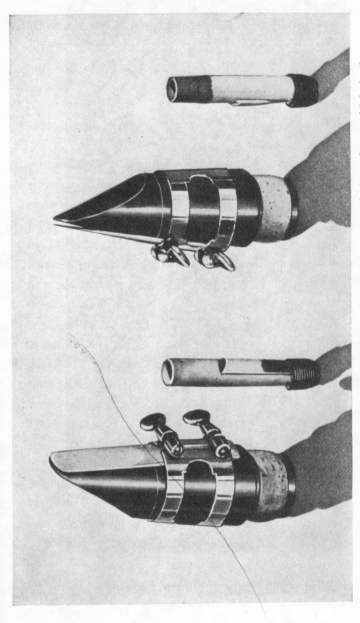

The clarinet mouthpiece and the primitive chalumeau mouthpiece from which it developed. Both have the single-beating reed. On the clarinet the reed is still made of cane, as it has been for centuries.

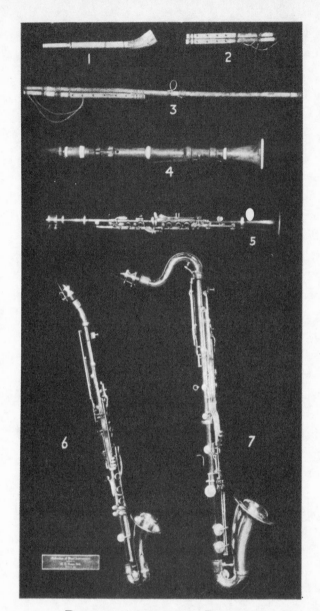

DEVELOPMENT OF THE CLARINET

(1) Razhok, primitive chalumeau from Russia. (2) Zooma'rah, primitive chalumeau from Egypt. (3) Urgun, primitive Syrian chalumeau. (4) Boxwood clarinet with five brass keys, used about 1800. (5) Modern Boehm-system soprano clarinet. (6) Modern Boehm-system alto clarinet in E♭. (7) Modern Boehm-system bass clarinet in B♭.

but those who have taken great pains to distinguish among these three types of instruments sustain the view that the single-reed chalumeau was a neglected instrument. The early Italian opera composers did not use the chalumeau in any of their compositions, although there were instruments of all kinds and descriptions in these loosely thrown together ensembles. Monteverde, who composed his famous "Orfeo" opera in 1608 and who continued to write until nearly the middle of the century, experimenting with all kinds of instruments and playing them in manners not thought of before, never once used the chalumeau. Another adventuresome composer was the Frenchman Lully. He tried a number of innovations, but he never used the chalumeau. Bach is noted for his curiosity about all kinds of instruments, and there are few instruments which he did not at one time or other give a trial. He even invented new instruments, apparently feeling the need of additional voices and colorings. But he never once used the chalumeau.

Handel, Bach's great contemporary, is said to have experimented with the chalumeau, although we do not have any of his original scores to prove it. Some authorities say there is in existence an incomplete overture in which two clarinets are used, but this is doubtful. Possibly the impression that Handel wrote for the chalumeau was due to the presence of clarinet parts in scores of the "Messiah," but these were added forty years later by Mozart. Other clarinet parts in some of Handel's other compositions were put there by Mozart, who could not endure the high clarion parts and rewrote them for clarinet. Mendelssohn performed the same service for Bach, changing high trumpet parts to clarinet parts, as in Bach's Suite No. 3 in D Major. Rameau is also said to have used the chalumeau in his pastoral play "Acante et Céphise," staged in Paris in 1751, but it is most likely that the so-called chalumeau parts were written for the clarion and not for the chalumeau, for it has been pointed out that not a note is in these parts which cannot be played on the clarion of the time. Here, again, it would seem as if the parts for chalumeau, as found in the scores, were originally clarion parts which were later played by the chalumeau. An even less well-established contention is the statement that Rameau used the chalumeau in "Zoroastre" in 1749. Neither the score as published that year nor the 1756 score contains any parts for the chalumeau, and we may conclude that none was written.

To be entirely ignored by such composers as Monteverde, Lully, Bach and Handel is almost enough to raise the question as to the very existence of the chalumeau. These men were noted for their willingness to try any instrument. No instrument, apparently, was too primitive and crude to be given a trial. They wrote for all kinds of lutes, organs, guitars, viols and other instruments now obsolete. They even wrote for the cornetto and the serpent, instruments which we know were very badly out of tune and very poor in tone quality. But they did not think sufficiently well of the chalumeau to write a note of music for it. This makes the chalumeau the ugly duckling of the wind-instrument family.

There were at least two men at this time who had faith in the chalumeau, and the fact that they actually wrote parts for it proves its existence. These two men were the German composer Keiser, who called for the chalumeau in his opera "Croesus," and the Italian composer Bononcini, who wrote parts for the chalumeau in his opera "Turno Aricino." It is a coincidence that both of these men wrote their history-making parts in 1710. The ugly duckling obtained definite recognition, and although for nearly one hundred years it was to take a place in the orchestra subordinate to that of the flute and oboe, eventually it was to share equal honors in the orchestra with these two instruments and to rise above them to become the most important woodwind in the concert band.

Johann Christoph Denner, instrument maker of Nuremberg, is usually given the credit for the invention of the clarinet in 1690. Although his invention consisted of little more than an improvement on the old chalumeau, he no less deserves the honor for which he is noted. Denner was a maker of flutes, oboes and bassoons and was a skillful and resourceful man. He took up the old riddle of the chalumeau and tried to find out why it would not "overblow" to the octave as did the flute, oboe and bassoon. He figured that if he could find out how to extend the compass of the instrument upward he could make it a valuable instrument. It had a tone quality which was different from that of either the flute or oboe, a tone quality which was equally as beautiful in its own way. He no doubt felt it was a shame to ignore an instrument with such possibilities.

Denner soon determined that this instrument did not overblow to the octave but to the twelfth; that is, when all the finger holes were closed and the lowest note, or the fundamental, was sounded, the next note to be obtained by increasing the blowing pressure and lip pressure was the twelfth note above instead of the eighth. He also discovered that this note came a lot easier if he bored a little hole up toward the mouthpiece. When this "speaker" hole was opened, the twelfth was overblown with greater ease. He no doubt was elated with this discovery, for it opened up to him some of the secrets of the chalumeau. But he was immediately beset with other practical problems. He could see that the overblown twelfth note would give him an increased range in the top of the instrument, but he did not see how he could bridge the gap in the scale between this top series of notes and the top of the then-known scale. This was a sticker.

After much experimenting he finally built a chalumeau which had a scale of one octave from G below the treble clef to G in the clef, to which he added notes at the bottom and at the top in an ingenious way. This octave G to G was played by covering and uncovering eight finger holes, just as if the instrument were an open-pipe instrument like the flute or oboe. Below the G was the bell note F, played with all fingers down. This gave Denner a series of nine notes, from F to G, but he still had a gap between his top G and the C obtained by overblowing. How could he connect his scale of nine notes with the new series of upper notes beginning with the overblown C? In the top of the scale above the eight finger holes Denner added two keys which were sprung shut over two holes drilled opposite each other. Apparently one of these keys was operated by the first finger of the left hand and the other on the back side by the thumb. When one key was opened, A was obtained, and when both were opened together, B was sounded. This gave Denner eleven notes, but the top key, or B key, gave him something else. This key also acted as a "speaker" key, and when it was opened (all other holes being closed), C and a whole series of notes above could be played with some of the same fingerings as those used on the notes in the lower series. Thus the baffling gap in the scale of this closed-pipe instrument was bridged, giving a scale from F below the treble clef to C in the treble clef and several notes higher, possibly to F in the top line, treble clef, or two complete octaves.

Drawing showing how Denner solved the problem of the chalumeau scale. Nine notes, from F below the staff to G in the staff, were played by eight finger holes and the "bell" note F. Notes from C in the staff upward were based on the overblown twelfth, or C, the individual notes being played by the finger holes. The stroke of genius was in obtaining A and B in the staff. These two notes he obtained by two keys covering holes located opposite each other. By opening one he obtained A; by opening both he obtained B. The B key also served as a "speaker" key to assist in overblowing to the twelfth.

Later J. Denner, no doubt a son of J. C., lengthened the clarinet and added a key at the bottom of the chalumeau for obtaining low F, low E coming from the bell with all holes closed. This made the first series of notes from E below the treble clef to B♭ in the staff, with the second series of notes beginning on B♮. This was the famous three-keyed chalumeau known during the first half of the eighteenth century. The next two keys added were those for low F♯ and G♯. Credit for these two keys is usually given to Barthold Fritz of Brunswick, and since it is known he died in 1766, these keys were in existence sometime before this date. This chalumeau with five keys is no doubt the instrument with which Haydn, Mozart and Beethoven were familiar.

It is not known when the chalumeaux first were called clarinets. This has led to considerable confusion. One instance concerns the exact time when composers ceased to write for the chalumeau and began writing for the clarinet. The sane way to look at this question is to allow for some confusion in names which naturally would exist during such a transition. Some people hold that immediately after Denner made his improvements to the chalumeau, this instrument became known as the clarinet. When they see clarinet parts in a score written after 1690, they immediately conclude that the composer had in mind the clarinet. The parts written in 1710 by Keiser and Bononcini, they say, were for clarinets and not for chalumeaux.

It is more likely that when chalumeaux are indicated in various scores, actually Denner's clarinets were used, for no doubt the chalumeau as improved by Denner was for some time called a chalumeau.

In 1751 or 1752, Haydn wrote his first Mass, and he called for two instruments which we believe to have been chalumeaux, but we are not sure. Men who have made a serious study of this point say that the first undoubted reference to clarinets in musical scores was in 1762, when Thomas Arne scored for clarinets in his "Artaxerxes." A year later Johann Christian Bach, son of the great Johann Sebastian, used a clarinet in his "Orione," performed in London in 1763. Gluck is said to have scored for the chalumeau in 1762, when he wrote his Vienna score of "Orfeo." This chalumeau was said to have had eight finger holes and two holes for the thumbs. When Gluck's Paris score of "Orfeo" was published in 1774, however, clarinets are indicated instead of chalumeaux. The whole question of names is not of importance, since the clarinet after all was only an improved chalumeau and not a different instrument.

The name clarinet was given to the chalumeau because in

tone it resembled somewhat a small clarion; hence clarionette, afterward shortened to clarinet, although the English still spell it "clarionet." The small clarion was high and shrill of voice, and the upper part of the chalumeau scale was likewise high and shrill; this resemblance suggested the word clarinet. Mozart must have helped establish the clarinet name, because he rewrote clarion parts for the clarinet. Handel's music was full of clarion parts, for the clarion was at its height during Handel's time, but Mozart could not endure the shrill voice of the clarion and adapted many of these clarion passages to the clarinet. This direct comparison must have helped in saddling the clarinet name upon the chalumeau, and probably marked the time when the chalumeau became generally known as the clarinet. The word chalumeau, however, has been preserved by naming the lowest register of the clarinet the chalumeau register.

Mozart showed the world how to use the clarinet in the orchestra, although Haydn and Gluck and others had been using clarinets for some time before Mozart. Gluck was not certain of himself in handling this new voice of the orchestra and at first considered it as a kind of substitute for the oboe and flute, or at least only a supplement or reinforcement for them. He hesitated to use the clarinet as a solo instrument as he did the flute and oboe, and confined himself to using it as a harmony instrument. Haydn had two clarinets in his Eisenstadt orchestra from 1776 to 1778, but he did not understand their possibilities until some years later, after Mozart had demonstrated their great resources. Mozart was attracted by the clarinet when only a child, having written a symphony for strings, bassoons and clarinets in 1765 while visiting in London. This fact raises an interesting and plausible conjecture that Mozart's interest in the clarinet was inspired by hearing Arne's "Artaxerxes," performed for the first time in London in 1762, and J. C. Bach's "Orione," performed for the first time in London in 1763. When Mozart visited the great orchestra at Mannheim in 1777, he was already familiar with the clarinet, and if he did not learn anything about its actual use from the Mannheim orchestra, he was to demonstrate eleven years later in his E♭ symphony, composed in 1788, that the clarinet was a musical instrument of the greatest promise. This symphony is often referred to as the clarinet symphony because of the prominence given to the clarinet. In it he even excluded the oboe entirely in favor of the clarinet. This was a common practice for some years, but after 1800 the proper place of both instruments was well determined. Five of Mozart's symphonies contain parts for clarinet, as do the majority of Mozart's operas. Haydn, who taught Mozart many things but learned from Mozart how to write for the clarinet and other woodwinds, included the clarinet in several of his later symphonies and in many of his operas.

Beethoven used the same orchestra in his first symphony, the C Major, in 1800, and in his second symphony, the D Major, in 1803; and this orchestra included two clarinets. In the first of these compositions, however, the clarinet was used as a harmony instrument or to add to the volume in tutti passages, all the important solo passages being given to the flute and oboe. In the second composition, Beethoven used the clarinet with the bassoon but showed he had not yet become acquainted with the resources of the instrument. In his famous "Eroica" symphony, written in 1804, the clarinet came into its own, being used to state important themes and to take solo parts, just as the long-established flute and oboe. From this time on, Beethoven wrote hardly anything in which he did not give the clarinet an important role. He was partial to the upper register and seemed to avoid the lowest, or chalumeau, register. Mendelssohn, on the other hand, seemed to avoid the upper register and was partial to the chalumeau register. Good examples of this type of writing are seen in the opening notes of "Elijah" and in the introduction to his "Scotch" symphony. Schubert used the clarinet often and was evidently fond of it. The same was true of Schumann. Weber shows an unusually keen knowledge of the resources of the clarinet, in the supernatural music of "Der Freischutz" and in several of his concertos with orchestra. Critics say nothing finer has ever been written for clarinet than these early concertos, some of them composed as early as 1811. After the first quarter of the nineteenth century the place of the clarinet was clearly understood and firmly established.

Although the great German composers wrote mostly for the three-key and five-key clarinets, there were developments going on in France which were destined to give the clarinet chromatic resources of which these great old masters scarcely dreamed. Some of these inventions happened during the lifetime of Haydn and Beethoven, but news did not travel fast in those days, and inventions were only slowly adopted. Keys were added from time to time until in 1810 Ivan Muller, great clarinet virtuoso of Paris, brought out his celebrated thirteen-key wonder. The technical resources of the instrument were increased by the more elaborate mechanism. Notable among the various keys contributed by Muller were the key for covering the F-C hole, and several trill keys.

The tone holes were also relocated, and the number increased to twenty-two. Although this feature improved the accuracy in the scale, it harmed the tone quality, for it is a well-established fact that the more holes there are in the body of the instrument, the poorer the resonance and tone quality.

Apparently other inventors recognized this principle, for after this thirteen-key model of Muller's, other inventors came out with improved models having fewer keys. All of these so-called improved models used the basic Muller system. Among such clarinets were the Gassner five-key model of 1849, the Kastner six-key and nine-key clarinets of 1848, and the Von Gontershausen thirteen-key model of 1855. This basic system survived for many years and is still found on clarinets used in some military bands. It made its last stand in the Albert system clarinet but is rapidly being supplanted by a superior system, known as the Boehm system, invented in 1843 by Klosé.

Klosé had the euphonious name of Hyacinthe Eléonore Klosé, and he was one of the greatest clarinet soloists of his day. Striving always for better performance, he eventually saw that his instrument stood in the way of greater achievement. The twenty-two-hole clarinet of Muller lacked resonance, and even the thirteen keys did not give facility of playing in certain key signatures. Manufacturers of the day did not seem equal to the job of improving the instrument, so Klosé added to his role of clarinet player that of clarinet inventor. He had seen what great improvements the Boehm system had made on the flute, and he had an idea that this system would improve the clarinet. He no doubt found considerable opposition to his ideas, because the Boehm system was created expressly for the flute, which is an open-pipe instrument and overblows to the octave, whereas the clarinet is a closed-pipe instrument and overblows to the twelfth. Wise men said it couldn't be done. They spoke with great decisiveness about the theoretical principles which precluded it. To make a chromatic instrument playable in all keys was difficult enough on an open-pipe instrument; on a closed-pipe instrument it was impossible. There were already twenty-two holes in the Muller clarinet; there would have to be many more holes in the Boehm-system clarinet. There were even some objections to the fourteen holes necessary for the Boehm-system flute because of the harmful effect on tone. To adapt the Boehm system to the clarinet would require many more holes and a mechanism that would be so complicated nobody would be able to play it.

Klosé still believed in his idea, and although he was not a mechanic himself he decided such a clarinet as he had in mind should be built. He finally went to August Buffet, Jr, famous woodwind maker in Paris. Buffet had already gained fame for his inventions on the flute. In 1835 he had invented the needle spring. Later he invented the "clutch" for articulating ring keys together, and the "sleeve" which permitted reverse-acting keys to be mounted on the same axle. Buffet listened to Klosé's ideas and finally built a clarinet. It was a great success, much to the surprise of the know-it-alls who said it couldn't be done. Instead of having more holes than the twenty-two on the Muller thirteen-key clarinet, it had only eighteen holes! The ingenuity of construction is even more remarkable when it is considered that only eighteen holes were required for the twenty-three keys. The clarinet was now playable in all signatures. Many trills before impractical or impossible were now playable with ease. Certain bad spots on the old clarinet, such as bridging registers, were made much easier. Klosé traveled over Europe with his new invention and astonished everybody with the great technical display made possible by the improved mechanism.

The mouthpiece of the clarinet has a story of development all its own. Although it retained the old principle of the single-beating reed found on the original chalumeau, it was refined and made more efficient. As the chalumeau and clarinet entered the orchestra, they were built in different keys. The change of keys was made possible by barrel joints of different lengths. The clarinet was made in five pieces: bell, bottom, top, barrel and mouthpiece. When a player bought a clarinet in those days, it came with two or three barrel joints which were interchangeable and which put the instrument in different keys, but all barrel joints used the same mouthpiece. Some of the mouthpieces on these old clarinets are very crude. They were whittled from a block of wood or were made from two blocks of wood held together by two pieces of metal tacked along the side. They had already assumed the shape of the modern mouthpiece and used a separate reed, which was tied to the mouthpiece with string. About the time Muller brought out his thirteen-key wonder, it became the custom to hold the reed on the mouthpiece with a metal band, or ligature, which could be clamped tightly to the mouthpiece with a screw. The reed was held on top of the mouthpiece and was controlled by the upper lip. In France a new school of players sprang up which advocated the reed on the bottom so it could be controlled better by the lower lip. This style of playing spread to other parts of the Continent and to America, but the old school of playing persisted in Italy and is sometimes called the Italian school to distinguish it from the French school. In America almost all players use the reed on the bottom.

Hardly any other instrument has been made in as many keys as the clarinet, unless it is the French horn. Along about 1800 there were in use as many as twenty different keys of clarinets. Denner started the tendency by making clarinets in both C and high A. Johann Christian Bach called for clarinets in Bb and D. Mozart wrote for clarinets in low A, Bb, B and C. There were also clarinets in high E and F, although they were more important in the band than in the orchestra. As if these were not enough, an instrument maker called Horn, of Passau in Bavaria, invented the basset horn in F, in 1770. Thus was the alto member of the family introduced. It was improved by Lotz of Pressburg in 1782 and also by Ivan Muller in 1812. Mozart was the first to use it, scoring for the instrument in his "Magic Flute" and also in his "Requiem." Beethoven became convinced of its merit and used it with good effect in his "Prometheus" overture. Mendelssohn followed by calling for the basset horn in his "Scotch" symphony. Soon after the middle of the nineteenth century, the old mechanism on the basset horn was supplanted by the Boehm system, the pitch of the instrument was changed to Eb, and it became known as the alto clarinet.

The bass clarinet is generally credited to Heinrich Gresner of Dresden. The date of the invention was 1793, but apparently no composer used the instrument until 1836, when Meyerbeer introduced it in his "Huguenots" opera, in Act V. Dumas, goldsmith to Napoleon, is said to have made a bass clarinet in 1805 and to have presented it to the Paris Conservatory. The bass clarinet used by Meyerbeer was an improved model made by Antoine (Adolphe) Sax. In 1838

Sax brought out a still better model with twenty-two keys, which is praised by Berlioz in his *Modern Instrumentation and Orchestration* for its "perfect precision of intonation, an equalized temperament throughout the chromatic scale, and a greater intensity of tone." These clarinets were made in B♭ and were straight like the soprano, so that the player had to stand up to play them. The bell reached nearly to the floor, with the result that the sound was muffled. Sax remedied this defect by making a concave reflector which was placed directly beneath the bell and which served to deflect the tone upward with greater volume. Later this defect was remedied by curving the instrument into the shape of a letter S. Sax also made double-bass clarinets in E♭ and BB♭. His double-bass clarinet in BB♭ was a failure, though, and it remained for M. Besson to bring out a satisfactory instrument of this kind, in 1891. Although Meyerbeer was the first to use the bass clarinet, Wagner was the first to show what really could be done with the instrument, and since Wagner it has been found in practically all opera music and in most symphonies.

The clarinet family today consists of the B♭ soprano, the E♭ alto and the B♭ bass. In various symphony and opera compositions the A soprano clarinet is called for, and, less often, the C soprano. In military bands the E♭ clarinet is used, but only occasionally is it found in the orchestra, its voice being very shrill. Berlioz once used it in the finale of his "Symphonie Fantastique." While the E♭ and the C sopranos are shrill, the B♭ soprano is brilliant in tone without that piercing quality which has caused many to dislike the higher-pitched instruments. The A soprano is pitched a half-tone lower, and there are many who believe it has a more mellow and richer quality for this reason. If the actual facts were known, no doubt this so-called superior quality would be found in the mind only. When the old masters wrote for A clarinet, there may have been greater difference than there is now, due not so much to the half-tone difference in pitch but to the difference in perfection of the two instruments. Conductors who demand the A clarinet just because the original scores called for it have been embarrassed many times when they could not distinguish the A clarinet and the B♭ clarinet apart. A classical example is the case of Meyerbeer, when he was conducting his own operas at Stuttgart. He found the clarinet player using the B♭ instrument, whereas Meyerbeer had written the part for the A clarinet. Being one of those who are sticklers for the A clarinet and believing the A clarinet possessed a tone quality which could not be produced by the B♭ clarinet, Meyerbeer insisted that the clarinet player use the A instrument. The clarinet player laid his B♭ clarinet down, fumbled around a bit, and then picked the B♭ clarinet up again. He then proceeded to blow through the instrument to warm it up a bit so it would be up to pitch and then nodded to Meyerbeer that he was ready. After the A passage had been played (on the B♭ instrument!) Meyerbeer beamed at the orchestra and said, "There, gentlemen, that is the color I had in mind."

It is not only the conductors who insist that parts originally written for the A clarinet be played on the A clarinet: many of the old-time clarinetists believe the same. When they buy a B♭ clarinet, they buy a pair—a "matched" pair— one in B♭ and another in A. Many other fine clarinetists, though, use only the B♭ clarinet, playing all clarinet parts on this instrument by transposing them. Berlioz objected strenuously to this practice, and this has led some to take the same stand; but many of these persons misinterpret Berlioz' objection. He points out that the lowest note on the A clarinet is the low E, which sounds C♯. The lowest note on the B♭ clarinet is also low E, but on the B♭ clarinet, due to its pitch, this note sounds a half-tone higher than C♯ or D. If the B♭ clarinet cannot play this C♯ in the lower octave but has to play it in the octave above, the music suffers. Few will dispute this point, but the resourceful Antoine Sax changed all this when, a little before the middle of the nineteenth century, he added to the B♭ clarinet a low E♭ key. With this key the player of the B♭ clarinet can transpose any A-clarinet parts and play them as the composer wished them to sound. The objection of Berlioz is overcome, for the B♭ clarinet player can now play the low C♯ with ease. Berlioz, probably, would find no objection to transposing A-clarinet parts on the B♭ clarinet, since his objection has been met.

While the bass clarinet is used in both band and orchestra, the alto clarinet is more of a band instrument than it is an orchestra instrument. This is probably due to the fact that in the band the clarinet is the most important instrument. It holds a place in the band of the same relative importance as does the violin in the orchestra. As the violin family is complete in the orchestra, with violins, violas, cellos and basses, the clarinet family is complete in the band, with soprano clarinets, alto clarinets and bass clarinets. As the most important instrument in the orchestra has a complete choir, so the most important instrument in the symphonic band has a complete choir.

The clarinet is often called the dramatic soprano of the woodwinds, to distinguish it from the other two woodwind sopranos: the coloratura flute and the lyric oboe. In its low-est, or chalumeau, register, its tone is sonorous and mellow but a little hollow and nasal. In its intermediate register its tone is somewhat weak but is effective in soft passages. These notes from F to Bb in the staff are the famous throat notes which no manufacturer has been able to bring quite up to the excellence of the rest of the scale. The middle register is the best part of the scale. Here the tone is clear, sweet and strong, penetrative and expressive. This part of the scale is capable of the greatest "crescendo al diminuendo" to be found on any woodwind. The upper register is naturally brilliant and sometimes is inclined to have a "reedy" quality.

Few wind instruments have such a wide variety of tonal colorings as the clarinet, and none except the flute can sur-pass it in agility. Flowing scales and arpeggios, trills and tremolos, legato and staccato playing come easy on the clarinet. In fact, there is scarcely anything which cannot be played on the clarinet, its possibilities being limited by the player more than by the technical resources of the instru-ment. While this is particularly true of the soprano clarinets, it is also true of the alto and bass clarinets in a degree, de-pending upon the size of the instrument. The reed and keys on the alto and bass are larger and respond less quickly and easily, but the key system is the same on all sizes of clarinets, and the player of one can pick up any of the others and play them with little trouble.

In the symphony orchestra, two or three soprano clarinets are used and one or two bass clarinets. Often an alto clarinet and a double-bass clarinet are called for. In the band many more than this are used. In a band of seventy-two pieces, from 25 to 40 per cent of the instruments will be clarinets.

There usually will be twenty-four B♭ sopranos, one or two E♭ sopranos, from two to four altos and a pair of bass clarinets, with possibly a double-bass in either E♭ or BB♭. As the size of the band increases, the proportion of clarinets increases.

With this array of clarinets, the symphonic band has great resources in tonal colorings. The soprano clarinets can ascend into their top register and terrify with their shrill and strident voice. In their lower register they can blend with the top register of the alto clarinet to sing sweetly and dramatically in a great variety of emotional moods. The lower register of the alto blends in with the top register of the bass clarinet to express sonorous beauty of a solemn and sometimes weird character. The bottom notes of the bass are used to express that which is mysterious, foreboding, sepulchral.

Today clarinets are made of grenadilla wood, of vulcanized rubber, and of metal, usually nickel silver. The first clarinets were made of boxwood, but warping of boxwood made this material unsuitable when the key mechanism included long hinges, for when the wood warped the keys would stick. Grenadilla wood was finally found to be the most suitable, and today the finest clarinets are made of this material. This wood is found in Mozambique, South Africa, and in the large island to the east called Madagascar. The grenadilla wood tree grows in desert areas, and it takes years to grow a tree large enough to be used commercially, for the growth is very slow. The wood, naturally, is very close-grained, hard and heavy. Originally dark brown with streaks of dark purple through it, it becomes darker with age, and after being soaked in oil it becomes black. The best wood is seasoned in unheated wood lofts for from five to ten years and even longer.

This aging process is carried on so the grain will become settled and stable. Cracking and splitting, shrinking and swelling are the bane of the clarinet player, and manufacturers use every effort to build clarinets of wood which will not have these faults.

In spite of the greatest care, some grenadilla-wood clarinets split, especially when used carelessly and in changeable climates. This has led to the use of ebonite, or vulcanized rubber. Other clarinets are made of metal, the first on record having been made by C. G. Conn in 1887 and patented by Mr Conn on May 23, 1889. Flutes were made of metal by Theobald Boehm in 1847, in Europe, but there is no record of a metal clarinet before 1887, either in Europe or America. This invention was ahead of its time, and it is only within the last ten years that metal clarinets have been used extensively. They meet the same criticism as Boehm's metal flutes had to contend with. Some musicians claim a metal clarinet does not have as rich a tone quality as a wood clarinet. Numerous blindfold tests have been conducted in which musicians used both wood and metal clarinets. The best musicians, both players and listeners, have repeatedly been fooled by these tests, showing that they could not tell the difference between wood and metal clarinets. The prejudice is strongly in favor of wood, however, and it will probably take years before the metal clarinet is universally accepted. Materials do unquestionably make a difference in tonal quality, but few ears are keen enough to distinguish between wood and metal, and there are tremendous advantages in durability, permanence of adjustment, and manufacturing cost in building clarinets of metal. Furthermore, who can say that the wood-clarinet tone is more "beautiful" than the metal-clarinet tone? They may be different (although even this point is heatedly debated), but by what standards can we say one is more "beautiful" than the other? The wood clarinet may be more mellow, while the metal clarinet may be more brilliant, but is one, therefore, more "beautiful" than the other? If the argument narrows down to a question of whether the "true" clarinet tone can be produced only on a wood or on a metal clarinet, who can say what is the "true" clarinet tone? There are pronounced differences of qualities in different registers on the same clarinet, differences much greater than those between wood and metal clarinets, taken register for register. Only time and usage will tell, as they did in the argument about wood and metal flutes. Today a wood flute is a curiosity, and possibly the same will be true of the wood clarinets in a decade or two.

CHAPTER VII

The Saxophones

THE SCAPEGOATS OF JAZZ

MENTION JAZZ MUSIC and for some strange reason nine out of ten people think of the saxophone. Strange, because many other instruments are much more closely identified with jazz than is the saxophone. Much more of a jazz instrument is the cornet, trumpet, clarinet or trombone; and long before the saxophones entered jazz, the piano, violin, string bass, guitar and banjo were old-timers at it.

The first jazz instruments were not the saxophones but the cornet and trumpet; in fact the germ idea of jazz music was originated on these two instruments. It all seems to have happened down in New Orleans about 1900. It was the custom to hire bands for advertising purposes, and these bands would travel around the city in a band wagon, much as bands are used today during political campaigns. Their repertoire was often meager, and when once a selection had been learned it was given an intensive workout. In these bands the leader was often the cornet or trumpet player, as in the silver-cornet bands. Being the best musician in the band, the cornet player would relieve the monotony of these few stock numbers by

adding obbligatos, according to his inspiration. These obbligatos became more and more elaborate, and playing
obbligatos became a sort of new art—at least this form of
obbligato. As the number would be played again and again
by the band, the cornet player would play one obbligato
after another, each one impromptu and each one different.

There grew up considerable rivalry among these obbligato
artists, particularly in the colored bands. Each band thought
it had the best obbligato player. Often these bands would
fight against each other to see whose obbligato artist was
the better. That cornet player who could play a chorus the
greatest number of interesting ways, and who could play
it the loudest and highest, was considered the best. This
activity was called "bucking" or "carving." Improvising
music of this kind required musical ideas and highly developed musical technique. Somewhat as the great old masters developed their music by stating a theme or idea and
then restating it again and again in different forms, so these
Negro musicians started with a melody and then played it
over and over in endless variations. The form of the variation
was original, however, and is the great contribution of the
colored race to music. Whether or not one likes jazz or
"swing" music, one has to admit that this type of performance is something different in the history of music. There is
a sort of wild barbarity, a spontaneity, a "swing" to this
music which no other music has. As Duke Ellington says in
a song of his, "It don't mean a thing, if it ain't got that
swing."

This new idea "caught on," and it wasn't long before the
colored dance bands were taking over the style. Not only
did the cornet player improvise, but the other instrument

players took their turn, or two or three would improvise to-gether. One of the best of these early jazz bands was known as King Oliver's band, and it became famous in New Orleans from 1915 to 1918. The instruments were at first clarinet, trombone, violin, string bass and drums. Later the instru-mentation was changed and consisted of two trumpets, clarinet, trombone, banjo, drums and piano. But there were no saxophones.

White musicians used to drop in and listen to King Oliver and his band "go to town." These musicians realized they were hearing something new in music, and they were fasci-nated. They finally formed white bands and played this new type of music. One of the most famous of these early white bands was called the "Dixieland Jazz Band," organized and led by a trumpet player known as Nick LaRocca. This band came North in 1917, toured as far as New York and then went to England. It created a sensation, for this was the first time most people of the North and England had heard jazz music. The instruments in this band were trumpet, trombone, clarinet, drums and piano. But there were no saxophones.

Colored jazz bands used to play on the river boats as they traveled up and down the Mississippi, and some of these bands left the boat and played jobs in the towns along the river. One of these early colored bands which ventured to come North was the "Original Creole Orchestra." This organization is said to have made a trip North as early as 1911. It consisted of cornet, trombone, clarinet, string bass, violin and drums. Later a guitar was added, but no saxo-phones were used.

The North did not see a famous colored band until King

Oliver brought his musicians to the Dreamland Café in Chicago in 1918. The "Dixieland Jazz Band" had met with such success up North that the colored boys decided they would try it. Their engagement was a success, for people liked this new kind of music. In 1921 this band made some recordings of their music for the phonograph, the first great jazz band to be recorded. The instruments in this popular jazz band were two cornets, trombone, clarinet, banjo, piano and drums. But there were no saxophones.

It was not until the third decade of the century and of the history of jazz music that a saxophone was introduced into the jazz band. One of the first bands to use a saxophone was called "Joe Kayser and his Novelty Orchestra." About 1921 this band was comprised of violin, piano, banjo, drums and a C-melody saxophone. Two years later we find the "New Orleans Rhythm Kings" playing in Chicago. The instruments used were clarinet, trumpet, trombone, string bass, piano, drums and a C-melody saxophone. Later a banjo was added. The "Wolverines" were another famous jazz outfit, organized in Chicago in 1923. It was comprised of cornet, played by Bix Beiderbecke, acknowledged the greatest of all jazz players; also clarinet, string bass, piano, banjo, drums and tenor saxophone. A year later the band was reorganized, and a trombone was added.

Although there were beginning to be saxophones in the jazz band, this instrument was not generally accepted in the jazz band, as can be seen from the fact that when the great Bix organized his own band in 1924, he did not use a saxophone. This band, known as "Bix Rhythm Jugglers," was comprised of a cornet, trombone, clarinet, piano, drums and banjo. While it was evident that the typical jazz band required cornet, trumpet, trombone, clarinet, drums and piano, with string bass, guitar, violin and banjo often called for, the saxophone was looked upon as a sort of novelty instrument. Whenever a saxophone was called for it would usually be the C-melody. Not until considerably later were the alto, tenor and baritone saxophones found in the jazz band.

That the saxophone was not used more in the jazz band is all the more remarkable when it is considered that there was a saxophone craze in America from 1919 to 1925, reaching a peak in 1923 and 1924. In these two years it is estimated there were one hundred thousand saxophones made and sold in·America annually, besides those imported. During those six or seven years of the craze, the total saxophones sold in America ran well over a half-million instruments. Yet, in spite of this great popularity among amateurs, there were astonishingly few saxophones used in the jazz band. This fact, as much as any other, would stamp the saxophone as anything but a typical jazz instrument.

Selling the saxophone to the American public has often been credited to Tom Brown and his famous saxophone sextet. He it was who taught America that the saxophone can moan, laugh, cackle, titter, squeal and grunt. To many uninitiated, this perversion of the saxophone talents is synonymous with jazz, although it really has nothing to do with it. There is good reason to believe that much of the general misconception about the saxophone's being a jazz instrument can be traced to this wrong notion. Tom Brown organized his saxophone sextet in 1911 and continued it until 1926, reaching a peak of popularity about 1924, which through more than a coincidence was the peak of the saxophone craze. After this date, both Tom Brown and the saxophone slumped in popularity, which shows how the popularities of both were interlocked.

Tom Brown's saxophone sextet had many imitators. The vaudeville stages from 1915 to 1925 were crowded with them. They cavorted around the stage with a successful combination of antics and music which pleased the audience. Much of the attraction of the saxophone for early audiences before which Tom Brown performed was the comparative novelty of the instrument. Outside of a few concert bands the saxophone was hardly known. But Tom Brown was a great showman, and he made the saxophone the most-talked-of instrument in America. After a few years there were scores of acts like his, and within a few years thousands of people began buying the C-melody saxophone because they yearned to play this amazing instrument. They also bought altos and tenors and sopranos and baritones and formed amateur saxophone ensembles and saxophone bands. And although the American people seemed clear that their own amateur playing was not jazz, they seem never to have properly distinguished between Tom Brown's antics on the saxophone and the antics of the real jazz player.

Many lovers of the saxophone now wish the instrument had been introduced to the American public through the concert band rather than through Tom Brown and his imitators. It no doubt would have taken much longer, but the reputation of the saxophone would have been much more favorable. E. A. Lefebre played the saxophone for Gilmore's band with great virtuosity. Other great legitimate artists were Jean Moeremans, soloist with Sousa, and Ben Vereecken, soloist with Pryor. H. Benne Henton, saxophone soloist with Sousa, showed thousands that the saxophone could be played with artistry as great as that expected in singing or playing the violin. It was he who was chosen by Richard Strauss to head the saxophone quartet which played the Strauss "Domestic Symphony" when the great German composer toured America.

The almost fatal reaction from the so-called saxophone craze, when C-melody saxophones squawked in every block, was that anyone could pick up the saxophone and play it after a few hours of practice. The saxophone is surprisingly easy to play in a simple way, but although the rudiments can be picked up quickly, it takes years of diligent study under competent teachers to master the instrument and play it with artistry. Only recently, more than ten years after the craze, has this sane view of the saxophone become at all general. The saxophone is finally taking its place as a serious instrument alongside the trumpet, trombone, violin or cello.

By 1926 it was customary for the regular dance band to use two or three saxophones, but dance bands are by no means all jazz or swing bands. The tendency for the dance band is to grow larger and larger, but the typical jazz band remains small; and while today there are some fine swing bands with ten to a dozen players, the true "jam" band— the jazz or swing band of the purest type—seldom numbers over six or seven. In such bands there may or may not be a saxophone, but there usually are a cornet or trumpet, a trombone, a clarinet, a string bass or drums and a piano.

There is no more reason for dubbing the saxophone a "jazz instrument" than there is for applying the same term to the violin. Did anyone ever play purer swing music on the saxophone than Joe Venuti plays on the violin? Why pick on the saxophone when the clarinet figures so prominently in jazz? Did anyone ever "swing" better on the saxophone than Benny Goodman and Peewee Russel do on the clarinet? And why hold the saxophone up to ridicule and say nothing of the trombone? Did ever a saxophonist get "hotter" on his instrument than Jack Teagarden and Tommy Dorsey do on trombone? And what about Louis Armstrong and Bunny Berigan on cornet? Earl Hines and Teddy Wilson on piano? Gene Krupa on drums? Vic Berton on tympani?

On the other hand, who is prepared to say that Lucien Cailliet, first saxophone of the Philadelphia Orchestra, Rolland Tapley, first saxophone of the Boston Symphony, Leonard Schaller, first saxophone of the Chicago Symphony, Carroll Gillette, first saxophone of the San Francisco Symphony, or Maurice DeCruck, formerly first saxophone of the New York Philharmonic-Symphony, is less of an artist than flutists, violinists or cellists are on their instruments? Whoever has heard any of these great artists play the troubadour song at the castle, in "Pictures from an Exhibition," by Moussorgsky-Ravel, is willing to class the saxophone among the most beautiful of musical instruments. Other convincing proof is the saxophone solos in Ravel's "Bolero" and Debussy's "Rapsodie" for saxophone, as played by any one of these fine saxophone artists. It is not the instrument at all, but the way it is played, which makes it legitimate or jazz.

Practically every instrument has been used in jazz, and the only reason all of them are not used is that many of them do not have what it takes to play jazz. One of the characteristics of jazz or swing music is a most vigorous attack. The cornet, trumpet, trombone, clarinet, saxophone, drums, piano and string bass all have the "sock" necessary for this attack, but how could a player "wham 'em out" on the flute, oboe, English horn, bassoon, French horn, viola or harp? Even the violin, though often used, is not a good jazz instrument because it lacks the punch necessary. If it is true that the saxophone got into bad company, the only reason the other instruments escaped is that they were too weak and timid.

When Adolphe Sax invented the saxophones in 1840, he expected them to take their place in the symphony orchestra and concert band along with other legitimate instruments. In France particularly, and also to less extent in Germany, the saxophone was readily adopted and was given important parts in opera and symphony music. In France, Meyerbeer, Massenet, Berlioz, Bizet and Saint-Saëns have used the saxophone to good effect, while in Germany Richard Strauss has been a champion of the saxophone, using a quartet of them in his "Domestic Symphony" and other compositions. Modern composers in Russia, Italy and America are giving more thought to the use of the saxophone resources, and considerable good music is being composed for this worthy instrument.

In the concert band, too, the saxophone is earning a solid place for itself. Sousa always used from four to eight saxophones and said one time, "There is much to be done in standardizing the saxophone, with its strange sweetness of tone and its variety of effects." Composers and arrangers are beginning to recognize that the saxophone family holds a unique place in the tonal spectrum, between the woodwinds and the brasses; for the saxophone is a strange blending of these two colorings, partly woodwind and partly brass. They serve a most useful purpose of blending the woodwind choir and the brass choir together.

The invention of the saxophone, by Antoine (commonly known as Adolphe) Sax in 1840, was an accident. Sax was conducting some experiments with the ophicleide, an old type of cup-mouthpiece instrument then in use but now obsolete. This instrument is more completely described in the chapter on the tubas. It was made of brass, the holes were closed by keys much like today's saxophone keys, and it was played with a cup mouthpiece. Sax was curious to learn what would happen if he played the instrument with a clarinet mouthpiece.

The strange blending of the brass and reed tone fascinated Sax. It was somewhat brassy, from the brass body, but it did not sound like the old ophicleide. It was reedy, from the clarinet reed mouthpiece, but it did not sound like a clarinet. It did not behave like a clarinet, either, for while the clarinet has only the odd partials in the scale, this new cross between a brass instrument and a clarinet had both the even and the odd partials. Sax realized he had produced a new tonal coloring among musical instruments, and after further experiment, during which he gave the saxophone body inside dimensions different from those of the ophicleide, he produced the instrument known today as the saxophone.

This crossbreeding of the clarinet with the ophicleide produced an instrument which not only had both even and odd partials, but which sounded a fundamental, or lowest, note whose wave was only twice as long as the instrument. In the chapter, "How Music Is Made," it is pointed out that the clarinet can sound a low note whose wave is four times the length of the instrument. This latter difference is not as important as the former, for in the saxophone, which has both even and odd partials, the key difficulties found on the clarinet are eliminated. While the distance between the first and second partials, or open notes, is a twelfth on the clarinet, it is only an octave on the new hybrid saxophone. The complicated mechanism necessary to bridge the gap between these two widely spread notes on the clarinet is not necessary on the saxophone. The fingering for the first octave can be repeated in the second octave by simply overblowing to the octave above, the same as on the flute and oboe. This enables the maker to build a key mechanism which is less complicated than the mechanism on the clarinet. It is this comparative simplicity of the key mechanism which partly accounts for the great popularity of the saxophone during the saxophone craze.

It is one of the mysteries of instrument making why the clarinet mouthpiece on the clarinet produces an instrument with the characteristics of the closed pipe, while the same mouthpiece on the saxophone produces an instrument with the characteristics of the open pipe. Why should the clarinet have only the odd partials and a fundamental whose wave is four times the length of the instrument, while the saxophone has both even and odd partials and sounds a fundamental whose wave is only twice the length of the instrument? This can be explained only in rather technical terms, which are out of place here. But some hint of the principles involved can be given here by pointing out that the body of the clarinet is cylindrical while the body of the saxophone is conical. Delicate acoustical apparatus has shown us that the even partials are actually present on the clarinet, but they are so weak they cannot be used. It seems that the cylindrical tube of the clarinet in some way dampens out the even partials. Some of these upper partials are quite strong, such as the eighth and tenth. In fact, these two even partials are of practically the same strength as the odd ninth. One theory advanced is that the natural frequency of the reed is approximately the frequency of the eighth and tenth partials and that the reed frequency strengthens these two and makes them stronger than the other even partials. The natural frequency of the reed is that sounded when it is struck or when it is blown on the mouthpiece unattached to the instrument. Under both these conditions, the pitch is high and lies near these two even partials. However, the partials which could be useful, such as the second and fourth, are so weak they can scarcely be detected by the ear. On the other hand, the conical tube of the saxophone shows no preference for even or odd partials and produces both with equal strength.

The mouthpiece is also an important factor to be considered in comparing these two instruments. The flute, which also has a cylindrical body the same as the clarinet but a different mouthpiece, produces both even and odd partials. If a clarinet mouthpiece is inserted on the flute, the even partials drop out and the instrument takes on all the characteristics of the clarinet. The single-beating reed of the clarinet closes the end of the instrument and makes it a closed pipe. The end of course is not closed all the time, for the reed opens and closes alternately. But on the clarinet, with its cylindrical tube, the single-beating reed acts as if it closed the tube. The reed vibrates in a similar manner on the saxophone, with its conical tube, but on this instrument the effect is not that of closing the tube. This is explained by acoustical

Over five hundred separate parts are necessary to make one alto saxophone. Approximately eleven hundred operations are required to make one set of alto-saxophone keys. Skilled labor is the big ingredient which goes into the making of the saxophone, for the raw material is only five and a quarter pounds of metal worth less than five dollars.

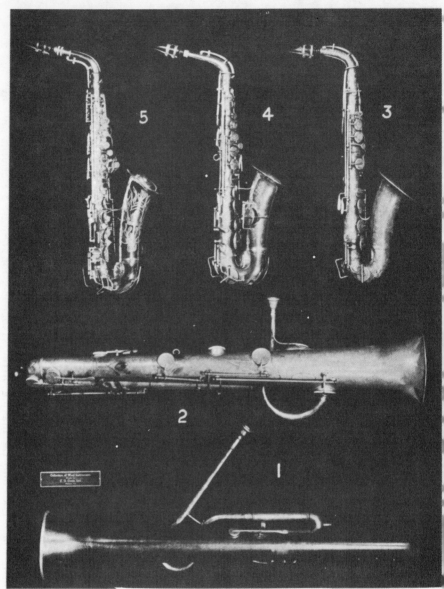

DEVELOPMENT OF THE SAXOPHONE

(1) Military serpent used in Europe first part of the eighteenth century.
(2) Ophicleide. Instruments of this type were used at the Battle of Waterloo
in 1815. (3) Original Adolphe Sax saxophone, invented by Sax in 1840. (4) First
saxophone built in America, by C. G. Conn in 1887. (5) Modern alto saxophone
in E♭.

engineers by the degree in which the reed closes the tube of each. The reed on a clarinet, vibrating at the same frequency as it does on the saxophone, seems nevertheless to render the tubing closed more of the time than it is open, and gives the clarinet the characteristics of the closed pipe.

We speak of the clarinet mouthpiece and of the saxophone mouthpiece as if they were identical. They are not identical, but only similar. They are alike in having a single-beating reed which opens and closes a chamber in the mouthpiece. The chamber in each, however, is slightly different in shape and size. These small differences have been developed as refinements in each mouthpiece to favor the scale and re-sponse of each instrument, but both mouthpieces remain alike in principle.

The inventor built a large family of these instruments, including, according to Berlioz, the following: the high E♭ soprano, the B♭ soprano, the E♭ alto, the B♭ tenor, the E♭ baritone and the B♭ bass. Other members of this prolific family today are the C soprano, the C tenor, more familiarly known as the C-melody; and the F alto, also called the F mezzo-soprano. There are also a few contrabass saxo-phones in E♭, but these are rare. Add to these distinctly different members of the family some different shapes for some of them and you have a large family. Among these varieties with different shapes are the straight and curved B♭ sopranos, the straight and curved F mezzo-sopranos, the curved E♭ alto and the E♭ alto which is mostly straight but turns up at the end something like a clay pipe or hockey stick.

Although made in this great variety of keys and shapes, the most useful members of the saxophone family are the middle voices: the E♭ alto, the B♭ tenor and the E♭ baritone. Next in importance are the B♭ soprano, the F mezzo-soprano, and the B♭ bass. The other members of the family are not commonly found in bands and orchestras. Occasionally the little E♭ soprano is used for special oriental effects, and some jazz musicians prefer the C-melody, but they are heard rarely.

It could hardly be expected that this new family would become popular overnight, but gradually the composers came to appreciate these instruments and give them parts in both orchestra and band. In America there was little known of the saxophone from 1840 to 1880. Only a few were imported from Europe, and these were practically useless from lack of music. About 1885 C. G. Conn began to make a few saxophones in America. His cause was greatly helped when E. A. Lefebre, great saxophone virtuoso of Europe and personal friend of Sax, came to America and toured the country as soloist with Patrick Gilmore's celebrated band. In 1895 Lefebre was employed by Mr Conn to supervise the manufacture of the American saxophone. Thirty years later, as previously related, America was buying more saxophones in a week than Antoine Sax ever dreamed would be sold anywhere in a year.

It was this tremendous demand for saxophones which brought about a unique condition in their manufacture. The American genius for quantity production was turned to the manufacture of the saxophone. In former days the saxophone had been made slowly by hand, piece by piece. When the great demand for saxophones hit the country, modern methods had to be employed. Precision machines were developed, new processes were invented and new accuracy and speed obtained. Today, although the demand has lessened, saxophones are still the largest-selling family of wind instruments. These modern manufacturing methods have been continued and refined, and the manufacture of the modern saxophone in America is now an interesting process, which amazes those who see it for the first time. Few people who play or listen to a saxophone realize it is made of over five hundred separate and individual parts, efficiently and accurately assembled into a fine musical instrument. Among these parts are over five dozen small key castings, four dozen knobs for holding the key hinges, four dozen hollow hinges of various lengths, four dozen springs and pads of assorted sizes and kinds, and over five dozen screws, from long ones nearly ten inches in length to tiny ones weighing 1,240 to the ounce!

The five and a quarter pounds of raw material in a high-grade saxophone are not worth over five dollars, but the finished instrument retails to the musician for over one hundred dollars. The greatest cost which goes into a saxophone is that of the labor of skilled and long-experienced craftsmen. For example, there are thirty-three keys on the common alto saxophone, and on each key there are, on the average, thirty-four separate and distinct operations, such as casting, polishing, milling, drilling, brazing, locating spring hooks, buffing—making a total of over 1100 separate operations to produce a single set of keys for one alto saxophone. Nor can a saxophone be cut out and sewed together like a suit of clothes or be kneaded by the hands into shape like a loaf of bread. Saxophones are made of brass, and hardly any operation can be performed without some expensive lathe, drill press, screw machine, punch press or other special machine, for brass cannot be worked by hand but only by accurate machines which can shape it into a finished product. The cost of these tools and machines runs into thousands of dollars.

The saxophone today is substantially the same as it was when Sax invented it nearly a hundred years ago. Of course it is more efficient and more accurate, but in appearance and general features it has changed but little. At first the saxophone was built only down to low B, but now nearly all instruments go down to low B♭. At first the top note was D; now nearly all members of the family can play up to F. The first saxophones were provided with two octave keys; now nearly all saxophones have the single automatic octave key. On the modern saxophone, also, are many improvements in mechanism which make difficult passages easier, especially rapid trills.

If Antoine Sax could see and hear the modern saxophone played today by a "hot" jazz artist, he would look at it and say, "That's my invention, all right, but I never dreamed it could do things like that." If he could see and hear it played by a great soloist in the symphony or concert band, he would say, "That unquestionably is my saxophone, but I never hoped it could sound so beautiful." And if he could see it being made in a modern American factory, he would say, "I never thought of making them that way. But tell me—what on earth do you expect to do with them all?"

CHAPTER VIII

The Trumpet and the Cornet

SIXTY CENTURIES OF RIVALRY

MOST LAYMEN don't know the difference between a trumpet and a cornet, but among musicians the trumpet versus the cornet is a subject which calls for heated argument. For centuries there has existed a bitter feud between these two instruments. First one would rise to the ascendancy and then the other. When one would be rising in favor, the other would be declining. Before long the tables would be reversed and the second choice would find itself swept upward on a wave of acclaim, while the other would decline in popularity. This seesaw feud has gone on for hundreds of years and is no nearer solution now than it has ever been.

As is true in most feuds that are especially bitter, this is a blood feud. The closer related by blood certain families or tribes may be, the more bitter the feud, and this is true of the contest between the trumpet and the cornet. When closely related in this manner, the only way to carry on a heated feud over a long period of years is to keep the fancied issue clearly defined; otherwise common blood and common interest will cause the hatred to cool off, and the feud will die a natural death. In order to understand the feud between the trumpet and cornet we must first understand why two instruments so similar can find enough difference between themselves to make a good fight.

The trumpet is the blue-blood in this feud. It points with

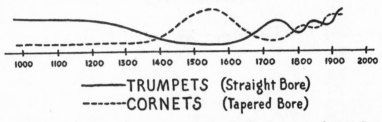

——————TRUMPETS (Straight Bore)
--------CORNETS (Tapered Bore)

Trumpets with their straight bore held the ascendancy for centuries over the cornets with their tapered bore. Late in the thirteenth century the rival cornets appear in churches and in early opera and reach great popularity in the sixteenth. At this time the trumpets languish. By 1750 the cornets give place to the oboes, and the trumpets steal a march in the roles given them by Bach and Handel. In 1800 trumpets wane when clarion parts are given to clarinets. The keyed bugle takes a sharp rise right after 1800, a triumph for the tapered cornet, but before it could rise high, the piston valves put the trumpet into the ascendancy again. During the era of the cornet virtuosi, just before and after 1900, the cornet was the favorite, but as the silver-cornet band gave way to the more modern concert band, the trumpet arose to claim popular favor. Now it looks as if the cornet were staging a comeback.

great hauteur to its ancient ancestors among the Chinese, Egyptians, Greeks and Romans. The genealogy of the trumpet can be traced in the records of the kings and princes, because for centuries the trumpet was the badge of royalty and could be used only by royalty or in royalty's service. Even as late as the Stuarts of England, the unauthorized possession of a trumpet was a serious offense. Present at all court functions, celebrations of great martial victories and important affairs of state, the family tree of the trumpet grew side by side with the family tree of royalty.

The lineage of the trumpet can be traced through its cylindrical bore. From two thirds to three fourths of its length was of uniform diameter with the opening at the mouthpiece end. At the opposite end was a length of tubing of increasingly larger bore, ending abruptly in a bell. The tone of the trumpet was brilliant and martial. It spoke in a commanding and confident manner, as the king spoke.

During these early centuries there undoubtedly existed another instrument similar to the trumpet but having a conical, or tapered, bore. Little has been written about such an instrument, as would be expected in the case of such a commoner. This instrument was much like our common bugle in bore and tone quality. It was small at the mouthpiece end and had a wide angle taper in the bore which flared out at the opposite end in a bell. Its tone was round and mellow, better suited to singing than to commanding.

Originally both the aristocratic trumpet and the plebeian bugle were a single, straight tube. Both were played with a cup-shaped mouthpiece. There was little in outward appearance to distinguish one from the other. Later it became the custom to bend the trumpet in the shape of the letter S. The bugle-type instrument was quick to follow this custom, and again the aristocrat and the commoner were difficult to distinguish apart. Still later the trumpet was bent in a sort of flat loop, like that characteristic of the ordinary bugle of today, and the commoner was not far behind in adopting this shape. Outwardly these two instruments were similar. Their musical natures, however, were different: the aristocratic trumpet was cylindrical in bore, the plebeian bugle-type instrument was tapered, or conical, in bore. This was the issue between them which has kept alive the blood feud for sixty centuries or more.

Even as the army lords, kings and priests held undisputed sway over the common people for many centuries, so the trumpet held sway over the bugle-type instrument. But along in the Middle Ages something happened both to the common people and the plebeian bugle. Just about the time the English barons struck for the common people against the oppression of kings and forced King John to sign the Magna Charta at Runnymede, the bugle-type instrument overthrew the oppression of the trumpet through a kind of intermarriage with royalty. The pure blood stream of the trumpet became contaminated with the blood of the common bugle, and the bastard cornet was born. And woe has been the lot of the trumpet ever since. This crossbreeding seems to have produced a surprisingly virile offspring. The old bugle-type instrument had not been able to contend at all successfully with the blue-blood trumpet, but the half-breed cornet seemed to incorporate some of the virtues of each which gave it a better chance in the long feud with the trumpet. The cornet adopted a bore which was partly straight and partly tapered. Its tone was not as round and mellow as that of the old bugle-type instrument, nor yet as brilliant and piercing as that of the trumpet. It could sing like its plebeian ancestor, although not with such a golden, mellow voice; and it could speak like its royal ancestor, although its voice lacked some of the silvery brilliance and nobleness.

By the fifteenth century the trumpet had been crowded

into second place for the first time in history. The pure tapered-bore instrument had never been able to do it, but the bastard-bore cornet had been more successful. By the sixteenth century the cornet had all but put the trumpet into obscurity. Everywhere the cornet flourished—in the choirs and churches and in the first orchestras started in Italy by the creators of opera. This continued until the beginning of the eighteenth century, when a double blow all but knocked out the cornet. The oboe became suddenly a very popular wind instrument and usurped the place of the cornet. About the same time or a little later, high-pitched and florid trumpet parts became popular, reaching their greatest vogue during the time of Bach and Handel. While the oboe ran the interference and blocked the cornet, the trumpet raced on to score a touchdown, to use a football metaphor. But by the end of the century there was a reaction against these shrill, piercing trumpet fireworks, and clarinets were used instead of trumpets, notably in the music of Mozart. While the trumpet was staggering from this blow, the cornet took a new lease on life when the keyed bugle was invented in the early nineteenth century. Many musicians acclaimed this new instrument as destined to transform band and orchestra music; but its popularity was short, for the piston valve was invented a few years later, and both types of instruments shared in this great improvement. In less than a hundred years, though, the cornet had again climbed to first place in popularity, through the great virtuosity of such well-known cornet soloists as Levy, Liberati, Hoch and Bellstedt. The pendulum then swung quickly to trumpets, and cornets have had to take a back seat for the last twenty-five years. At the present time, however, there are many indications that the cornet is about to stage one of its celebrated comebacks.

And what happened to the old, original tapered-bore instrument? Did it get completely put out of the running by the tough competition of its ancient rival, the trumpet, and its own bastard offspring, the cornet? No; trailing comfortably behind the two more popular instruments, the tapered-bore instrument adopted the piston valves and has finally settled down to a modest but important job in the concert band as the fluegelhorn.

This synopsis of the blood feud between the royal trumpet on the one hand and the plebeian bugle and the bastard cornet on the other gives an idea of the rocky road over which have come the two sopranos of today's brass choir, to say nothing of the mezzo-soprano fluegelhorn. But such a synopsis necessarily omits the drama and thrills of this desperate struggle among themselves and the common battle they waged against other instruments along the way.

The beginning of the story of the trumpet and cornet is something like the beginning of the story of the human race. The best authorities now agree that man did not descend from a monkey but from some primate which was the ancestor of both man and the monkey. Likewise, we are able to trace the history of the trumpet to a common ancestor from which descended not only the trumpet but also the cornet, horn and tuba. The animal horn or the elephant tusk, hollowed out and cupped at the small end, may have been this common ancestor; or it may have been a giant shell of some sea nautilus, or merely a hollowed-out piece of wood. The only essentials of such an ancestor are a tube with a cup-shaped mouthpiece at the small end and a flare or bell at the opposite end. The mouthpiece served as a fixture across which the lips of the player could be stretched, and the tube and bell served to amplify and give resonance to the weak, thin buzzing of the lips.

One of the first things early man devised after rising above the Stone Age into the age of metals was a metal trumpet. Ancient ruins reveal trumpets made of bronze, iron or other metals. At first these instruments resembled the animal-horn and the elephant-tusk prototypes which our ancestors copied in metal. Gradually they became more slender and longer as the primitive craftsmen became more familiar with the metal medium. From a foot long they grew to be three and four feet long, sometimes longer. Convenience in carrying and comfort in holding limited the length of these primitive trumpets, but we can imagine that the pitch of the note also had something to do with it. The fundamental, or lowest, note of a four-foot trumpet was approximately an octave below Middle C; and the next note, probably the "pitch" note, was Middle C, somewhere near what would be desired when used in the temple or on the battlefield. Such a trumpet had a range strikingly similar to the range of a male voice. A tube twice as long would have as its fundamental, or lowest, note the C two octaves below Middle C, which was too low to be of practical use. The second note, probably the "pitch" note, would be one octave below Middle C, also too low for usefulness. Of course, higher notes could be sounded on these longer tubes, but we can imagine that the second open note was the easiest to blow on such crude instruments (just as it is on the ordinary bugle of today) and that this was the note most often used. On the other hand, difficulty of blowing high notes on shorter trumpets probably restricted the shortness of the tubing. For instance, a trumpet only a foot long would sound as its fundamental note the C which is an octave above Middle C; and its "pitch" note might be an octave higher, due to the smallness of the instrument and the difficulty of playing the fundamental. To blow a note of such high pitch would be difficult, especially on an instrument as crude and inefficient as this was.

So we see that physical conditions—convenience in carrying and holding, and limitations of the player's lips and lungs—naturally restricted the length of the early trumpet to about four feet. It is more than a coincidence that trumpets and cornets of today are about that length. The B♭ trumpet is the most used today, and the length of its tubing is just about four feet. The C and D trumpets are sometimes played, and occasionally the E♭ trumpet is called for, but these shorter trumpets are hard to play, as any trumpet or cornet player can testify. Of course, cup-mouthpiece instruments are made much longer than four feet these days, but this has come to pass after centuries of experimenting with proportioning the bore and refining the workmanship so that it would be possible for the player to make these longer tubes sound more easily. These instruments with longer tubing are used for musical purposes and are not restricted to uses in the temple or on the battlefield, as were the early trumpets. Low, sonorous notes are desirable for effects and colorings in music but were not suitable for signal purposes and for exorcising evil spirits.

In China and India two or three thousand years B.C., we find trumpets being used to scare away evil spirits. These instruments had to be loud in order to be useful. They were usually over a foot long and less than four feet. Trumpets are mentioned often in the Bible. The Hebrews possibly learned about the trumpet while they were captives in Egypt, but it became rapidly popular, if we are to believe the Hebrew historian Josephus. He wrote that during Solomon's time there were two hundred thousand in use. Such trumpets were about twenty-one inches long, and some were made of precious metals. They were used mostly in religious worship but were also employed on the field of battle. The classic instance of this is the taking of Jericho, whose walls are said to have crumbled while trumpeters marched and played around the city.

The Greeks have a historical example of the use of the trumpet which is equally famous. During the siege of Troy the Greek trumpet, called the salpinx, shared honors with the spear of Achilles and the chariot of Agamemnon in taking this ancient city and rescuing the beautiful Helen. The Greeks had six varieties of trumpets and horns, but the salpinx was the best known. Trumpet playing became a favorite art with the Greeks, and Timoeus and Crates, two trumpet players, have made their names immortal by winning the musical contest at the Olympian games in 396 B.C. The Romans had a small-bore trumpet called the lituus. It was a straight, cylindrical tube for most of its length, but near the bell end it flared out at right angles like a hockey stick. In 1827 excavators of a tomb at Cerveterie discovered one of these ancient trumpets, and it is now preserved at the Vatican.

When the Roman legions conquered Gaul they showed the natives some of the finest metal trumpets these barbarians had ever seen. Other Europeans who missed this musical treat later trekked down to Rome and saw for themselves. When they sacked this great city they carried back with them some fine specimens of trumpets. During Chaucer's time the trumpet was familiar to all, as is seen from the many times he mentions it. In the Canterbury Tales he has the knight talk about the "trompes" and "clariounes." In the same collection of stories he has the squire refer to the "trumpette" and the "claryon clere."

Out of the maze of names used to refer to these instruments we conclude that there were two kinds of trumpets. There was the large trumpet, or buzine—also called trombe, tromp, trompe—which later became the sackbut, or trombone. It was a straight tube about six feet long, to which a slide was later added. The other variety of trumpet was the clarion, an instrument shorter and of smaller bore. The words we use today to refer to these instruments are much more definitive. One we call the trumpet, which was formerly spelled "trumpette" and means, in Italian (*trombetta*), "little trumpet"; the other we call trombone, which means, in Italian, big trumpet. The trumpet and trombone are so similar in bore and tonal quality that they really are little and big brother of the same family.

During or a little before the fourteenth century, while Chaucer was making immortal in his writings the names trompe and clarioun, a new instrument put in an appearance in Europe which was destined to challenge the supremacy of these aristocratic instruments. In Germany it was called the zinke, and in England it was called the cornetto. If ever an instrument belonged to the lower strata of society, the cornetto did. It was originally made of wood and covered with leather. It had six finger holes in front and a thumb hole behind and was played with a cup-shaped mouthpiece made of wood. The tone was dull and windy, but for some strange reason it became extremely popular. In the fifteenth and sixteenth centuries it became the most popular wind instrument in Europe. It was employed, along with the sackbut, to play with the soprano voices in the church choirs. In the old account books of the churches of the time there are many records of payments to this or that cornetto player for his services. When the music-loving King Henry VIII died in 1547, he left a noble collection of twenty of these odd instruments.

Possibly one reason for the popularity of the cornetto was the ease and cheapness with which it could be made. Anyone with a pocketknife, a stick of wood, a piece of thin leather and a gluepot could make one. Two pieces of wood were hollowed out and glued together to make a conically shaped horn. This crude wooden horn was then covered with leather, and holes were drilled into the side. The mouthpiece was equally simple to make, being similar in shape to today's mouthpiece for the cornet, only it was made of wood. There were three sizes in use in England, the smallest being the treble cornetto in F, about eighteen inches long. The next in size was the cornetto in C, about two feet long. The largest was the great cornetto in G, nearly three feet long. In Germany these instruments were made in other keys, the small treble zinke in D being a common one. This member of the family was just about a foot long and was unusually difficult to blow and poor in tone quality.

When opera began to develop in Italy, toward the close of the sixteenth century, it was only natural for the composers to look to the cornetto as an instrument for the orchestra. The chief form of music before opera sprang up was church music, and the cornetto was one of the star performers in the choir. It is not surprising that in 1565 Striggio and Corteccia used four cornettos in their odd assortment of about two dozen instruments, used to accompany light plays. This newcomer among musical instruments, with a background of less than three hundred years, had crowded out the celebrated trumpet, which had lived with kings and princes for several thousands of years. No trumpets were allowed in this motley group of lutes, flutes, flageolets and violins, although four trombones were admitted.

In 1600 Jacopo Peri composed "Euridice," the first opera ever performed in public. In the same year Emilio del Cavaliere produced his previously referred to oratorio, "La Rappresentazione dell' Anima e Corpo." Although neither the cornetto nor the trumpet was called upon to perform in the orchestras which provided instrumental music for these productions, this was more of a reflection on the trumpet than upon the lowly cornetto. Eight years later, however, Monteverde called for two cornettos, one small clarion and three trumpets, as well as four trombones. This was quite a "brass" section, even though there were about twenty stringed instruments in the orchestra. The interesting part about the use of trumpets was that Monteverde called for them to be played with mutes. This is thought to be the first time mutes were used. After Monteverde, Legrenzi of Venice wrote for two cornettos, while Lully, the French composer, preferred the trumpet, using it for volume and color effects. Bach used the cornetto sometimes but was more familiar with the trumpet, usually writing for three of them. Handel, Bach's contemporary, apparently did not think so

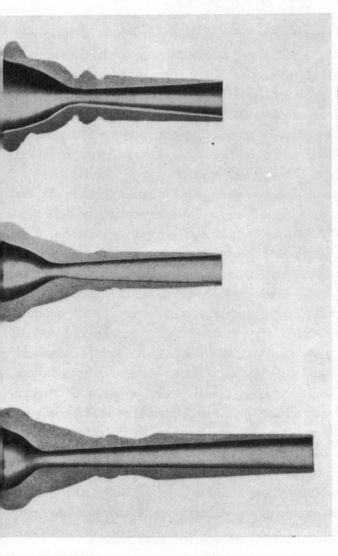

(*Left to right, cross sections*): Trumpet, cornet and flüegelhorn mouthpieces. Note that trumpet mouthpiece is small and shallow, cornet mouthpiece is deeper and more conical in shape, while flüegelhorn mouthpiece is large and deep. These differences contribute much to the differences in tone quality among these three instruments, graduating from brilliant to a darker and more mellow quality.

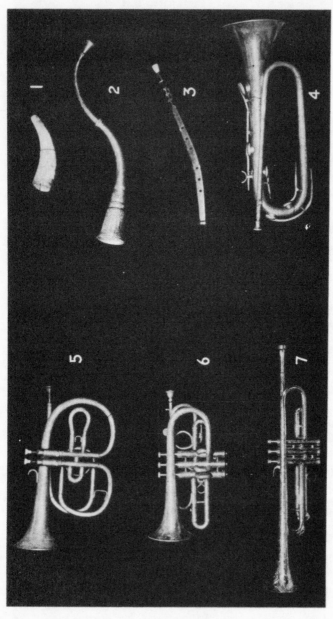

DEVELOPMENT OF THE CORNET AND TRUMPET

(1) Hebrew shofar, made from animal horn. (2) Chinese trumpet. (3) Soprano zinke in D, used in Germany in sixteenth century; ancestor of cornet. (4) Keyed bugle, invented and used about 1800. (5) Cornopean in E♭, showing two piston valves, invented about 1815. This instrument was used about 1825. (6) Cornet, made in 1877. (7) Modern trumpet.

highly of cornettos, for it is said he experimented once with them and that was enough.

The cornetto declined toward the close of the seventeenth century. In England it was supplanted by the oboe, and by the middle of the eighteenth century few were left. In Europe it survived until Bach and Handel. Gluck was one of the last composers to use this type of instrument, the zinke being found in some of his later scores. Few cornetto or zinke parts are to be found in any scores later than 1780 to 1795. Although the soprano of this type of instrument became obsolete at this time, the bass member of the family, the serpent, or ophicleide, survived until well into the nineteenth century, no doubt because there was no other and better wind bass to take its place.

As the cornetto declined, the trumpet increased in popularity, until it reached a peak during the time of Bach and Handel. Monteverde at the beginning of the seventeenth century started the style of scoring for one small trumpet, or clarion, and three regular trumpets. Later it became the custom to write for first and second clarions in the upper parts and for trumpets in the lower parts. Stradella and Pallavicino, two Italian composers, further developed the vogue of writing specially high parts for the clarion, and by 1700 Scarlatti, Purcell and others had established the manner of featuring the clarions in extremely high and ornamental solo passages. This custom reached its peak during the time of Bach and Handel, but after their time this practice declined rapidly.

This era is of especial interest to the trumpeter. Many of the trumpet, or clarion, parts written during these years are almost impossible to play today on the regular trumpet.

This has caused much conjecture about how such music was originally performed, if it were really performed at all, on the trumpet. To meet the demands of the composers in those days certain players, fitted to the task, became clarion players, while others became trumpet players. The typical clarion was a short instrument of small bore and was played with a small, shallow mouthpiece. Clarion players developed a freak lip, practising only in the very top of the scale and attaining a proficiency and skill especially for playing these extremely high notes. Trumpet players today know that they can increase their range upward by special practice and by using small and shallow mouthpieces, but by specializing on these high notes and by using a small, shallow mouthpiece they lose the ability to play well in the lower part of the trumpet scale.

In the time of Bach and Handel, the clarion player was required to play only in the top of the scale. He was a specialist. Lower parts were given to regular trumpet players. This explains why these high parts today are so difficult, if not impossible, for the regular trumpet player. No one attempts to play these parts on a regular B♭ trumpet, and even on the C or D trumpet they can be played only after gruelling practice. Occasionally the small E♭ trumpet is brought into service in an attempt to master these high clarion parts. Many trumpeters bless Mozart and others for taking some of these parts away from the trumpeter and giving them to the clarinetist. Mozart had a special "peeve" against the clarion, and even against the trumpet, for his sensitive ear could not endure the piercing, shrill voice of these instruments, especially in the upper register. Mendelssohn and other composers seemed to agree with Mozart that pity should be taken upon the trumpet players—to say nothing about the audience—and have arranged much of this clarion music so these extremely high trumpet parts have been eliminated. Conductors go still further today by delegating such high parts to oboes or clarinets in orchestras where the trumpeters are not equal to the task.

Although some authorities assume that the clarions used to play these high and florid passages were all short instruments, others point out that some of this music could not be played on a short instrument because some of the notes written are not present on such an instrument. For instance, the German composer Steffani in 1695 composed a march in "I Trionfi del Fato" for four trumpets in C. Many of the notes in these parts are diatonic, some are chromatic, and they were written over one hundred years before the trumpet was made chromatic through the invention of either keys or valves. The only notes on trumpets of the time were open notes, such as are to be found on the bugle. As will be shown more in detail in later chapters, the successively higher notes on a bugle are increasingly closer together. For instance, the second open note is an octave higher than the first, while the third is only a fifth higher than the second. The fourth is only a fourth higher than the third, the fifth only a third above the fourth, and so on, until between the sixth and seventh there is only a step and a half. There is a whole step between successive notes until we reach the eleventh and twelfth, where only a half-step exists. This is also true between the thirteenth to the sixteenth partials.

It is obvious that if diatonic notes are to be played on a simple trumpet without valves, they must be played in the top part of the range, where the notes are close together.

In order to play the notes written, it has been pointed out, it would be necessary for the player to use a trumpet which was eight feet long and which sounded as its fundamental the C two octaves below Middle C. It would then have the natural scale shown below, starting at No. 1:

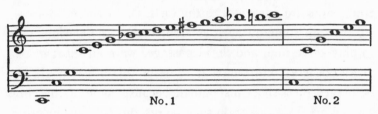

No. 1   No. 2

On such an instrument it is clearly seen that the following music by Steffani could be played, because the notes necessary are to be found on such an instrument:

If the instrument were only four feet long, having as it would a fundamental only an octave below Middle C, its natural scale would be as shown above, beginning at No. 2. It is at once obvious that there are gaps in such a scale which would make it impossible to play Steffani's music, D and F# being absent. Instruments of higher pitch, and consequently of shorter length, would have still greater gaps in the scale and would be even less adequate for playing this music.

This is conclusive proof that some of the trumpets used for some of the high and florid solos of the late seventeenth and early eighteenth centuries were eight-foot trumpets. These instruments must have been very small in bore and must have used a small mouthpiece. Even so, it surely taxed to the utmost the powers of the players in those days to play such music. A survey of much of the music of these times shows that the first clarion player was regularly required to play up as high as the sixteenth partial. This is substantially the job of the French horn player, who is required to play up to the sixteenth partial on his horn. The notes on the horn, however, are not nearly so high in pitch, since the horn's fundamental is considerably lower than that of the eight-foot clarion, the horn being nearly thirteen feet long. Praetorius, writing about 1619, says the clarion in D was called upon to play from the seventeenth to the twenty-first partial. This range is almost unbelievable. The second clarion player was regularly required to play up to the tenth and eleventh partials. The third part for regular trumpet was written in the middle range, from the third or fourth to the sixth or eighth, the seventh being flat and seldom used.

Praetorius says all trumpets of his time were built in D and that they were small in bore, short in length, and used a small mouthpiece. In this he is probably correct, except for the undoubted fact that eight-foot trumpets were often used. He was no doubt right in describing the bore, mouthpiece and pitch of the instrument as D, for this was generally the key in which they were built. They were also found occasionally in C and sometimes though rarely in G. Monteverde in "Orfeo" scored for five differently pitched trumpets, but composers since his day did not follow this lead. When the trumpet became a regular member of the orchestra it was usually built in F, with crooks for changing the pitch to E, E♭, D, C, B♭ and A. Sometimes trumpets were called for also in G, G♭, B, A♭ and D♭.

While the trumpet was attaining great popularity in the orchestra, it was also gaining great favor with kings and princes. Today the rank of leaders of the nation is shown by the number of cannons fired in their honor. In former times the rank was shown by the number of trumpeters who accompanied the royal personage. The royal bodyguard of Edward III was composed of seven trumpeters, while seventeen trumpeters saw to it that Charles II was given proper respect on all occasions. When the Prince of Orange journeyed from Holland in 1677, five trumpeters attended him. When the Earl of Mulgrave visited Tangiers in 1680, two trumpeters were assigned to attend him and signify his rank. Two trumpeters and one drummer were assigned to Prince Rupert in 1664. When these dignitaries alighted from their carriage to enter a building, warning of the approach of their excellencies was given by a fanfare of trumpets. When they boarded ship, the gangplank was cleared of common people by a blast from the trumpets. Whenever they walked in public thoroughfares, day or night, a flourish from the trumpets commanded respect for these distinguished personages.

It was often common for drummers to accompany trumpeters in such duties. A roll on the drums and a fanfare on the trumpets were calculated to arouse the proper respect for royalty. This association of the drum and trumpet was also found in the orchestra. Very often, when trumpets were called for in some of the earlier scores, drums were also used. In the early days of the orchestra, the trumpet and drum were associated in the composer's mind with things military. Usually when a military idea occurred in the composition, the trumpet and drum were called upon to play together. This was before the trumpet and drum were fully understood and before their wide range of colorings and effects was realized.

After Bach and Handel, trumpet playing declined. Haydn, the great successor of these two masters, did not do well with trumpets. When Haydn entered the service of Prince Esterházy, music-loving prince of Austria, his orchestra at first did not include trumpets at all. As late as 1766, the regular personnel of this orchestra, one of the foremost in Europe, consisted of six violins and violas, one cello, one string bass, one flute, two oboes, two bassoons and four horns —but no trumpets or cornets. Several years later the resources of the orchestra were enlarged so that trumpets and tympani could be added when needed. Even when Haydn did use trumpets, he scored for them so they played an octave or a sixth above the horns. To this thin arrangement he added drums for accompaniment. He probably felt the need of filling in with something, and the drums seemed the most appropriate.

Mozart, who was at first Haydn's pupil but whose genius lifted him to a place above his master, seemed to share Haydn's dislike for trumpets. This antipathy for trumpets was due to an extremely sensitive nature. Until Mozart was ten years old, the sound of the trumpet was excruciatingly painful to him, and he could not endure it. As an adult he found little pleasure in trumpets, and he used them sparingly. In 1788 he wrote his three greatest symphonies, but in only two of them did he use the trumpet. He could not endure the high clarion parts written by Bach and Handel. He even rearranged some of this music, giving the high clarion parts to the clarinets.

Beethoven generally wrote for two trumpets and often used them as solo instruments. This can hardly be interpreted to mean that Beethoven was particularly fond of the trumpet, for it was a known custom of his to score as much as possible for all players in the orchestra and to pass around the solo parts in order to keep them all interested. In general he followed the custom of Mozart and Haydn in handling the trumpets, writing for them parts which were an octave, a sixth or sometimes a third above the horns, all to the accompaniment of the pounding of the tympani.

Although it probably was just as well that the trend was away from the high clarion writing of Bach and Handel, the composers who followed failed to invent any writing for the trumpet which was as interesting. Bach and Handel and their predecessors made the trumpet one of the most interesting instruments in the orchestra. They no doubt went to extreme lengths and exhausted the possibilities along this line, but they have to be given credit for resourcefulness and inventiveness. When composers after Bach and Handel abandoned this style of writing, they failed to bring forth anything to take its place. They used the trumpets much as bugles are used today in drum corps. The trumpet parts were thin chords whose poverty of design was covered up in the noise of the tympani. They apparently did not think well of the long trumpets on which it was possible to play chromatically in the upper registers. This kind of playing was a man killer for the trumpeters, but it did have possibilities which some feel were not fully exploited. These old masters also knew about adding crooks to the simple trumpet, in order to obtain, by jumping from one trumpet to the other, something approximating chromatic playing. Wagner's success with this type of instrument shows well enough that Mozart, Haydn and Beethoven overlooked possibilities in the trumpet of their time. Instead of taking advantage of the long trumpet with its diatonic and chromatic upper registers, and instead of using the trumpet with crooks as did Wagner, they contented themselves with writing thin tonic and dominant chords for these instruments.

Possibly it is expecting too much, even from such geniuses as Haydn, Mozart and Beethoven, to look for trumpet writing beyond the thin chords based on the tonic and dominant. After all, although Wagner did great things on the simple trumpet without valves, he had set before him the example of piston-trumpet performance. He chose the simple trumpet because he preferred the tone to that of the valve trumpet, but the example of the valve trumpet must have suggested the superior trumpet writing for the simple trumpet. To appreciate what Haydn, Mozart and Beethoven were up against, we need only examine what sort of music is written for the regular military bugle today. Bugle calls are limited to five or six notes. Other notes are possible, but these five or six are the best in quality and the easiest to blow. Below are shown these notes (⌀), with other notes which are possible but seldom used (•). The numbers indicate their relative position in the harmonic scale, or scale of open notes.

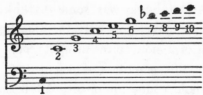

The obstacles in making music with these notes are obvious. They have wide gaps between them, and their range limits the music to a monotonous span. In the upper part of the scale the notes are closer together and have greater musical possibilities, but these notes are hard to play and can be blown only by a few powerful individuals. Even with the accurately built instruments today, many players cannot hit the ninth and tenth partials; on the crude bugles two hundred years or more ago it is doubtful if many players could go beyond the sixth. It is little wonder that early composers did not think seriously about the musical possibilities of such instruments.

It was to overcome such limitations and bridge the gaps in the natural scale, that the Kent bugle was invented in 1810. This invention is often credited to James Halliday, an Irish bandmaster, and it became known as the Kent bugle in honor of the Duke of Kent, who became much interested in it. There is evidence, however, that Kolbel of St Petersburg built a keyed bugle in 1770 and that Weidinger of Vienna also made such an instrument in 1801. These instruments were said to have five holes in the side which were opened and closed by five keys, similar in appearance and principle to the keys now found on saxophones. The inventors concluded, correctly enough, that they could make this instrument chromatic by using keys, just as the woodwinds had been made chromatic by the use of this device. Playing the keyed bugle was somewhat like playing the saxophone, a later invention, only the mouthpiece was cup-shaped instead of a mouthpiece using a reed.

Immediately this invention was hailed as one likely to change the whole course of music. All brass instruments played with a cup-shaped mouthpiece could now play music just as a flute, clarinet or oboe. Instead of being neglected except for a few scattered chords, the trumpet and cornet could now take their place alongside the instruments which had been accepted for years in the orchestra and band. Abandonment of the high clarion writing of Bach and Handel was no longer regretted. Trumpet players would no longer have to choose between blowing their lungs out on the high notes or taking a back seat and playing only thin chords. They could now play their parts as did players of other instruments. A new voice, a new coloring had been added to the orchestra. Great prophecies were made about the benefits that would come to all the brass instruments as a result of this invention.

The principle of using keys to bridge the gaps in the scale of cup-mouthpiece instruments was found to be better adapted to conical-bore instruments than to cylindrical-bore. For this reason, the keyed bugle became the most popular, with the keyed cornet less popular and the keyed trumpet not popular at all. This was a victory for the conical-bore instrument in its struggle with the cylindrical-bore trumpet. The demand for the keyed bugle increased suddenly, while the keyed trumpet dropped into the background.

Unfortunately for the inventors, but fortunately for music, Blumel, an oboe player from Silesia, invented the piston valve in 1815, and the great keyed-bugle invention was quickly forgotten. Blumel may have obtained his original idea from an ingenious Irishman named Clagget, who in 1788 rigged up two trumpets—one in D and another in E♭— jointed together so they could be played with one mouth-piece. By means of a change valve either trumpet could be connected with the mouthpiece. The advantage of this device is somewhat similar to that now on double French horns. By selecting the D or E♭ trumpet, it was possible to obtain the open notes on either and thereby play a scale with fewer

gaps in it than are found on a single trumpet. It is said
Clagget also experimented with a valve similar to that developed twenty-two years later by Blumel, but if he did,
he did not develop it to a practical stage.

Blumel's device consisted of a sort of pump which could
add a length of tubing to the main length, sufficient to lower

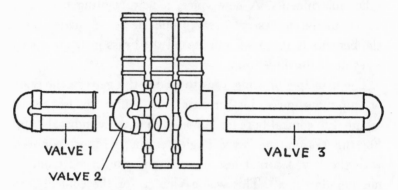

VALVE 1

VALVE 2

VALVE 3

Showing the comparative lengths of the three valve slides of the
cornet and trumpet. The first valve controls a length of tubing equal
to a whole tone; the second, a semitone; and the third, a tone
and a half, or three semitones.

any open note a half-step. To the five or more open notes,
such as were shown to be the only notes available on the
simple bugle or trumpet, were added an equal number of
notes through this piston device. This gave twice as many
notes as before, and although the ability to flat all the open
notes a semitone did not give everything desired on the
trumpet or cornet, the principle was to be expanded so that
all the gaps would eventually be bridged and the trumpet
and cornet would be made truly chromatic. Blumel sold his
invention to the German instrument maker Stolzel of
Breslau. Stolzel carried the invention still farther by adding
a second valve capable of adding a length of tubing to the

main length sufficient to lower the tone of any open note a full tone. The two valves could be combined to add a step and a half. In 1830 Müller of Mayence saw the need of a third valve and added one controlling a length of tubing capable of adding three semitones. This is the modern arrangement of valves and makes the scale completely chromatic above the second partial or open note.

To understand how this valve worked we need only take the bugle scale, which is the scale for all simple horns. If we start with the G above the staff, we can bridge the gap to E below by adding first the half-step tubing (bringing us

Open notes are shown as half-notes and are playable without valves. Notes played by using the valves are shown as quarter-notes. Numbers under notes indicate which valve or combination of valves is used, the valves being numbered starting with valve nearest mouthpiece. The numbers in parentheses indicate notes not playable on two-valve instrument, but made playable after the third valve was added in 1830.

down to F♯) and then the whole-step tubing (bringing us down to F). The next note is open, so we play chromatically from G to E by pushing down the half-step valve, then the whole-step valve, and then playing E open. To go on down to C chromatically is done in the same manner: push down the half-step valve and sound D♯, then push down the whole-step valve and play D; finally push down both valves, thereby adding to the open E a step and a half, and C♯ will sound. Since C is open, the next half-step is reached without any valve.

With the two valves it is not possible to bridge the gap between this open C and the open G below, for it is obvious that the two valves and their corresponding tubing can take us down below C only a step and a half, leaving us stranded on A♮. It is not possible to play G♯. Also, there is a gap between the open G and the open C below, for it is possible to play down from G chromatically to E♮, leaving a gap of D♯, D♮ and C♯. But the third valve was added, controlling one and a half steps. By pushing down all three valves and using the tubing of all three, six semitones are made available. These are sufficient to bring us down chromatically from open G to the open C below. This makes the entire effective range of the trumpet and cornet chromatic. Of course, the fundamental of the instrument is an octave below this lowest open C, but this is impossible for all but a few artists to play. By using the six semitones, it is possible to descend below this open C to F♯ below the treble clef, but these notes are not very musical at best and are obtainable only by a few players with unusual lips. This still leaves a gap between F♯ and the C below, but this does not present any problem to the trumpet and cornet player, for he does not care to go down that far anyway. This problem does present itself to the tuba player, and a fourth valve has been added, as will be related in a later chapter.

It would be supposed that composers would seize upon the new valve trumpet immediately and would score for it intensively, it being a newcomer to the orchestra and consequently offering new resources never used before. At least it would be supposed that the new valve trumpet would outmode the old simple trumpet. Such was not the case, at least not immediately. It was twenty years before the valve trumpet was called for to any extent. Beethoven and his contemporaries seem to have ignored it. With a few rare exceptions, there are no trumpet notes written in the scores of this time which could not be played on the simple trumpet. It is possible that even these were written for the keyed trumpet.

It is surprising how the simple trumpet with crooks hung on after the valve was invented. Scores called for the trumpet with crooks until nearly 1900, but the F trumpet and the Bb-to-A trumpet gradually became standard. The chief crooks used were C, D, Eb, E and F, those common in the music of Mendelssohn and Schumann. Other crooks were called for, in practically every key from low Ab to high C. The valve trumpet is said to have been specified in a score for the first time in 1836 by Meyerbeer in "Les Huguenots." Another contender for the honor is Chelard, whose "Macbeth" was performed in Paris in 1827 and whose score is said to call for valve trumpet. With Schumann, Wagner and Berlioz, the valve trumpet became rather generally accepted, so that by the latter part of the nineteenth century it was no longer necessary for the composer to specify "valve trumpet" or "piston trumpet" to distinguish from the simple trumpet, the word trumpet meaning by then the trumpet with pistons, or valves.

In England the valve trumpet had a difficult time in gaining any acceptance, owing to the popularity of the slide trumpet. This instrument was hardly known outside of England, but it had a tremendous vogue for about a hundred years, beginning with the close of the eighteenth century. Some authorities have confused this instrument with the treble trombone, but it is distinctly different. It was usually built in F, the same pitch as the classical F trumpet. Coming onto the scene before either keys or valves had been added to the trumpet, it was of course a simple trumpet, but it had a slide which was capable of lowering any natural, or open, note a half- or a whole tone. This slide was something like a slide on a trombone, except it was shorter and worked in an opposite way. Instead of being pushed forward to lower the pitch of a note, it was pulled backward toward the player. Its position was approximately where the first valve slide on the modern valve trumpet is now located and was rigged up with a spring so that when the slide was released after being pulled out to flatten a note, the slide jumped back into closed position.

Although there were some famous performers on the slide trumpet, it was difficult to play. It could add only a half-tone or whole tone to the open notes, which was not sufficient to make the trumpet chromatic, any more than a trumpet with a half-step valve and a whole-step valve could be chromatic. Serious gaps were left in the scale which dampened the ardor of its many admirers. The intonation was bad, too, especially when the trumpet was played with crooks. When played in F, the intonation was fairly good, but when crooks were added, the slide was not long enough to add a whole step to the open notes, because of the longer interval required for a whole step in the lower reaches of the scale. When the trumpet happened to be in higher pitches, such as B♭, C or D, the positions of the slide were so radically altered that only the most skillful players could play the trumpet in tune. Although the slide trumpet delayed for over fifty years the introduction into England of the more efficient valve trumpet, eventually, along toward

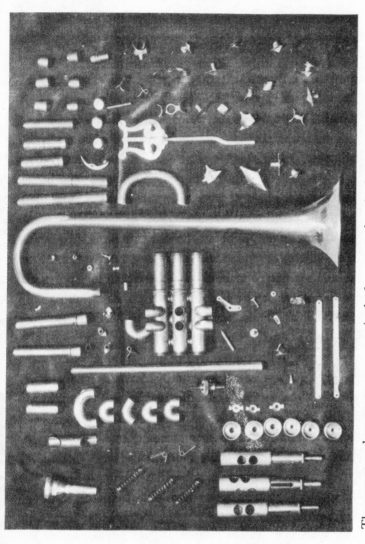

The cornet and trumpet are comprised of over two hundred separate parts and must be carefully assembled to make an instrument. The largest single piece is the bell, an important part of any cup-mouthpiece instrument.

the close of the nineteenth century, the valve trumpet began to displace the slide trumpet, and after 1900 it was mostly a historical relic.

Wagner is given credit for being the first composer to score well for the trumpet. He usually used three and sometimes he used four trumpets. He became acquainted with their resources, appreciated their colorings and conceived effective ways of scoring for them. It was a long time, however, before Wagner abandoned the old custom of scoring for trumpets with crooks to throw them into various keys. There was a belief in those days that trumpets in different pitches possessed different qualities of tone. This is difficult for us to understand, because today the trumpet player uses the B♭ or C trumpet and transposes all music written for variously pitched trumpets. Nobody seems to think that any desirable tonal coloring is lost by this method. Possibly the trumpets in Wagner's day were not nearly so accurate in intonation, and it may be there was some justification for his practice. One thing is sure, his method of writing worked a severe hardship on the trumpet player. A classical example is the ninety-six bars in the opening of the introduction to "Lohengrin," where ten crook changes are marked. The rate at which these ten changes must be made is indicated when it is considered that only two and a half minutes are consumed in playing these ninety-six bars. This averages a change of crook every fifteen seconds. Trumpet players began to revolt against such practices. They found they could easily transpose the music, and they preferred to transpose rather than to change crooks. This is the universal practice today.

Following the invention of the keyed bugle in 1810, keys

were added to both cornets and trumpets. It was not long, however, until piston valves were installed in both cornets and trumpets. Although trumpets were much the more popular, cornets were scored for to some extent, especially by French composers, notably Berlioz and Bizet. This instrument was known as the "cornopean." Usually they were called for in addition to trumpets, and not as trumpet substitutes. If they did not exclude the trumpets, they did all but obliterate the old keyed bugle and later the piston bugle. In the middle of the nineteenth century this instrument had quite a vogue in the form of the well-known saxhorn. The saxhorn was the invention of Antoine Sax in 1842. There were seven instruments in the family, from a high soprano in E♭ to a contrabass in B♭. In bore they were all conical, and their tone was especially mellow and of singing quality. These instruments are still used in some of the European brass bands, but they are rare in America. After inventing the saxhorns, Sax invented another family of instruments, called the saxtrombas. Instead of having a conical bore, they had a bore more like that of the cornet; that is, they were only conical in part of their length, the rest of the bore being cylindrical. Although there are many who regret that the saxhorns did not survive, rather than the saxtrombas, the brass instruments in use today are more like the saxtrombas than the saxhorns. Those who prefer the saxhorns say the saxtrombas are so nearly like the trumpets and trombones as to lack contrast necessary for best musical effects.

Although in the larger horns, such as baritone and bass, only the saxtromba bore has survived, in the soprano instruments we have retained one of each type. We retain the old trumpet with its cylindrical bore, shallow cup mouthpiece and bright tone. This is the brass soprano of the orchestra. We also retain the cornet, with its partly cylindrical, partly conical bore, its deeper cup mouthpiece and its mellow quality of tone. This is the brass soprano of the concert band. The more nearly conical in bore bugle and saxhorn have survived in the fluegelhorn. Its bore is conical in shape, its mouthpiece is larger and deeper than that of the cornet, and its tone is broader and more mellow than that of the cornet. Some have called the fluegelhorn a mezzo-soprano, and that is really what it is. It is found in the band and serves to blend the tones of the cornets and trumpets with the altos and French horns.

The classical trumpet was built in F, a fourth below the Bb in which trumpets are usually built today. Being lower in pitch, this instrument had a more beautiful lower register. On the other hand, its top register was not as good as that on the Bb trumpet. As the tendency was to write higher and higher for the trumpet, the Bb instrument came to be the standard pitch for both trumpet and cornet. This tendency to write higher and higher for the trumpet has led to the use of the C trumpet, and even trumpets in D and Eb. Occasionally brass bands call for the Eb cornet also.

Although built in Bb, most trumpets and cornets have a slide which can be pulled out, bringing the pitch of the instrument down to A. The majority of compositions for band are written in flat signatures, and such signatures are easier to play by using an instrument built in a flat key. For instance, a composition written in three flats has only one flat for the Bb trumpet. Orchestra music, on the other hand, is usually written in sharp signatures. This makes it helpful to use an instrument built in a sharp key. For example, a composition written in three sharps has a part in C (no sharps) for the A trumpet. This explains why trumpets and cornets are built in B♭ with slide to A.

Although players often refer to "blowing" the cornet or trumpet, such instruments are not "blown" at all. If a person picks up a trumpet and blows into it, no sound comes out. The instrument is made to sound by setting up a vibration of the air inside the tubing. This vibration is made by pressing the lips against the cup-shaped mouthpiece and blowing between them. Teachers often describe the lip action as that required by spitting a hair from between the lips. The weak buzzing sound produced by the lips when air is forced between them is picked up by the instrument and amplified, as will be shown more fully in closing chapters.

Although the orchestra has become almost classical in most respects and has changed little in recent years, the American concert band has been undergoing great changes. The old brass band is practically a thing of the past, and in its place is evolving the concert band. This has had an important bearing on cornets and trumpets. In the old days the soprano section of the brass band was composed almost entirely of conical-bore saxhorns and later of cornets. The altos and tenors and baritones and basses were also conical-bore instruments of the saxhorn family. Gradually woodwinds found their way into the band. More and more were admitted, and the brass was pushed back to give room. Eventually there were more clarinets in the band than cornets or saxhorns. At first the clarinets were grouped to the left of the director, with the cornets on the right. Lately, however, first clarinets have been stationed on the left of the director, just as are the first violins in the orchestra. On the right of the director are second clarinets and other woodwinds, such as bassoons, oboes, alto and bass clarinets. Back of these, with the trombones, will be found a group of cornets and trumpets.

Following the era of florid cornet soloing by such virtuosi as Levy, Liberati, Hoch, Smith and Bellstedt, the cornet band became popular. It was seldom that a trumpet could find a foothold in the band. Gradually the trumpet came to the front and bands were filled with trumpets, almost to the exclusion of cornets. Along with the growing popularity of the woodwinds has come a realization that cornets are better fitted to be the brass sopranos of the concert band than trumpets. The American Bandmaster Association has specifically recommended that the cornet be used in the band instead of the trumpet. There is no objection to having a couple of trumpets in the band to give contrasting coloring for effects, just as occasionally two or three cornets will be used in the orchestra for effects; but the cornet has very definitely become the principal soprano of the brass choir of the band. Since there are several times more soprano voices used in the brass choir of the band than there are used in brass choir of the orchestra, the cornet can be said to have achieved an edge today on the trumpet in the age-old feud which has existed between them for several centuries.

Although the differences among trumpet, cornet and fluegelhorn are generally accepted to be as given in the foregoing pages, actually today these differences have become greatly minimized in manufacture. The generally accepted definitions that the trumpet is two-thirds cylindrical and one-third conical, while the cornet is one-third cylindrical and two-thirds conical, are really not true. Actually the only part of the trumpet tubing which is straight is the valve and tuning slides, but these likewise are the only straight tubing on the cornet. The mouthpipe of the trumpet used to be mostly straight, but today even it is generally tapered. The actual sliding part of the tuning slide is cylindrical, but on most trumpets the side joining the mouthpipe is smaller than the side leading to the valves, thereby giving it a general taper. It is distinctly true, however, that the *degree* of taper is different among the three instruments. There is less taper in the trumpet, more in the cornet, and most in the fluegelhorn. The mouthpiece receiver on the trumpet is larger than the receiver on the cornet, while the bell is usually smaller, thereby allowing more taper between mouthpiece and bell in the cornet than in a trumpet, both of the same bore through the valves. Therefore, although the two-thirds-to-one-third relationships do not hold, actually there is an effective difference among them which still defines their tonal qualities.

CHAPTER IX

The French Horns

GRADUATES OF THE CHASE

FIVE GENERATIONS OF PEOPLE existing at one time call for a photograph and a write-up in the local newspaper. Sometimes a span of ninety or a hundred years is covered by such a group of prolific and long-lived persons. The modern French horn wins all the honors for such distinctions among musical instruments, for the horn's remote ancestor —the Hebrew shofar—stands beside it today, hale and hearty after sixty centuries of recorded history.

The Hebrew shofar is the oldest type of horn of which we have any authentic record. It was used in religious ceremonies by the Hebrews six thousand years ago and is still used today in Jewish ceremonies connected with the New Year and the Feast of Atonement. No other instrument can point to such a long record of continuous use. Hundreds of generations of rams have furnished horns from which the shofar has been made, but during all these ages this ancient instrument has not changed. It is the same today as it was six thousand years ago when the fathers of Abraham introduced it into their religious ritual and ceremony, even to the sharp rim of the cup serving as a mouthpiece.

The shofar is made by cleaning out the inside of the horn of a ram and making a sort of funnel or cup-shaped opening at the small end to serve as a mouthpiece. This cup often has a sharp edge, as has been found out by a number of today's French horn and trumpet artists who have tried to blow this instrument. Their lips are accustomed to the wide, smooth rim of a metal mouthpiece, and when they participate in the Jewish services, as they sometimes are called upon to do, they find the sharp edge of the ancient shofar most uncomfortable.

Of course instruments were made from the horns of animals a long, long time before the recorded history of the Jewish race. All primitive peoples made and still make instruments from the horn of rams, cows, buffaloes. Tusks of the elephant are also a favorite material. This crude kind of musical instrument no doubt is the common ancestor of all cup-mouthpiece instruments, including trumpet and trombone with cylindrical bore, but the French horn is the true son of the ancient instrument made from an animal horn, because it is conical in bore like the animal horn. The natural horn without valves carried a taper from the mouthpiece to the bell, and the valve horns of today are tapered throughout except through the valves.

It is conjectured that the Queen of Sheba was greatly entranced by the shofar when she visited King Solomon and carried many of these instruments back home with her; in any event, the ancient Ethiopians used a similar instrument in their religious ceremonies which was known as the kenet. The Greeks also used the kegas to announce sacrificial offerings and to call the people together for various religious and secular gatherings. Alexander the Great is said to have used a great horn for assembling his troops, and tradition has it that such a mighty blast could be blown upon it that it could be heard for two miles. A similar horn is said to have been used by Roland, famous warrior nephew of Charlemagne. When leading a division of Charlemagne's great army, Roland upon several occasions used this horn to signal his uncle, miles away, for assistance when the tide of battle turned against him.

Chaucer furnished an early record of the horns in England. There are many passages in his writings which refer to the "bemes," the term for horns. In one passage he implies that they were made of many materials but were not any too musical:

"Of bras thay broughten bemes and of box [wood],
Of horn, of boon [bone], in which thay blewe and pouped,
And therewithal thay shryked and thay houped."

Such horns were used mostly in war, in the chase, and for different kinds of signaling. Henry VIII seemed to consider them genuine musical instruments, for he left twenty-two horns of various kinds in his collection of musical instruments.

It was in France, though, that the horn met its great opportunity and where it started its rise into the ranks of orchestral instruments. It is because of the prominence given the horn in France that it has come to be known as the French horn. It started its apprenticeship as a hunting horn, but served it so well it was finally accorded a place in the orchestra. It found favor with the French king Louis XI, who reigned in the latter part of the fifteenth century. At that time the horn was made of metal and was bent in a circular shape, inscribing about three fourths of a circle. The mouthpiece was deep and shaped like a funnel, as are the horn mouthpieces of today. Being short in length, the horn had fewer notes than it possessed later. Its repertoire consisted of a few short blasts which served as simple signals. Louis XIII, who ruled during the first half of the seventeenth century, used a longer hunting horn which was curved in circular form and described a complete circle with some overlapping. Having more possible notes, the horn was given a larger repertoire. Short, simple notes in a series were sounded instead of single blasts, to signal certain information to the hunters. One of the most elaborate was an abbreviated melody of several notes which indicated that the fox had been apprehended.

These calls seemed to please the French kings and their nobles, and new calls were added and old ones made more elaborate. This quest for more musical calls resulted in making the horn longer and longer, to afford more and more notes. By the middle of the eighteenth century, Louis XV was using a horn consisting of three complete circles of tubing, the instrument encircling the body and resting on the shoulder. Many complicated calls were used, and it became necessary for the hunt master of Louis XV to systematize the growing repertoire of calls. The shorter, more simple calls were reserved for such ordinary tasks as cheering the hounds, signifying the progress of the hunt and asking for aid in case of emergencies. A second group of more elaborate calls was used to signify the kill. They were so systematized that one call indicated a deer, another a fox, and so on. They could even indicate the color of the animal, the number of antlers and other descriptive information. These calls were a kind of telegraphic code set to music. The third group of calls was the most elaborate of all. These calls were in reality musical airs. They were played after the hunt was over as a means of celebrating and rejoicing. Many of them were of a high musical order and later were incorporated in orchestral scores much as they were played originally in the hunt. It was this group of horn calls which bridged the way for the entrance of the lowly horn of the chase into the orchestra.

Even before Louis XV, the hunting horn had impressed certain composers well enough that they wrote orchestral parts for them. Lully, an Italian by birth, is given credit for being the first to do so. He wrote parts for the "trompes de chasse" in his "Princesse d'Elide," performed in Paris in 1664. Apparently this was done as an experiment, and that Lully was not any too well pleased with the results is indicated by the fact that he didn't continue using the hunting horns. These instruments did not become regular members of the orchestra until nearly a hundred years later. When Rameau used two horns in his "Zoroastre" in 1749, the hunting horns were coming into their own as orchestral instruments. Rameau used these two horns in a kind of duet, which consisted partly of hunting calls and partly of sustained harmony passages. Grossec scored two horns to play an obbligato for some arias written in honor of Sophie Arnould's debut in Paris in 1757.

Although the horn was first introduced into opera in France, it was in Germany that it first attained prominence as an orchestral instrument. Lully was bold enough to try the hunting horn in 1664, but it was not seriously considered in France until nearly a hundred years later. In Germany, however, it became an instrument to reckon with early in the century. It was known in this country as the waldhorn, or "forest horn," and was first used in the orchestra by Keiser in his opera "Octavia," performed in Hamburg in 1705. This composition called for a pair of horns in C. Six years later two horns became regular instrumentation in the orchestra of the Royal Theater of Dresden. Not to be out-done, the Imperial Opera orchestra in Vienna the following year added two horns. From this time on the horn was a popular instrument in Germany, especially in the northern part, and a historian writing in 1713 about musical instruments in Germany said the horn was in considerable demand, not only in theater orchestras, but also in small ensembles and in churches. In 1721 Bach called for two horns in his first "Brandenburg Concerto," and the position of the horn was assured.

To Bach's countryman and contemporary, Handel, goes the honor of introducing the horn into England, in 1715. This event is not as English as it might seem, for Handel, the English king and the horn were all three from Germany. Handel was chief musician to the Elector of Hanover, in Germany. He secured permission from the Elector to go to England for a short visit, but once in London, he tarried many months, which greatly irked the Elector. At the end of two years the Elector of Hanover was made king of England, much to the embarrassment of Handel, who was still in England. As a means of gaining back the favor of his former German patron, now English king, Handel composed his "Water Music." It was in this series of compositions that Handel introduced the German waldhorn. Apparently his efforts were pleasing to George I, for he welcomed Handel back into his favor. Five years later Handel used two horns in D, in the London performance of "Radamisto." From that time on, the horn's place in the orchestras of England was accepted, for every great composer since Handel's day has used this instrument.

The horn was also used in Italy by the early composers of opera. Scarlatti seems to have been one of the first Italians to appreciate the horn, for in 1715 he wrote parts for two horns in F, in his opera "Tigrane," performed for the first time in Naples. He wrote mostly in the upper register of the horns, in order to have at his command sufficient notes to compose simple melodies. Later as he learned more about the use of horns he wrote harmonies more in the modern style of composing.

The horns of this early period, up to the time of Bach and Handel, were played with the bell up. The mouthpipe was horizontal with the mouth, then the tubing made a couple of turns, ending with the bell opening straight up. The Germans were responsible for reversing the position of the horn, turning the bell downward to its modern position. This position was arrived at in their efforts to subdue the harsh tone of the horn by partially stopping it with the hand. In order to do this the bell was turned downward so it was possible to place the hand in the bell. They also muted the horn with mutes made of wood and cardboard.

The horn at this time was about seven and a half feet long, and various pitches were obtained by inserting crooks of various lengths in the mouthpipe. Some of these crooks were longer than the main length of the horn itself, the longest being twelve and a half feet. Even short crooks inserted in the mouthpipe threw the intonation off, and it can be imagined how terrible in intonation were the horns with these long crooks. At first horns in D and F were mostly used. Later horns in C and G were common. Still later crooks were added to throw the horns into E♭, E and A. Then longer crooks were added to give low B♭ and low A♭. Short horns were also constructed to give high B and even high C. In 1755 Johann Wernern, second horn of the Imperial Opera orchestra of Vienna, used what was called the "improved" horn. It had a total of nine crooks, giving him horns in the following keys: low B♭, C, D, E♭, E, F, G, A and high B♭. Even this was not enough for some horn players, and it is said that they finally packed around with them a total of sixteen crooks, ranging from low A♭ to high C. To divide this great number of crooks among several horns was bad enough, but to supply sixteen crooks with one horn was almost criminal. Such a horn could not possibly be made to play in tune.

It is no wonder that horn players revolted against such practices. Hampel, a horn player in the Dresden orchestra, was the first to do anything about it. He schemed around and finally discovered that less serious difficulties would be experienced if the crooks were inserted in the body of the horn, rather than in the mouthpipe. In 1753 he brought out his celebrated "Invention horn," also called the "Machine horn." This horn was devised so that movable slides could be inserted in the body of the horn, somewhat as tuning slides are inserted in the horns of today. Acting in self-defense, Hampel did a great service for his fellow horn players.

Hampel was a man of genius and continued his experiments. He noted that oboe players were accustomed to inserting a wad of wool in the bell of their instruments to soften the harsh tone. Horns in those days were not any too sweet and smooth in tone, and he conceived the idea that this trick might do the horn some good, too. What he found out led to a new era of horn playing. He found that this device not only softened the tone of the horn but raised the pitch a semitone. Later the wad of wool was abandoned and the hand was inserted into the bell of the horn. By raising the pitch of the horn a semitone, it was possible to sharpen by a half-step all the open notes in the natural scale, thereby adding a complete new series of notes and making the horn chromatic in the upper part of the scale where the open notes were close together. This discovery was made in 1760, and although used quite extensively by most horn players, composers did not write regularly for the "hand" horn until early in the nineteenth century.

Other attempts were made to fill in the gaps of the open scale. Notable among these was the invention of Kolbel, a Bohemian horn player at the Chapel Royal of Russia. Kolbel in 1770 conceived the idea of placing a key on the bell. By opening this key, the effective length of the horn could be reduced sufficiently to raise the pitch of all open tones a semitone. The idea seemed to win favor, and by 1801 the number of keys had been increased to five keys, making the horn chromatic, except between the two lowest open tones. A few years later the sixth key was added, giving a chromatic scale from low C to the top of the scale. Only the bell series of notes was of good quality, however; the other series of notes came from the holes and were not as clear and resonant. The difference in quality was generally recognized and led to the practice of detaching the bells altogether. The horn without the bell produced a harsh tone, and although not desirable musically, the practice was adopted more or less generally for certain effects. Composers wrote notations for such passages specifying "bells off." An instance of this is found in Mehul's duet for horns in "Euphrosyne et Coradin."

Horn players can thank the oboist for the invention of the stopped horn, as already noted. They can also thank the oboist for another and even greater improvement to their instrument—the valves. In 1815 Blumel, an oboe player of Silesia, invented the piston valve. By this device, a length of tubing could be added to the length of the horn by pushing down a piston, or pump. The length of tubing so controlled was sufficient to add a half-step to the open notes, giving a whole new series of notes. The ease with which this could be done appealed to horn players and also to the players of other cup-mouthpiece instruments. The invention was sold to Stolzel, a German, who refined the invention and added a second valve which controlled a length of tubing sufficient to lower all open tones a whole step. In 1830 Müller of Mayence added a third valve which operated a third loop of tubing sufficient to lower the open tones one and a half tones, making the instrument chromatic. Ten years later Stolzel's inventive genius produced the sub-ventil valve, so called because the valve tubing came out at the bottom of the valve. This was hailed as the last word in valve construction, but modern instruments have gone back to the valve whose valve slides come out at the side.

Blumel was not satisfied with the piston valve, believing that the travel of the piston was too long and clumsy. He finally hit upon the rotary valve in 1827. This valve consisted of a little rotor or drum which revolved on an axle.

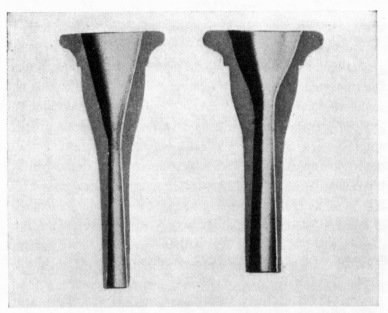

Cross sections, showing the difference between the French-horn mouthpiece (*left*) and the mellophone mouthpiece (*right*). Note that the horn mouthpiece is deeper and more funnel-shaped. This difference in shape has much to do with difference in tone quality.

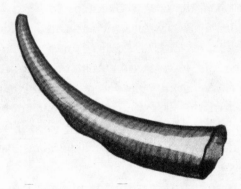

THE ANCESTOR OF THE FRENCH HORN
The Hebrew shofar, still used in religious services after sixty centuries.

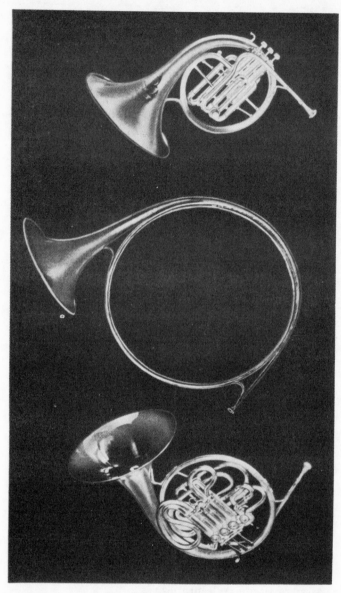

(*Left to right*): Modern double French horn in F and B♭. Simple or natural horn, used in the chase. Modern mellophone, used as French-horn substitute. Valves of French horn are played with the left hand, valves of mellophone are played with the right hand, as are all other valve instruments except French horn.

Slots were milled in the side of the rotor so that when it was turned the air column was switched into valve slides, thereby adding various lengths of tubing for lowering the open tones. It was another ingenious device for accomplishing the same effect as that of the piston valve. Although the piston valve has survived in France and England, the rotary valve is popular in Austria, Germany and also in Italy. In America, the rotary valve has found favor on only the French horn, most French horns using this type of valve. The action of the rotary valve is shorter, faster and more delicate than that of the piston valve, and fine French horn players almost universally prefer this type of valve to the piston type.

Although the advantages of the valve horn are obvious, its adoption was long delayed because of custom and the general reluctance of musicians and composers to adopt anything which is different. It was twenty years after the invention of the valve before it was generally specified. Beethoven, Weber, Schubert and Rossini used the old hand horn freely, and it was not until about 1835 that the valve horn was really accepted. Even then it was the custom to use two hand horns with two valve horns. There was a feeling that valve notes were not as good as the open notes on the hand horn. After valve horns were generally used, composers often called for hand horns with crooks for certain passages where they wanted to display the French horn quality of tone to the best advantage. The valve horn did not win the battle over the old hand horn until toward the latter part of the nineteenth century, and it was not until the final quarter of the nineteenth century that the hand horn was entirely abandoned in favor of the valve horn.

Today it is customary to use four horns, but when the

horn was gaining a foothold in the orchestra composers were undecided just how many were needed to produce the best effects. When Bach wrote the first of the "Brandenburg Concertos" in 1721, he called for only two horns. He seemed to be following the practice used in writing for oboes and bassoons, because a pair of these was usually used. Haydn in 1759 used two horns, along with two oboes, in his First Symphony, and we find he was still using two horns when he composed his D Symphony thirty-six years later. It is true that in 1766 his famous orchestra at Eisenstadt included four horns, but this orchestra was distinctly an opera orchestra and not a symphony orchestra.

Mozart's three great symphonies written during the summer of 1788 all call for two hand horns. Three years later when he wrote the opera "Idomeno," he employed four horns. In this he was merely following the custom of the time. Two horns were used in symphony, and four horns were often used in opera. Usually two of the horns were in one key and two were in another key, giving in this way more open notes than if all four were in the same key. The melody or harmony was passed from one pair of horns to the other in order to use the notes available on them. Generally Haydn and Mozart wrote from the second open note up to G or A above the staff, the twelfth or thirteenth note in the open scale. Occasionally they wrote up to high C, using the fourteenth, fifteenth and sixteenth open notes, but this depended upon the key of the horn, for these extremely high notes were not possible on the horns of high pitch. Although hand stopping had been discovered some time before, only a few stopped notes were called for.

Beethoven started out writing for two hand horns, as in

his C Major symphony composed in 1800, but five years later when he composed his great "Eroica" symphony he called for three horns. This is the first time three horns had ever been used in the symphony. The fourth horn was added to the symphony in 1824, when he called for a quartet of horns in his Ninth Symphony. That four horns were an innovation not generally accepted is shown by the fact that Schubert, Schumann, Mendelssohn and others who immediately followed Beethoven used sometimes two horns and sometimes four. These composers were obviously thinking in terms of two instruments, for they generally gave to the two horns two notes, to form a chord with two bassoons, giving the lower notes of the chord to the latter two instruments. When they did write for four horns they usually gave the two upper notes of the chord to the first and second horns, and the two lower notes to the third and fourth horns. It was not until later that they fell in with the custom, almost universally adopted now, of giving the two top notes to the first and third horns and the two lower notes to the second and fourth horns.

All composers have not adhered to this rule, however. Various French composers of the nineteenth century, among them Saint-Saëns, very often had the third and fourth horns play the higher notes and gave the lower range to the first and second. Recently composers have considerably changed the writing for French horns, and this tendency is becoming more and more common. They are learning to use them in rotation, 1-2-3-4. In many instances, the doubling of the first horn is done by the second and the doubling of the fourth horn is done by the third, just opposite to the custom adopted by the classic composers. The second horn of today must have a good upper range, and the third horn must have an easy and good lower range.

Although these composers wrote during the era of the valve horn, they almost always used the hand horn. Schumann was one of the first of the great composers to use the valve horn; for instance in his Third and Fourth symphonies. Although Schumann was not as good an orchestrator as Schubert and Mendelssohn, it is to his credit that he saw, better than they, the value of this new invention.

Rossini did a great deal for horn playing by demonstrating its possibilities as a solo instrument. He experimented with highly florid passages and showed that the horn was entirely capable of this type of playing. He undoubtedly enjoyed advantages not possessed by his contemporaries, for his father was an expert horn player, and he was brought up on a diet of horn music. He knew the horn intimately and was a recognized authority on the instrument. He is reported to have rebuked his father for bad performance one time while his father was playing under his direction. The orchestra was rehearsing one of Rossini's operas in a small town in Italy when his father hit a "sour" note. Rossini looked over gravely at his father and said, "You may go right home!"

Weber is celebrated for his beautiful handling of the horns, as in "Oberon" and "Euryanthe." One of the most famous passages for the horn is the noble horn quartet in "Der Freischütz." Meyerbeer demonstrated new possibilities for the horn in the masterful way in which he delegated melody and thematic material to four horns. Berlioz believed a good way to treat the horns was to pitch them in four different keys, thus affording a great number of open notes. He recommends this form of writing in his famous *Instrumentation and*

Orchestration. He also makes a plea for the natural horns without valves, but toward the close of his treatise on horns he has to admit that the valve horns have advantages over the old hand horn. Berlioz, along with all other Frenchmen, was backward in his attitude toward the old hand horn. After all other nations had discarded the hand horn, France was still using it, but finally had to give in and adopt the valve horn.

Wagner followed the practice of his time by using both hand and valve horns, using the latter for first and second parts, and the former for third and fourth. Not until "Lohengrin," finished in 1848, did he abandon the natural horn for the valve horn. In the "Ride of the Valkyries," finished in 1856, he wrote for eight horns in an effective manner. Using eight horns probably suggested the need for carrying the horn harmony down lower in the chord, for we find him advocating a sort of bass French horn. He had a quartet of these made, called tubens. There was the tenor in B♭ and the bass in F. They were of long, small tubing and were played with a funnel-shaped mouthpiece. Such instruments, however, do not achieve the true French horn quality and never became widely used. Horn players say they are very difficult to play in tune but that they respond easily. A very tight embouchure must be used because of this freedom of response. To make a bad situation even worse, Wagner wrote for two pairs of tuben in the opposite key. Parts for the tuben in F were written in B♭ and parts for the B♭ tuben were written in F; and both parts were written in the bass clef!

One of the very first to use the tubens was the Chicago Symphony Orchestra, under the celebrated Theodore Thomas. Max Pottag, French horn in this orchestra, recalls that Theodore Thomas had been using tubens long before Mr Pottag joined the Chicago orchestra in 1907, and ever since, he has been playing the tuben parts when called for. Anton Bruckner employs eight horns and four tubens in each of his Seventh, Eighth and Ninth symphonies. The Chicago Symphony Orchestra horn quartet played the four tuben parts in Wagner's "Ring" for years with the Chicago Civic Opera Company, when Campanini was impresario. Other symphony orchestras using genuine tubens are the Philharmonic-Symphony Society of New York and the Philadelphia Orchestra, but in many other orchestras the tuben parts are given to other instruments.

Wagner wrote a great many beautiful horn passages. One of the most dramatic is the famous horn call of Siegfried. At one place in the opera this stirring call is supposed to be heard in the distance. To achieve this effect, the horn player sounds the call backstage. Arthur Berv, first horn of the Philadelphia Orchestra, relates an almost tragic experience when he was called upon to play this well-known passage with the orchestra while on tour. To produce the far-away effect, he chose a spot just outside an exit door, permitting the horn music to reach the audience through this passage-way. Standing there ready to play the call, with just a few bars to wait, he was accosted by a custodian of the theater. The custodian told him in no uncertain terms that fire regulations or some other rule required that this door be kept closed. Mr Berv's frantic explanations seemed to mean nothing. Just at the point where the custodian threatened to close the door by force, he relented and permitted Mr Berv to play his call; but during the altercation the cue was missed, and although the call was finally given, it was a bar too late.

THE FRENCH HORNS

After the concert Mr Berv hastened to explain to the conductor why he had come in so late, and the conductor, at first somewhat irritated because of the tardy horn call, broke out into a hearty laugh when he learned of the poor horn player's predicament.

This Siegfried horn call is constantly getting into trouble. Once in Boston the horn player was out backstage waiting to play the passage, when a stagehand spotted him. Being new on the job and very zealous about his duty, he refused to permit the horn player to give his call. Remonstrating with the horn player, the stagehand said, "You can't play here. Why, can't you hear?—there's an orchestra playing in there." The cue came and went, but the horn call never was sounded.

No other instrument of the brasses can equal the French horn in velvety tone, playing range, dynamic expression and variety of effects. Not only is it one of the most expressive solo instruments of the brasses, but it has a unique quality of tone which blends well with strings, woodwinds or brasses. When played mezzo forte, its tones melt into those of the strings or woodwinds, and when played forte it can give a good imitation of the trumpet or trombone. It can match tones with the delicate flute or with the deep-voiced, dark-colored bassoon. It is difficult to describe the tone quality of the horn to those who have never heard it. It has rare tonal tints which no other instrument has and which no one can ever forget after having once heard them. It is mellow but highly penetrating and expressive when played naturally, but when forced it becomes bold and powerful. The muted notes, when played naturally, produce beautiful far-away and echo effects, but when forced they give peculiarly demoniacal or terrifying effects and are often used to depict themes of this nature. An example of the latter occurs in Gounod's "Faust." The very voice of the devil comes from the horns as the aged Faust is inveigled into selling his soul for youth. These sounds from the "blasted" horns make the flesh creep. Terrifying are the "blasted" horn notes written by Wagner to signify the death of Siegfried in "Götter-dämmerung." No other instrument can quite imitate these dreadful, ghastly sounds.

In the middle register, from B♭ below the treble-clef staff to F top line, the French horn can be depended on for almost any demands. It can play extreme pianissimo and swell to powerful fortissimo and die back again into pianissimo with the most surprising smoothness. Both legato and staccato playing come easily for most players, as do trills, especially in the upper part of the scale. These are made both with the valves and also with the lips. Because of the close spacing of the open notes, lip arpeggios are very fine on the horn.

While all other valve instruments are played with the right hand, the French horn is played with the left. The reason for this is to be found in the history of the horn. When Hampel discovered how to obtain an additional series of notes by stopping the horn, he naturally employed the right hand because it was more facile than the left. This very important job of stopping the horn was most naturally delegated to the right hand, leaving the left hand nothing to do but hold the horn. Later, when Blumel invented the piston and rotary valves, stopping the horn was still very important. In fact, when the valves were first used, the natural hand horn was called for as much as the valve horn. The player would be asked to use first the hand horn and then the valve horn. Even today, stopping the horn is still important. There never was, therefore, a distinct break between purely hand-horn playing and valve-horn playing. The right hand continued to be used to stop the horn, and that is the way we find it today. Stopping is not as important as it used to be before good valves were manufactured and before satisfactory mutes were developed, and there is no question that greater speed could be developed in operating the valves with the right hand, but custom decrees that the valves shall be operated by the left hand. If some manufacturer should get the courage to make a French horn in which the valves were operated by the right hand, it is extremely doubtful if it ever would be used. The French horn probably will always remain the one exception to the use of the right hand to operate the valves.

There is considerable confusion about stopping. About half the treatises dealing with the French horn say that stopping the horn raises the pitch, and about half say that stopping the horn lowers the pitch. In the less critical of these, no distinction is made between partial stopping, such as half- and three-quarter, and full-stopping. It is pretty well agreed among most horn players that partial stopping does flat the open notes. From this well-established fact, many jump to the conclusion that full-stopping must also flat open notes, only more so. Some contend that since an act carried only part way flattens the open notes, it is illogical to believe that this same act carried further should have an opposite result. The subject is really one without practical value, since some of the finest teachers and some of the finest horn players in the world have enjoyed great success while believing that when they full-stop the horn, the pitch is raised. For all practical purposes this is true.

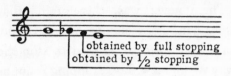

G on the second line is open, and so is E on the first line. G♭ is obtained by half-stopping, while F is obtained by full-stopping. Now, the burning question is this: is F (which everyone admits is obtained by full-stopping) the result of flatting the open G one full tone or the result of raising the open E a half-tone? Most French horn players contend that the open E is raised a half-step. This view seems to obtain strong support from instruments having "stop valves." These stop valves are used in order to add tubing sufficient in length to flatten any note a half-step. When the horn is full-stopped, the whole instrument plays a half-step sharp, and the stop valve is used to compensate for this half-step sharpness, so the player can play the stopped horn in tune. If full-stopping the horn did not raise the pitch, it does seem exceedingly strange that players could succeed so well if their playing were based on false principles. Someday a sound engineer or other acoustical expert may demonstrate that full-stopping actually does flatten open notes, but in the meantime—and afterward, too—horn players will play just as beautifully, regardless of whether full-stopping flats or sharps the open notes.

The French horn is considered difficult to play, and for this reason the mellophone is sometimes used as a substitute. Both are built in F, and both play the same music. Since both are voiced the same, one would naturally suppose they were the same in length, but the French horn is twice as long as the mellophone, the former being about 147 inches long, the latter being about seventy-one inches long. How then can they play the same music?

The scale of open notes in the French horn is as follows:

The C an octave below Middle C is the second note in the scale and not the fundamental of the horn. The diameter of the horn tubing is so small in proportion to its length that this lowest note is not used. The length of the horn is sufficient to give a fundamental an octave lower, but the tubing is so small that this note is not obtainable. The eleventh, thirteenth, seventeenth and nineteenth notes of the scale are badly out of tune with evenly tempered scale and are not used. These are shown above as solid notes, the open notes all being in tune and used.

The scale of open notes on the mellophone is as follows:

The lowest note on the mellophone is the same as the lowest on the French horn, but it is the fundamental, or first open note, of the mellophone and not the second in the scale, as is true on the horn. The horn plays upward from its second open note, while the mellophone plays upward from its first open note. This explains why these instruments, although of unequal length, play the same music.

The respective scales of open notes also explain why the French horn is more difficult to play than the mellophone. It has been observed in several previous chapters that the open notes in the scale become closer together the farther up in the scale these notes are found. By comparing the scale of open notes of the French horn with that of the mellophone and noting particularly the difference in the spacing between the notes from C in the staff to C above the staff, it is clear that the notes on the French horn are close together, while on the mellophone they are comparatively far apart. In the octave just cited, there are only five notes on the mellophone, but there are nine on the horn. If there were nine bottles lined up on a box just a yard long, it would be more difficult to hit any one bottle than if there were only five bottles on the box. It would require a better marksman to pick out any one bottle among the nine than it would among the five bottles. That is somewhat the case in playing the French horn. The notes are so close together that it requires a well-trained embouchure, or playing lips, to reach up among this cluster of notes and pick out just exactly the one required. On the mellophone the job is comparatively simpler because the notes are farther apart and more easily located.

Although somewhat easier to play, the mellophone can never be a substitute for the French horn. The quality of tone is not there. The larger-bore tubing of more abrupt conical shape lacks the richness of the small, gradually tapered tubing of the horn. The mouthpiece of the mellophone is larger, more cup-shaped and consequently easier to control. The mouthpiece of the French horn is small, funnel-shaped and more difficult to blow. But no instrument can take the place of the French horn, and players are glad to devote themselves to the pleasant, if exacting, task of coaxing the velvety tone from the horn.

CHAPTER X

The Trombone

THE DR JEKYLL AND MR HYDE OF THE MUSICAL WORLD

FOR CENTURIES THE TROMBONE was merely a big trumpet, and its history is inextricably bound up with the early history of the trumpet. In fact, its name trombone means, in Italian, "big trumpet." It is cylindrical in about two thirds of its length and conical in the other third, somewhat as the trumpet. Its tone is bright and noble, suggesting a trumpet of lower pitch. But it became an individual instrument on that distant day when somebody added the slide feature.

There are many delightful stories about the origin of the trombone. One of the most widely related is that the Spartan bard, Tyrtaeus, invented it in 685 B.C. He is supposed to have obtained his idea from playing a trumpet with a tuning slide. To support the story of early invention, a trombone is supposed to have been found some years ago in excavations of the ruins of Pompeii, which was destroyed in 79 A.D. None of these stories has been definitely verified, and most authorities have ceased to regard them seriously. The best information obtainable is that the trombone slide principle was invented in northern Italy during the early part of the fourteenth century.

THE TROMBONE

Nobody will ever know exactly who was responsible for this great invention or just how it came about. It is conjectured that the idea grew out of the use of a tuning slide. But tuning slides themselves must have been a rare device on a musical instrument and may have been a product of the same locality during the same era as that which produced the trombone slide. Granting that the idea arose from the use of a tuning slide, it is obvious how this device would suggest the slides now found on trombones. The player probably noticed that when he tried to tune his instrument while playing, the pitch was lowered when the slide was drawn out and was raised when the slide was pushed in.

If this fourteenth-century player were an especially intelligent musician he probably worried much about the limitations of his instrument. He no doubt wished it were possible to play on his big trumpet all the notes which the wandering troubadour could play on his fiddle. He also, no doubt, felt his instrument inferior to the simple flute, with its many holes in the side of the body. To try to make music with a half-dozen solitary notes was a disappointing task. The simple trumpet was all right for military bugling, but as a musical instrument it had serious shortcomings.

On this occasion when the slide idea was born, the trumpeter noted that moving the slide gave additional notes. The half-dozen which he had become so tired of playing suddenly multiplied. If the slide happened to be of such a length that when it was drawn a note was flattened a semitone, the player probably observed that he could play, with the use of the slide, the flats of his half-dozen notes, giving him a scale of a dozen notes. He also clearly saw that if the slide were long enough to lower the tone a whole step, he could obtain the half-step by drawing it only halfway out, and then could obtain the whole step lower by pulling it out the entire length.

Here was an idea which had great possibilities, one which was to have tremendous results for future music. To obtain more and more notes for bridging the gaps in the scale of the half-dozen open notes, the slide was made longer and longer. At first, though, it is believed the slide was long enough for four semitones. To lower the B♭ tenor trombone four semitones would require a slide about fifteen inches long, since each of the semitones would require about three and a half inches to four inches. This was sufficient for bridging the gaps in most of the scale then used and made the scale chromatic from the lowest note (the second open tone) to the top of instrument, except for a slight gap of two semitones between the second and third open tone. The player could go down the scale from open F in this order: F (open), E, E♭, D, D♭, using the four semitones made available by the slide; but the player could not play chromatically down to open B♭, because there was no way of playing C, B♮.

This section of the trombone scale shows the open notes of the scale as whole notes, the numbers below denoting their order in the natural scale. The first of these was probably not playable on the early trombone. The solid notes show the notes playable by using the four positions of the slide. The X's indicate the missing notes, later added when the slide was lengthened.

But why want too much! The four semitones gave such great improvements over anything ever known before that it seemed tempting fate to ask for more, or even to think for a

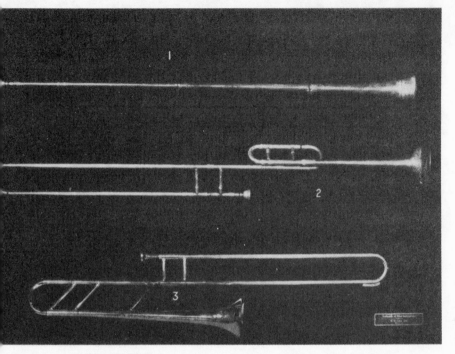

DEVELOPMENT OF THE TROMBONE

Clarion in B♭, used in Florence in early fifteenth century. (2) English sackbut B♭. Originated in northern Italy in fourteenth century and spread to Europe in fifteenth century. (3) Modern Conn Connqueror trombone with Vocabell.

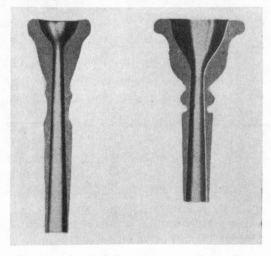

Cross sections of the trumpet and trombone mouthpieces. Notice the same general shape, the difference between them being mostly size. Similar shape helps give similar tone quality.

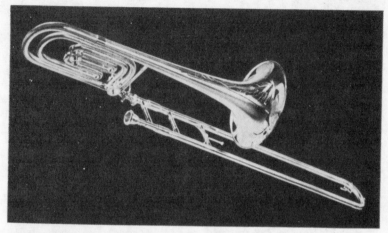

The bass trombone, with rotary-valve change to F and E, bridging the gap in the bottom of the scale of open notes.

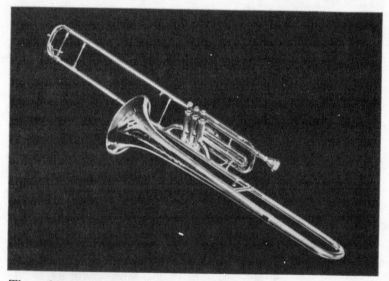

The valve trombone, developed after the invention of the piston valve in 1815. Very little used in America. Sometimes called the Italian trombone because of its use in Italy.

moment that this great slide trumpet with an additional four semitones for every open note was not indeed perfect!

This instrument with the slides was introduced into England before the fourteenth century closed and was given the name of sackbut. This name was apt, being derived from Spanish and meaning "a pump." Henry VII was fond of band music, made up of crude oboes, flutes, trumpets and drums, and according to one account his band in 1495 contained four sackbuts. Henry VIII increased the number of sackbuts to ten, which would seem to indicate they were a kind of favorite of his.

As the sackbut was used more and more, this gap in the scale between the second and third open notes seemed to many musicians a hindrance to the full development of the musical possibilities of the instrument. Finally "perfection" was again reached by increasing the length of the slide about four inches so an additional semitone could be added. Virdung, one of the earliest European historians on musical instruments, wrote in 1511 that there existed at that time a marvelous instrument with a slide long enough to add five semitones to the natural, or open, scale. This extra semitone probably seemed at the time more than enough for all musical purposes, just as, in the development of the flute, the first three or four keys seemed all that could ever be needed. But these five semitones could lower the scale chromatically from open F only to C♮, leaving the B♮ unplayable. But, again, what was one semitone! It was some years later before the sixth semitone was provided by making the slide longer. This is the number of semitones possible on the modern tenor slide trombone, and it makes the scale chromatic from the second open note to the top of the instrument.

In 1520 the Brescian school of violin making became famous as a source of fine violins, and, by a strange coincidence, in this same year the Hans Menschel family of Nuremberg became famous as a source of fine trombones. Another parallel between the violin and the trombone is the fact that they are the two outstanding instruments which can be played in perfect tune. Instruments with keys and valves have certain inaccuracies in their scale, but the ability to place the finger any place on the string of the violin and to place the slide in any desired position on the trombone enables the musician to play a true and accurate scale on these two instruments. This parallel makes us wonder if the fact that fine instruments of each type were first built in 1520—the violin in Italy, the trombone in Germany—is not more than a coincidence. Possibly each was the flowering of the great musical urge which was working in both of these countries at this time.

In Germany, in 1558, a composer named Kruger published a volume of four-part chorales, for four and six trombones, to be played along with the organ. No doubt some of the fine trombones made by the Menschel family were used by musicians to play these compositions. More than likely Kruger was inspired to write this music because of the fine trombones which were made available to trombone players by Hans and other members of this family. Composers do not write for instruments which do not exist, nor beyond the known capacity of existing instruments, but they are quick to employ new instruments which seem to have musical possibilities.

In Italy the creators of opera were using trombones. Two of the earliest, Striggio and Corteccia, used four trombones in 1565, along with cornets and other instruments. In France, Balthasarini gave a performance in 1581 of his "Ballet Comique de la Reine," and in the odd assortment of instruments used for instrumental accompaniment trombones were used, as well as cornets. Monteverde, an ingenious Italian composer who was quick to recognize merit in musical instruments, called for five trombones in the performance of his opera "Orfeo," given in 1608. These five trombones were divided into three voices: two altos, two tenors and one bass. Praetorius, writing about this time, said the trombone family consisted of an alto in D, three tenors in A, E and D (the latter an octave below the alto), and a bass in A, an octave below the tenor in A.

Although Bach and Handel used the trombone occasionally, they showed no improvement in the use of this instrument over their predecessors. Bach didn't seem to care a great deal for the instrument and used it only sparingly. Handel used the trombone probably less than Bach, but when he did write for it, he wrote effectively. No doubt, one of the reasons Bach and Handel did not write more for this instrument was that they were so engrossed with their high clarion writing. They were not even content to write in the range of the soprano trumpet—they concentrated on the sopranino clarion. With their attention turned toward the high sopranos, it is no wonder they minimized the tenor voice of the brass family. The most effective writing Handel ever did for the trombone was not for the tenor but for the alto in A, which was really a soprano in A, being of the same pitch as today's A trumpet. This effective writing can be heard as the obbligato to the voice which sings "The Trumpet Shall Sound," in the "Messiah."

During the latter part of the eighteenth century, the composers of opera first learned the effective use of the trombone.
Gluck was one of the first and one of the greatest masters of
the instrument. Up to his time the instrument had been used
chiefly as a volume maker to strengthen the choral or instrumental ensemble in tutti passages. It doubled trumpet parts
or played along with the voices an octave below. Gluck saw
greater possibilities for the instrument. He liked its coloring
and felt it could sing a song of its own. He began giving
melodies to the trombones and scored for them in three parts.
This three-part harmony was tied in with the lower voices
by giving the fourth note of the chord to the bass instruments
or having them double the third-trombone part an octave
lower. This finely knit style of writing, rich in colorings and
varied in pattern, set the style of trombone writing from that
time until today. Opera composers adopted this style almost
immediately, because they saw its superiority over what had
been done before, but it was not until Beethoven's time that
it was used in the symphony orchestra. This form of part
writing for the trombone section first made its appearance in
symphony, in the Finale of Beethoven's famous Fifth.

Gluck was a German but wrote in France during most of
his life. Gossec, however, is given credit for introducing
trombones into French opera, when he used them in 1770, in
his opera "Sabina." Gluck and other German composers
usually called for three trombones—the alto, tenor and bass
—but French and Italian composers ordinarily used only
the alto and tenor. It was not until the latter part of the
nineteenth century that it became fairly general for composers in all nations to use three trombones, but they were
not the alto, tenor and bass of Gluck and other Germans, but

two tenors and a bass. The small alto fell into disfavor, and a second tenor trombone took the top notes. The range of the trombone trio was extended into the bass, and the bass member of the family became more important.

In England the adoption of the sackbut in the orchestra was delayed because of its association with the cornetto and its consequent decline along with this instrument. The cornetto and sackbut were usually used together in English bands and church choirs, one cornetto as treble to three sackbuts as alto and tenors. When the cornetto lost favor after 1650, the sackbut also was neglected. For nearly a century there was little call for the sackbut, and it was late in the eighteenth century before some of its old popularity returned. It came back also with a new name—trombone.

During the period when the trombone was staging a comeback, it seems the English people went in for slide instruments in a big way. They not only became interested in the slide trombone but also in the slide trumpet, so much so that while other countries in Europe were welcoming the valve trumpet, England was too engrossed in the slide principle to get interested in the newly invented valves. The enthusiasm for the slide principle, not only in trombones but also in trumpets, delayed the use of the valve trumpet in England until well into the nineteenth century.

While the slide trumpet has been more fully discussed in the story of the trumpet, it is interesting here because of its slide principle. Far from being like the slide trombone, the slide trumpet is interesting in the discussion of the slide trombone chiefly because it is so different. Some have confused this instrument as being in reality a treble trombone. This is far from true. With the passing of the cornetto, which took treble parts with the trombone, the treble trombone did have a vogue. The "tromba di tirarsi" of Bach and Handel is a genuine trombone built in treble A or B♭, an octave above the corresponding tenors in these keys. Such treble trombones had a short period of popularity, but it passed after Bach and Handel. The slide trumpet, however, was different from this treble slide trombone. The slide on the trombone was pushed forward, or away from the player, in order to lower its tone. The slide on the slide trumpet was operated in exactly the reverse manner. To lower the tone, the slide was drawn toward the player. The slide on the trombone was out in front of the instrument, while the slide on the trumpet was placed toward the back of the instrument, somewhat as the first valve slide is now placed on the modern trumpet. The slide of the trombone can be extended to six positions beyond the closed position and can lower the pitch of the instrument six semitones. The slide on the slide trumpet was short and had only two positions besides the closed position and could lower the pitch of the instrument only two semitones.

This latter difference is the important difference between the trombone and slide trumpet. The two positions of the slide were used not so much as the trombone slide was used but more as the valves are now used. Instead of the second valve with its half-step of tubing opened by pushing down the valve, the same length of tubing was added to the open notes by pulling the slide out halfway. To lower the open note a full tone, the slide was pulled all the way out. In this manner a semitone or a full tone could be added to all open notes. Obviously, such an instrument was not chromatic, for there were gaps between the second and third, third and fourth, and fifth and sixth open notes which could not be completely bridged chromatically.

In Germany, France, Italy and England the trombone was used in early opera, but it was not admitted to the symphony orchestra until later. Bach and Handel availed themselves of the resources of the trombone in their operas and oratorios, but not in their symphonic compositions. Haydn used three trombones in his great "Creations," but refused to admit the trombone in his earlier symphonies. Mozart experimented successfully with the trombone in some stirring passages in "Don Giovanni" and apparently felt more at home with the trombone in his "Magic Flute," written about four years later. But in spite of Mozart's frequent and effective use of the trombone in his operas, he did not use trombones at all in his three greatest symphonies: the E♭ Major, the B Minor, and the C, or "Jupiter."

Beethoven was openly fond of the trombone; so much so that when he was buried in 1827, two of his "Equali" compositions for four trombones were played at his grave. Yet Beethoven did not use trombones nearly as often as might be expected. Apparently he was too bound by the customs of the times, which permitted the trombone to show what it could do in the opera but confined it to a back seat in the symphony. He ignored the trombone in his first four symphonies, written from 1800 to 1805. Finally, in 1808, the trombone got its first chance in symphonic music. In his great Fifth Symphony Beethoven is forced to call upon the trombones.

Developing this marvelous musical structure, theme following theme, Beethoven seems not to need trombones. Through three movements he gives utterance to the greatest of his musical thoughts without once bringing in trombones. But toward the close of the third movement, after a prolonged pianissimo of strings and tympani, when the air is supercharged with electric expectancy, suddenly there is a twitch of the strings, a change of the rhythm, and the theme of triumphant joy for the fourth movement is stated in one of the most remarkable passages in all music. Then apparently Beethoven seemed to realize the inadequacy of all other instruments or combinations of instruments to express the exultant joy which surged in his thoughts and soul. This great emotion broke through conventional form and expressed itself in noble, sustained chords from the trombones. What a triumphal entry for any instrument into the symphony! Although few instruments have been shut out from the symphony so long, no other instrument has ever had such a triumphal entry into these exclusive ranks. After this sensational debut, it is no wonder the trombone ever afterward found its place in the symphony secure.

Incidentally, two other novices were admitted into the symphony at the same time: the piccolo and the contrabassoon. When Beethoven's soul surged forward with its expression of hope and joy, he seemed to cast aside precedent and to think only of putting into musical form this great inspired feeling. Whatever musical coloring was needed, he appropriated. The trombones definitely characterized this supreme utterance, but the contrabassoon added certain purple tones at the bottom of the tonal picture, while the piccolo was needed to put the bright, silvery sharpness at the top. It was a moment in which the fetters of Beethoven's soul were broken, and the trombone, contrabassoon and piccolo for the first time found their own freedom.

Beeth
descripti
enough,
and Eight
symphonie
until sixtee
the Fifth th
compositions
1824. Probab
chestration w
orchestra. Or,
theme required
event, three tron

The cause for
teen years may b made
later by Mendelss wn regard for the
trombone. He said ed the trombone as too solemn
and noble an instrument to be used except on very special
occasions. Perhaps Beethoven felt likewise. Perhaps during
the writing of his first four symphonies he failed to find an
occasion important enough to use the trombones, and then
had to wait sixteen years after that sublime outburst in the
Fifth before another occasion came along in the Ninth
Symphony.

Schubert, Schumann and other composers who followed
Beethoven accepted the trombone as a regular member of
the symphony orchestra. Berlioz in his "Requiem" called
upon the trombones to perform the stupendous task of
simulating Gabriel's trumpet blast on the Day of Judgment.
He outdid all other composers by specifying sixteen trombones! Not only that: he demanded that the trombones

[notes which were
produce certain low notes A, G# and
He wrote pedal notes to thes
Realizing the conster
note. Realizing in t
when they came to
tions by writing in
instrument and th
Berlioz under
better th
served
ar]

not ordinarily played.
F, below the lowest open
tion of the trombone players
notes, he anticipated their objec-
he margin: "These notes are in the
e players must get them out." As usual,
stood the resources of the instrument even
n the players themselves, and this example has
to show all the musicians who followed him that these
legitimate notes on the trombone—at least on the trombone of larger bore.

Wagner usually wrote for three trombones, but in his "Ring" operas he wrote for four. Wagner was a past master in writing for trombones, as he was with all brass instruments, but he often seems to forget the usual duties of the first trombone and writes extremely low notes for it. To play these parts the first trombonist must have the thumb valve, or F attachment, on his instrument, an attachment usually used on only the bass trombone. Bellini does the same thing in his "La Somnambula," where he writes an E♭ below bass clef for first trombone, a note which can only be played with the F attachment. The functions of this attachment will be more fully explained later.

Shortly after the invention of valves by Blumel in 1815, valves were added to the trombone. This made it like a big valve trumpet in everything but appearance. It still retained the trombone appearance. But while the tone quality remained substantially the same, its style of performance was changed. It lost its perfection of scale, inheriting all the evils of faulty intonation found in valve trumpets, only more so. It lost the characteristic glissando effects which were due to the slides. It failed to achieve acceptance generally because it was considered inferior to the slide trombone. Strangely enough, about the only place where the *valve* trombone did meet with favor was in Italy, the birthplace of the *slide* trombone. The valve trombone has become so definitely identified with Italy that in America the valve trombone is often known as the Italian trombone.

Above it has been noted that Beethoven introduced the trombone into the symphony upon a very special occasion and waited sixteen years before he found another musical idea which seemed to warrant the services of this great and noble instrument. Mendelssohn frankly stated that he felt the trombone was too sacred to be used except upon the rarest occasions. Berlioz likewise held the trombone in great reverence. He protests against the indiscriminate use of the trombone, saying this "is to impoverish, to degrade a magnificent individuality; it is to make a hero into a slave and a buffoon."

Probably one of the finest, if not the finest, characterizations of the trombone is to be found in Berlioz' monumental work, *Modern Instrumentation and Orchestration*. In it he says:

"The trombone is—in my opinion—the true chief of that race of wind instruments which I have designated as epic instruments. It possesses, in an eminent degree, both nobleness and grandeur; it has all the deep and powerful accents of high musical poetry—from the religious accent, calm and imposing, to the wild clamors of the orgy. It depends on the composer to make it by turn chant like a choir of priests; threaten, lament, ring a funeral knell, raise a hymn of glory, break forth into frantic cries, or sound its dread flourish to awaken the dead or to doom the living. . . .

"The character of tone in trombones varies according to the degree of loudness with which their sound is emitted. In a fortissimo it is menacing and formidable. . . . Such is the terrific scale in D minor, upon which Gluck has founded the chorus of furies in the second act of his 'Iphigenia in Tauride.' . . . In simple forte, trombones have an expression of heroic pomp, of majesty, of loftiness. . . . Then they acquire—with enormously increased grandeur—the expression of trumpets; they no longer menace, they proclaim; they chant, instead of roar. . . . In mezzo forte in the medium, in unison or in harmony with a slow movement, trombones assume a religious character. Mozart, in his chorus of the priests of Isis, in the 'Magic Flute,' has produced admirable models of the manner of giving these instruments a sacerdotal voice and attribute. . . . The pianissimo of trombones applied to harmonies belonging to the minor mode, is gloomy, lugubrious—I had almost said hideous. If, particularly, the chords be brief and broken by rests, it has the effect of hearing some strange monsters giving utterance, in dim shadow, to howls of ill-suppressed rage."

Since the trombone, as Berlioz says, belongs to that race of instruments called "epic," we would naturally expect it to move through music at a majestic pace, and so it does, sometimes because of serious limitations. There are many musical figures which are impossible on the trombone. Trills, except some lip trills in the upper register, are entirely impractical; and even those which are practical are seldom played because they require lip training which is beyond most players. Pure legato is also impossible in some parts of the scale because of the limitations of the slide movement. Only if the notes played are based on the same fundamental can pure legato be accomplished. To play several notes in the lower positions of the slide and then have to bring the slide to closed position for the other notes, breaks the legato quality. It is also obvious that the rapid repetition of certain notes is impossible or impractical, where the slide must be moved from closed or first position to the sixth or seventh positions, or vice versa.

But there is one technical resource which the trombone has to the highest degree—this is glissando. With the slide it is possible to "smear" the seven semitones encompassed within the limits of the slide into one continuous, integral note of ascending or descending pitch. A less exaggerated form is the slur, which the trombone can do beautifully. While the slur is used legitimately in all music, the glissando is chiefly associated with the Negro minstrel show or hot jazz.

It is this glissando or "smear" effect which makes the trombone the Dr Jekyll and Mr Hyde of the musical world. Contrary to popular opinion, the distinction of being the jazziest instrument in the orchestra or band goes, not to the saxophone, but to the trombone. Known and admitted to be the most noble of all musical instruments, it is at the same time the jazziest of the whole lot. It depends upon the player. When played as a "slip horn," nothing can equal it as a means of expressing jazz. "Hot licks" come natural to this instrument. Its slide gives it unmatched resources for slurring, portamento and glissando, in which are all the suggestiveness, smirk and sensuousness for which jazz is noted. Modern muting and "wow-wowing" were early used on the "slip horn." It can moan, it can scream, it can seduce, it can laugh like a hyena. It is the most gifted of all instruments called upon to give expression to the worst type of jazz mania. But when Mr Hyde steps forward, all is noble, sacred, grand. Whenever composers wish to depict religious solemnity, or martial glory, they call upon the noble trombone. Wagner used it often in his allegorical and religious "Nibelungen." When Berlioz wished to portray Gabriel's awful trumpet announcing the Day of Judgment in "Requiem," he called for sixteen trombones! The trombone is like a great and gifted person whose talents may be turned to good or to bad, but in either case great achievement is assured through unusual capabilities.

Few laymen understand the mechanical operation of the trombone and fewer still its musical principle. Like the rube at the circus, the average person knows the trombone player doesn't swallow the slide, but beyond that he seldom worries. The heart of the trombone is of course the slide. The mouthpiece goes into one side of the slide, the other side connecting with the bell. These two straight slides are joined at the far end by a U-shaped piece of tubing called the outside slide, which telescopes over the two straight inside slides. It is this outside slide which is operated by the right hand, which pulls it in and pushes it out. When the slide is in, only the natural scale of the instrument is sounded, just as on the bugle or other simple horn. But when the slide is extended into each of the lower six positions, six semitones are added to each open note, as has been described earlier in this chapter in discussing how the trombone came to be developed.

No wonder the musical principle of the trombone is confusing. There seems little rhyme or reason to the instrument when the uninitiated watches it being played. The player may be performing a well-known tune, and the notes may descend gradually and slowly down and down, until the observer begins to anticipate the further lengthening of the slides as he waits for the descending notes. As the spectator waits for the slide to descend for the next lower note, he is puzzled to see the player pull the slide clear in to closed position—just where, by all the laws of relative position, it should not be. Vice versa, when the observer expects the slide to be drawn in for a higher note, he is nonplused to see the player shoot the slide out to full length. He knows that by all the laws of relative position the note cannot be out there, but it is. It is a puzzler.

Everything becomes plain when a little explanation of the musical principles of the trombone is given. In closed or first position, when no part of the outside slide is effective except the curved bow at the end, the natural scale of open tones is sounded by changing lip and blowing pressure, as follows:

The gaps in this natural scale are bridged by using the slide, as already explained, but the perversity of the slide can be understood only by charting some of the notes made by using the slide. Below is reproduced a section of the trombone scale. Open notes are shown by half-notes; notes made by using the slide are shown by quarter-notes. Under each note is shown the position of the slide, 1 being closed, 2 being the first extension of the slide, or second position, 3 being the next, etc.

Imagine a slow passage descending from D above the bass staff: the slide is dropped to fourth position for B, and just when you think the player is going to drop the slide to a still lower position for Bb, you are fooled, the player pulling the slide in to first or closed position, which you feel should by rights give a higher note! Then A is obtained by extending the slide about four inches to second position, G is obtained by extending the slide an additional seven or eight inches to fourth position; but just when you think you have everything figured out and when you expect the player to extend the slide seven or eight inches still further to sixth position for F, lo and behold, the player pulls the slide in, which you swear should give a higher-pitched note: but it doesn't, it gives a lower note! The interval between F and Bb in the staff gives a clear notion of just how the open note (F) is sounded and how the lower semitones are obtained successively by extending the slide first into second position, then into third position, and so on, to obtain the chromatic intervals between the gaps in the open notes of the natural scale. When the slide is extended to the seventh and final position and the player cannot descend any farther by using the slides, the

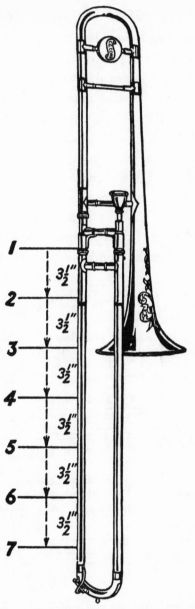

Showing the positions of the slides as used to bridge the gaps in the open-note scale. When the slides are placed in these positions, a chromatic scale is possible except in the bottom of the range. These positions are only approximate, correct intonation requiring certain variations.

next chromatic step is found to be another open note (B♭), played in first or closed position.

In this manner it is possible to descend chromatically to E below the staff, but this note is obtained by using the seventh and last position. Between this note and the next open note (B♭) is a gap of five semitones. On the regular tenor trombone, these notes cannot be played, but on a tenor trombone with a valve attachment added, generally known as a bass trombone, these notes can be played and the gap bridged chromatically. This is done by operating a valve with the thumb of the left hand which adds a length of tubing capable of throwing the trombone from B♭ into F below.

Gap of five semitones, not playable on the tenor trombone in B♭. These notes are played by putting trombone into F or E by means of valve operated by thumb of left hand. Such a trombone is usually called a bass trombone.

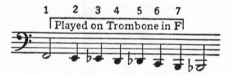

These notes, with slide positions marked above, are based upon open F of trombone when lowered to key of F by operating thumb valve. They serve to bridge the gap found on the B♭ tenor trombone.

If bass trombone is put into key of E by thumb valve, the E is open and the other notes down to B♮ are played by the slides in positions as marked above.

This length of tubing, which is added by opening the valve, really adds five or six semitones to the total length of trombone tubing. When in F, the F below the staff is open or first position. By keeping the trombone in F, it is possible to extend the slide first into second, then into third, etc., positions to play E, Eb, D, Db, C, B. When the player comes to B, he has run out of slide again, but by closing the F valve and putting the trombone back into the key of Bb, the player finds that the next chromatic note is open Bb, played with the slide closed. Then, by extending the slides, this fundamental can be added to and some so-called pedal notes secured. These are difficult to obtain, but are used as far down as the seventh position. This gives a chromatic scale from low E, below the fourth line under the bass staff, to D on the fifth line above the bass staff, a total chromatic range of nearly four octaves.

Adolphe Sax was the inventor of this valve for the trombone, according to Berlioz. Before this ingenious device, composers could bridge this gap only by using trombones of different pitches, selecting the notes from one to bridge this gap on the other. Although today such a trombone with thumb valve is called a bass trombone, when it was invented it was still called a tenor trombone, which in reality it is. The bore is large, it is true, but often is not any larger than some large-bore tenor trombones which do not have this device. The chief reason for calling such a trombone a tenor trombone was that in those days they used a true bass trombone which played an octave below the tenor. The name tenor had to be preserved for the tenor with the valve attachment in order to avoid confusion with the real bass trombone.

This bass trombone was a monstrous affair with double tubing for slides. On the tenor trombone, when the slide is extended about four inches to a lower position, eight inches of tubing is actually added, twice the extension. On the bass trombone, for every inch the slide was extended four inches of tubing was added to the trombone. The slides were so long that a handle had to be used for the lower positions. Although usually pitched in E♭, the same as the present E♭ bass tuba, there were some made in BB♭, the same pitch as the present contrabass tuba in B♭. Wagner calls for the bass trombone in some of his compositions, but since there are few such instruments being played today, these notes are either played on the contrabass tuba or played on the tenor trombone an octave higher.

In the regular dance and radio bands, trombones of medium bore are used, the tone being brilliant and cutting. Trombones in the symphony orchestra are of large bore, the tone being correspondingly bigger and broader. The first trombonist uses a tenor, while the second and third trombonists usually use the bass trombone with thumb valve for throwing the instrument into F or E♭. Usually both sides of the slide are of the same bore size, but in some models the side nearer the bell is larger; these are called duo-bore trombones. The former have a brighter, more solid quality and are generally found better for recording and radio work. The duo-bore trombones have a big, round tone but seem to sacrifice some of the brilliance usually associated with the true trombone quality. Control men in recording and radio studios find the straight-bore trombones better for recording and radio work than the duo-bore, because the latter have an uneven and jumpy quality, technically known as "spreading," while the former "cut through" with sharper and more solid quality.

CHAPTER XI

The Tubas

THE STORY OF LARGE FAMILIES

IN 1590 THE French churchman Guillaume of Auxerre invented the serpent, a queer-looking wind instrument about eight feet long. Its tubing was made in a shape suggesting a squirming snake which had been struck with a stick. For about two hundred years it flourished as an important bass instrument, but now it is chiefly known for its many and varied progeny. Among these are the ophicleides, a family of six; the saxhorns, a family of eight; the saxtrombas, a family of eight; the tubas, a family of nine; and the much-maligned saxophones, which have now grown to a family of nine.

Too much credit cannot be given Guillaume for his invention, because the serpent is little more than a bass member of the large family of cornettos, or zinken. These instruments put in an appearance in Europe in the fourteenth century. In England they were called cornettos and were built in three keys. The little treble cornetto in F was only about eighteen inches long and had a thin, weak tone. Another was the cornetto in C, about two feet long. The third was the great cornetto in G, approximately three feet long. In Germany these same instruments were known as zinken and were built in several keys, one of them being a high soprano in D which was only a little over a foot long. It is not definitely known how many different members there were in this original family of instruments, but there undoubtedly were quite a number.

The cornettos and zinken were the "poor white trash" among musical instruments. Not only were they cheaply made, but they were noted for their poverty of musical qualities. Constructed of wood and covered with leather, their tone was colorless, coarse and windy. Anyone with a pocketknife, a pot of glue and a thin skiver of leather could make one of these instruments. Two sides of the tube were whittled out and stuck together with glue. Then the tube was covered with leather to strengthen the thin wood. After this, holes were bored in the side of the tube and a cup-shaped mouthpiece was turned out of a piece of wood. The instrument was then complete. Making these ancient instruments was something like making the cigar-box fiddle or the slippery-elm whistle of today.

Nevertheless, these instruments became the most popular in Europe. In the fifteenth and sixteenth centuries they were heard in military bands and church choirs and were rated as the most important wind instruments of their time. Their number and variety multiplied. They swept over Europe somewhat as their famous offspring, the saxophones, later swept over America in the 1920s. Guillaume, no doubt, heard them from morning to night, not only outside his church but also in his own choir loft. Apparently Guillaume shared the enthusiasm of his contemporaries for these instruments. He decided the world would be further blessed if a larger and better zinke or cornetto were invented, and accordingly he brought forth the serpent.

Originally it was a conical tube about eight feet long with six finger holes and was played with a wooden cup-shaped mouthpiece. Later, keys were added and the mouthpipe and mouthpiece were made of metal. Its pitch was two octaves below Middle C or thereabout, and it furnished a deep voice for the military bands and for the church choirs. It found its place in musical circles much as might a bass singer in a college glee club which was without adequate bass voices. The only important wind bass at the time was the bassoon, and its reedy quality of tone did not seem to strike the fancy of the populace. The serpent, therefore, was looked upon as a much-needed addition to wind instruments, a great boon to music.

Fifty years before Guillaume invented the serpent, another churchman, Afranio of Ferrara, Italy, had invented the shape of the bassoon. He built it so its tubing was doubled back upon itself in parallel lines, which shape earned for the instrument the name of fagotto, or bundle of fagots. Guillaume apparently did not think well of his brother churchman's design, for the serpent was curved into a fantastic shape which resembled a reptile. It has seemed odd to some people that Guillaume, a divine, would make an instrument in the shape of the serpent, symbol of evil. Possibly it did not occur to Guillaume that he was giving the shape of a serpent to his instrument. Possibly he took his design from the fifteenth-century painting, "Angel with the Trumpet." In this painting, the trumpet is shown bent in the shape of a reversed letter S. Perhaps Guillaume was simply trying to carry this idea into the bass instrument and evolved his serpent shape. In any event, he produced an instrument whose shape has caused wonder and amazement for three hundred years.

Although Afranio's bassoon design lacked a certain amount of showmanship which Guillaume's serpent design possessed, the former proved the more practical and was eventually emulated by the serpent. After remaining curved like a snake for two centuries, the serpent finally changed to the bassoon shape along toward the close of the eighteenth century. Its eight feet of tubing was placed in two parallel lines, and it became known as the serpent horn, or military serpent. Although usually built in C or D, two octaves below Middle C, sometimes it was built long enough to play down to A or G. This was getting down into the bass territory of the modern bass tuba. In the beginning of the nineteenth century there appeared the metal serpent horn, known more generally as the serpentcleide, or ophicleide, both of which mean "keyed serpent." The first of these had seven keys, but later the number increased to eleven. It usually was pitched in B, two octaves and a semitone below Middle C.

Blood began to tell in this new tribe of instruments, for the number of ophicleides increased until there were six or seven. Besides the bass in B, there were also basses in C and B♭. Then contrabasses in F and E♭ were created. There were smaller ophicleides, too, for we find altos in F and E♭. The zinken and cornettos had long since passed from the scene, but their ability to propagate had been successfully carried in the blood stream of the serpent and passed on to the ophicleides. It is possible that had Guillaume failed to invent the serpent, the youngest and largest of the zinken, this race of musical instruments would have become extinct in the seventeenth century. All of the smaller members of the family did become extinct, but this race of musical instruments was saved from oblivion through the virility of the large serpent. From the seed of the serpent grew up the family of ophicleides, and dynasty after dynasty of related instruments grew up, only to give way to still another. Today we have zinken progeny in the form of tubas and saxophones.

Besides the popular acclaim accorded the original zinken, these early instruments found some favor with composers of serious music. The early Italian masters called for zinken in some of their operas. After the big bass zinke, the serpent, had served its apprenticeship in the military band and church choir, Handel scored for it in his "Water Music" and his "Fireworks Music." Mendelssohn wrote parts for the serpent in his "St Paul" and wrote freely for the later form of the serpent, known as the ophicleide. Schumann used it in his cantata, "Paradise and Peri." Even Beethoven wrote for it, no doubt because there was no other bass suitable for his needs. But Wagner was faced with no such compulsion, for there were several cup-mouthpiece basses available in his time; yet he wrote for the ophicleide in some of his early scores. It appeared in Wagner's scores for the last time in his "Rienzi," first produced in 1842. Meyerbeer, who died in 1864, used the ophicleide to the complete exclusion of the bass tuba. William Wallace in his opera, "Love's Triumph," written in 1862, provided parts for the bass tuba, whereas in all previous scores he had given the bass parts to the ophicleide.

During the first half of the nineteenth century the ophicleide held a place of some prominence in music, but the eventual doom of the ophicleide was sounded early in the century. In 1815 Blumel invented his piston valve, and although the keyed serpent continued on for another generation, it was only a question of time until it was supplanted by the valve bass. In 1815 the ophicleide was "going strong." It was probably at the height of its popularity. It was used in opera and in the church choir. It was a popular instrument in the military bands. Ophicleides were used in the bands of both French and English on the field of Waterloo. But the year which saw Napoleon go down to defeat was the fatal year in which sentence was also pronounced upon the ophicleide by Blumel's more efficient piston valve.

When the piston valve was first invented, few people realized that the day of the ophicleide was over. Twenty years after Blumel made his first model, there were important musicians who felt that the keyed serpent was still the last word in basses. The beginnings of the valve bass were not any too impressive. Naturally the soprano and alto instruments were the first to be given the advantage of the new valves. It was not until 1828 that Wilhelm Wieprecht, master of bands of the King of Prussia, produced his family of valve instruments. This family was not quite complete, but it included a small E♭ cornet, an E♭ trumpet, a B♭ tenor and a B♭ baritone. Later, it seems, the bore of the baritone was made larger, and it became known in England as the euphonium and in other countries as a bass tuba. This instrument was pitched in B♭, the same as our present baritone and euphonium tubas, but the bore was somewhat larger than our present euphoniums, and the instrument was generally referred to as the bass tuba. Bass tubas were built in other keys also, the F bass tuba being a popular one. Of the latter there seems to have been two varieties, both built in F, but one larger in bore than the other. Berlioz refers to one as the bombardon and to the other as the bass tuba.

By the middle of the century there were quite a number of bass horns of various kinds and types. In Berlioz' famous book on instruments, published in 1848, no less than seven basses of various kinds then in use—at least in France—are described. The ophicleides were still hanging on, for Berlioz calls attention to the bass in B, as well as the contrabass ophicleides in F and E♭. Then he takes up the newer bombardon, built in F and equipped with three valves. Similar to the bombardon, but built in larger bore and equipped with five valves, is the German bass tuba, a creation of Wieprecht. Although Berlioz praises the great sonorousness and low compass of the bass tuba in F, he hastens to mention that Adolphe Sax was at that time building a bass tuba in E♭, a whole tone lower. The old wooden serpent Berlioz mentions rather casually, with some caustic remarks about its "barbarous" tone quality. He also mentions the "Russian bassoon," an instrument even inferior to the serpent, and suggests that the art of music would not suffer in the slightest if it should disappear.

With such an array of bass instruments to select from, composers, directors and musicians must have been in a constant quandary. Times certainly had changed from the day when the only wind basses available were the bassoon and bass trombone. The serpent was welcomed with open arms when it appeared on the scene, but the world was soon to find out that it brought not so much a gift of music as of fecundity. In Berlioz' day, the old serpent was still hanging on desperately but was rapidly being suffocated by its many offspring which were growing up around it. Before 1590 there was only the feeble low voice of the bassoon, with an occasional low growl from the bass trombone, but before the middle of the nineteenth century there was a veritable babel of bass voices, a babel of the children of the serpent. It was time somebody made a housecleaning, and Adolphe Sax elected himself the man of the hour.

Adolphe Sax is familiarly known as inventor of the saxophone. He and his father, C. J. Sax, were instrument makers in Paris. These two men contributed many improvements to musical instruments, refining their response and intonation and inventing ingenious mechanisms which made them easier to play. Fresh from the triumphs attending his inventing and patenting the family of saxophones in 1840, Adolphe saw the great need of bringing order out of chaos among the cup-mouthpiece instruments, especially those of lower voice. The result of this work was his family of saxhorns, brought out in 1842. Owing to the lack of uniform terminology in Sax's time, it is rather difficult to describe this family, for sopranos were sometimes called altos, altos were often referred to as tenors, tenors were called baritones, and one is never sure whether a baritone was a euphonium or a bass. Six years after their invention, Berlioz discusses eleven different members of the saxhorn family, from very high sopranos to low double-basses in E♭ and drone double-basses in BB♭. But put into familiar terms which have come to be generally accepted today, this family of saxhorns consisted of a small E♭ soprano, similar to our high E♭ cornet; a B♭ soprano, similar to our B♭ cornet; an E♭ alto; a B♭ tenor; a B♭ bass; an E♭ low bass; and a contrabass in BB♭.

This logical organization of the cup-mouthpiece instruments was accepted more or less quickly, not only in France, but also in Germany, where Wieprecht had already made progress along this same line. England and Italy fell in line later, and finally America has come to use this classification of the various cup-mouthpiece voices, separated by intervals of fifths and fourths. With the invention of the saxhorn family, the miscellaneous serpents, ophicleides, bombardons and other odd tenor, baritone and bass instruments faded out of the picture.

As Haydn sounded the death knell to the rabble of instruments through his orchestrating, so Adolphe Sax silenced the Tower of Babel through his instrument making. The day of Haydn had been preceded by a lot of haphazard inventing of instruments of all sizes, kinds and descriptions. When Haydn appeared he selected with great insight those instruments worthy of a place in the orchestra and sent the rest of the rabble to oblivion, from which not a single instrument has staged a successful comeback. A century later Sax found a similar condition. The seed of the serpent had spread and sprouted and had produced a confusion of voices which irked the systematic, straight-thinking Sax. He looked them all over, found them all wanting in some aspect, and then substituted a new family of instruments, made up of a combination of the best of them all. Having salvaged the best from the lot, he saw no need of saving the remnants, and so he, like Haydn, dispatched the motley crew into oblivion.

Besides organizing the voices of the cup-mouthpiece instruments into a logical and limited number of instruments, Sax also made a contribution in new tonal color. The saxhorns are characterized by a conical bore of wide taper and a mouthpiece which is deep and bell-shaped. This construction gives to the whole family a distinctive tonal color which is round, mellow and on the dark side of the tonal spectrum. In America we hardly know what this tonal color is like, for our instruments have a straighter bore and are more brilliant in color; but the tapered bore is still much used in Italy and also in the military bands of France and England. The effect of a lot of these saxhorns playing together suggests a great pipe organ, because the tone is so full and mellow.

All the smaller instruments up to and including the alto were played in a horizontal position, as is the familiar cornet today, while the larger instruments were played in a vertical position, as is our bass or baritone. The Eb bass and the BBb contrabass were also made in a circular form, encircling the body and resting on the left shoulder. These were called helicons, a name originally given by Ptolemy to a geometrical drawing illustrating his idea of the eternal ratios existing between tone and color throughout the universe. Often there were two Bb sopranos, both in the same pitch but differing in the size of bore. The smaller bore was the soprano, while the larger and more tapered bore was the mezzo-soprano. They both sang in the same voice, but the larger and more tapered bore instrument had a bigger, more mellow tone. This mezzo-soprano has come down to us in the form of the fluegelhorn. The bore of the Eb alto was pretty well standardized, but the bore of the Bb instruments pitched below it fluctuated through a wide range. In small bore the Bb saxhorn had a tenor quality; when the bore was enlarged and the taper opened up, it took on a broader quality and became the baritone, or euphonium; when the bore was enlarged and opened up still more, it was deeply sonorous and became the bass.

This B♭ bass, only an octave below the cornet, became accepted as the bass voice. Because of this, when the E♭ bass, pitched a fifth lower, was added later, it was called the contrabass; likewise the B♭ bass an octave below the former B♭ bass was called the contrabass in BB♭. All the upright saxhorns, from the B♭ tenor to the BB♭ bass, are known as tubas: there are the tenor tuba, the baritone tuba and the various bass tubas. Today, however, it is unusual in America to call any instrument a tuba except the bass; in fact, the word tuba has become a synonym for the wind bass. This name tuba was taken from an old Roman instrument, but none of today's tubas resembles the Roman tuba, for it was a straight bugle only three feet long. About the only resemblance between the two kinds of instruments is the wide angle taper, but today's tubas have even lost this.

The baritone in B♭ was sometimes called a baritone and sometimes a euphonium. Sometimes the difference was only a matter of names, but sometimes there was a difference in bores and tapers. Today the word baritone refers to a small-bore instrument while euphonium refers to a large-bore instrument, both in the same B♭ voice. The baritone, having a small bore, does not possess the big, mellow quality of tone possessed by the euphonium, but its tone is broader and fuller than that of the B♭ tenor, which is still smaller in bore. The name baritone naturally comes from the word used to classify human voices, but those who christened the larger-bore instrument as euphonium went far afield for the name. The word in Greek means "sweet-sounding" and is apt enough from this standpoint; but it was probably stolen

DEVELOPMENT OF THE TUBA FAMILY

(1) The serpent. Invented by Guillaume of Auxerre in 1590. The ophicleide (see development of saxophone) was developed from the serpent, and the family of baritone and bass tubas was developed directly from the ophicleide. (2) Original sousaphone made for John Philip Sousa's Band in 1898. The modern bell-front sousaphone was first made in 1908.

INSTRUMENTS OF A BAND OF CIVIL WAR DAYS

All instruments are of "backfiring" variety, the bell extending backward over the shoulder and directing the sound to the rear. Useful in marching bands which played at the head of a moving column of men, but abandoned in favor of the bell-front instrument, which is better in concert work.

directly from another musical instrument which preceded it by two or three generations. In 1790 Ernst Chladni, a German, invented a musical instrument made of glass plates and rods, which also gave forth sweet sounds and was also called the euphonium. The wind euphonium, however, seems to have appropriated the name and probably has it for keeps.

While the smaller instruments usually had only three valves, the euphonium and basses generally had four and sometimes five valves. The reason for this goes back to the acoustical principles of open-pipe instruments. All open-pipe instruments have a natural, or harmonic, scale made up of the following intervals:

In the chapter on cornets and trumpets is shown how the three valves serve to bridge the gaps in the scale so it is possible to play chromatically from the second partial upward. It is possible to descend below the second partial to F♯ by using the three valves, but this leaves a gap between F♯ and the first partial, or fundamental. On soprano instruments this gap is unimportant, for the effective range of the instrument is above the second partial, and while these valve notes below the second partial can be played, composers and arrangers recognize they are not very good in musical quality and do not call for them often. Since the valve notes below the second partial are not of good quality, nobody seems to worry about the fact that still lower valve notes are not available on a three-valve instrument. This is true not only on sopranos but also on altos and tenors and baritones.

On euphoniums and basses, however, this gap is an entirely different matter. The bore on these instruments is so large that the lower notes are of good quality. In fact, the best notes on large-bore instruments are the lower, while the poor notes are the top notes—just the opposite of the soprano instruments. The valve notes below the second partial are of good quality on these larger-bore instruments, and it is desirable not only to play from the second partial down to F♯ but also to play on down to the fundamental, completely bridging with chromatic intervals the wide gap of a complete octave which exists between the first partial, or fundamental, and the second partial. But three valves with their six semitones are not sufficient. In descending from the second partial we use the second valve, first valve, first and second, etc., but when we have all three valves down and have descended chromatically as far as our three valves will allow us, we find outselves stranded on F♯. This leaves a gap between the fundamental C and F♯ of five semitones. To make these notes available, a fourth valve was used which was capable of adding sufficient length of tubing for lowering the instrument five semitones. This extra valve, in combination with the other three valves, allows us to play F, E, E♭, D and D♭. The next note is the open C, or fundamental, so chromatically we are able to bridge the gap of an entire octave between the first and second partials.

This addition of the fourth valve made the euphonium and bass saxhorns chromatic throughout their complete range. Later a fifth valve was added, not because it was necessary to bridge the gaps in the scale but in an effort to correct the intonation on some of the valve notes. This discrepancy in the intonation of some of the notes played with the valves touches on an inherent fault of all valve instruments. A full explanation of the problem would require a discussion too long and involved for the scope of this book. The fundamentals of the problem can be illustrated roughly by an analogy. Suppose there were a great stairway, the first step of which was high and large, the next step a bit smaller, the third still smaller, and so on gradually, until at the top the steps were low and small. Suppose the lower steps were so high and large that a small child could not climb them. To assist the child, a large block half as high as the first step could be made which could be placed at the bottom of the first step. The child could step up on the block and from the block could reach the first step. Then the child could pull the block up after him and place it at the bottom of the second step. This block, which was made just half as high as the first step, would be slightly more than half as high as the second; and after several steps the block would be nearly as high as or higher than each step, and no block would be needed at all.

The musical scale is like our imaginary steps: as we ascend, the steps grow smaller and smaller. A valve with its tubing is a sort of block which helps us span a step too long for us to make without it. Now it is perfectly obvious that, in the stairway analogy mentioned above, a block large enough to be just half as high as the bottom step would be more than half as high· for other steps on up, because each step is graduated smaller and smaller. Likewise, in music a valve with tubing which is just right to bridge a gap in the lower part of the scale would not be right for bridging a gap in the top of the scale. Valve tubing of proper length for the wide gaps in the lower part of the scale would be too long for the smaller gaps in the upper part; and, vice versa, valve tubing made the proper length for the small gaps in the upper part of the scale would be too short for the wider gaps in the lower part of the scale. For this reason, instrument makers calculate the length of valve slides so they will be in between and come nearest to a compromise up and down the scale. If the valve slides are all right for the middle of the range of the instrument, they throw the top a little flat because the slides are a bit too long; and they throw the bottom a little sharp, because they are a bit too short. This is more serious in the lower part of the scale, where the gaps are large, than it is in the top, where the open notes are close together. For this reason, some cornets and trumpets have adjustable first- and third-valve slides, so the slides can be lengthened when used for notes in the lower part of the scale.

The problem as outlined for cornets and trumpets is identical with that on euphoniums and basses, only it is considerably augmented in the case of the latter. In our imaginary stairway, it is easy to see that if we should add one or two steps at the bottom, each correspondingly larger than those above it, the discrepancy between each step would rapidly increase. Therefore the inadequacy of valve slides on large instruments like the euphonium and bass is greatly magnified. Valve slides which were of proper length in the middle of the scale would be far too long for the top and still farther too short for the bottom. For this reason, the fourth valve on basses and euphoniums is especially welcome, not only to bridge the gap between F♯ and C but also to use as an alternative for the combination of the first and third valves. The fourth valve is roughly equal to five semitones, but it usually is made somewhat longer than the combined length of the first valve (with its two semitones) and the third valve (with its three semitones).

Although the fifth valve is rare on American basses, double-bell euphoniums usually have a fifth valve, not for the purpose of affecting intonation but to control the smaller bell. The instrument normally uses the larger bell, but a fifth valve can be operated to bring the smaller bell into use. The smaller bell is used for trombone and echo effects.

Although our family of tubas is organized on the same basis as the saxhorns, it did not descend directly from the saxhorns but from the saxtrombas. This family of instruments, which is also an invention of Sax, was brought out about 1850, eight years after the saxhorns. There were eight members in this family, including the E♭ sopranino, the B♭ soprano, the B♭ mezzo-soprano, the E♭ alto, the B♭ tenor, the B♭ baritone, the E♭ bass and the BB♭ contrabass. The saxhorns were conical in bore and were played with a deep bell-shaped cup mouthpiece. These features produced a broad, mellow tone. The saxtrombas were designed with smaller tubing, about one third of which was straight, or cylindrical, the other two thirds being conical. The mouthpiece was not so deep as that of the saxhorns and was shaped more like a bowl. The resulting tone was brighter and more solid.

Most European countries prefer the saxhorn family because of its mellow tone. In Italy and England especially, the conical-bore instruments are used almost universally. In America the saxtromba family is preferred, or at least the modified saxtrombas which we have developed. The

American instruments are larger in bore than the original saxtrombas and are played with a more shallow mouthpiece. However, the fundamental principle in the bore construction has been followed, the bore having less taper than the bore of the saxhorn. While these later instruments of Sax's had no wide acceptance in Europe, they have come to be, in their slightly modified form, America's choice.

There were nine distinct members of this family which grew up on American soil. The small E♭ cornet used to be quite a popular instrument but has fallen into disfavor lately. The B♭ cornet is the favorite soprano of this big family. These two instruments are played in horizontal position, but the rest of the family are upright instruments. They include the E♭ alto and the B♭ tenor, both of which are now almost obsolete; the B♭ baritone; the B♭ euphonium; the B♭ bass, which is entirely obsolete; the E♭ bass and the BB♭ bass.

Along about the time of the Civil War a peculiar family of tubas was quite popular. This was the instrument which "backfired" over the left shoulder. The family was made up of soprano, alto, tenor, baritone and bass. All of them were played with rotary valves, rare in America on any instrument except the French horn. The idea behind their peculiar appearance was that the bell pointing backward over the shoulder would throw the music of the band backward. Since the band marched at the head of the army or parade, this seemed a logical idea. After the war, the military spirit died out, marching bands gave way to concert bands, and the backfiring instruments gave way to those with upright bells or bells projecting forward. They are now only interesting relics.

Although not belonging to the family of tubas, but rather to the French horns, the Wagnerian tuben were an interesting, if short-lived, invention. Wagner introduced these instruments in his "Nibelungen Ring" as a means of extending downward the French horn range. He apparently was not satisfied with the tone quality of the regular tubas as basses for the French horns, and he had the tuben built as an experiment. There were two—a tenor in B♭ and a bass in F— and they were played with a deep funnel-shaped mouthpiece like a very large French horn mouthpiece. There is no evidence that Wagner was not satisfied with his invention, but these instruments were not widely used by anyone else and soon became obsolete. Occasionally tuben are used in these Wagnerian numbers, but usually the tuben parts are played by the regular tubas.

Until after the Civil War there were no important tuba makers in America. The instruments were imported from England, Germany, France and Italy. Henry Diston, a famous cornet soloist from England, toured America with his three brothers shortly after the Civil War and finally was persuaded to head a band instrument firm in this country. The firm was established in Philadelphia, and although the instruments were supposed to be made in America, many were imported and merely stamped with the Diston name. Pepper also started a band-instrument factory in Philadelphia shortly after the war. Hall Bros. of Boston, inventors of the "pinched rotary valve," and Isaac Fishe of Worcester were other makers. The bulk of the instruments used in American bands, however, continued to be imported.

The split lip of a cornet player in 1873 started the band-instrument business in America. Captain C. G. Conn returned to Elkhart, Indiana, after the Civil War and started a grocery and bakery. He was a musician and played cornet in the silver-cornet band. One day the Haverly Minstrels visited the town, and during an altercation with a big bass player in the visiting troupe Conn received a badly split lip. This prevented him from playing the cornet, and to help remedy the situation he invented a mouthpiece with a rubber cushion. The invention became known, and before long Conn found himself in the mouthpiece business, making his mouthpieces on an improvised lathe made from a sewing machine.

In 1875 Conn started making cornets, with the assistance of a partner by the name of Dupont, an English horn maker. Experienced horn makers were secured from England, France and Germany. Early in his experience Conn obtained patents on several inventions, among them being front-action instruments with valve slides ascending from the valves and preventing water from entering the slides. This new family of tubas was called the "American Band Instruments," and it wasn't long before they were competing on a favorable basis with imported instruments. The first double-bell euphonium, now so familiar, was built by Conn in 1890. In 1898 Conn built the first sousaphone, a variety of helicon with the bell opening upward. The instrument was built especially for Sousa and was named in his honor. In 1908 the first bell-front sousaphones were made—and thereby hangs many a tale of mirth for the initiated.

The ignorance of the history of the sousaphone seems to be universal among movie technicians. It is a favorite sport of the few who know when this instrument was first created to watch the movie productions for uses of these modern instruments in historical scenes. British soldiers bound for the Boer War are serenaded by a band with a battery of bell-front sousaphones, at a time when there were only four sousaphones in existence and these had upright bells and were all four in Sousa's band. Spanish-American War fervor is made to live again in music from the sousaphone, at a time when no sousaphone had yet been built. The Boys in Blue and the Boys in Gray are both cheered on to victory or are honored in celebrations of triumph by bands whose bass parts are played on sousaphones, at a time when Captain Conn was merely a soldier and over a decade before he ever thought of making a band instrument. The gold rush to California, the completion of a railroad track by driving a gold spike, packet-boat races on the Mississippi are all occasions for parading sousaphones before the public, and nobody seems to worry about the fact that the first sousaphone was not made until 1898 and the bell-front sousaphone was not made until 1908.

Although the bell-front sousaphone is the most popular bass tuba in American bands, Sousa steadfastly clung to the original sousaphone with bell up—whether for musical reasons or for sentimental reasons, no one knows. Either would be sufficient justification in this instance. When Sousa died in 1932 and his band was dissolved, the four sousaphones were bought as noble souvenirs of a noble man. One of these original sousaphones from Sousa's band is now exhibited by the Museum of Science and Industry in Chicago. And as spectators gaze upon this interesting specimen they can reflect that they are gazing upon the latest offspring of the prolific serpent—although, if the strain runs true to form, certainly not the last.

CHAPTER XII

Percussion Instruments

TINKLE! JINGLE! BOOM! CRASH!

WHEN THE MOORS CROSSED from Africa into Spain in 711 A.D. they brought with them some queer drums which looked like the two halves of a large ball. Five hundred years later the Crusaders, returning from the Orient, rode across Europe with these same half-sphere drums slung across the necks of their horses. Today we have the giant kettle-drums, or tympani, which trace their ancestry directly to these ancient instruments.

It cannot be said that either the Moors or the Crusaders introduced drums into Europe, for the drum is an instrument which is indigenous to every soil and climate. There are no peoples on the globe, however primitive or cultured they may be, who do not play the drum in some form or other. There has never been a time in the history of the world in which the drum did not figure prominently. Today the wildest tribes in the heart of Africa beat their drums to accompany the ceremonies of war and death, joy and celebration. Today in the finest concert bands and symphony orchestras all over the world the drums boom out to sound a rhythm or punctuate a musical phrase.

PERCUSSION INSTRUMENTS

The warp and woof of music are rhythm and melody, and the drums are the rhythm instruments *par excellence*. It is easier to recognize a song by its rhythm without melody than it is by its melody without rhythm, which shows what a basic part of music is rhythm. Primitive music is more rhythm than it is melody. Some of this primitive music is tremendously expressive. Melody could add very little to the foreboding pulsations of the African war drums. In fact, melody would detract more than it would add. There is something in the constantly recurring rhythmical beat of the drums which pulsates in the blood. There is something in the incessant and ominous boom of the drums which pounds in the brain. Melody would relieve the tension, would break the spell. But the dread rhythm of the war drums, beating in the ears, booming in the brain, speaks a terrible message which could be spoken in no other way.

If it be a dirge, how little is melody missed when the drums begin their lament! With a rhythm peculiarly expressive of grief and sorrow, the drums beat out a mournful elegy which asks nothing of either words or melody. By contrast, what can be gayer than the castanets and tambourines of Spain or the bongas and maracas of Cuba? The quickened rhythm, the joyous accents of these instruments sing a song of gaiety and happiness which melody could scarcely supplement. What can the melody of the bugle add to the stirring rattle of the military drum, sounding assembly or commanding a charge? The weird, the mysterious, the terrible all can be portrayed with tremendous drama and reality by bare rhythm without melody.

It is no wonder that all peoples, from the most primitive and barbarous to the most educated and cultured, have been lovers of the drum and other percussion instruments. In earliest history we learn that the Egyptians, Assyrians, Hebrews, Greeks and Romans all used instruments corresponding to our kettledrums, tenor drums, tambourines and cymbals. Of these, the most important soon came to be the kettledrums. In early Europe they were used not only in military affairs, but in the court of Edward I as musical instruments. Later, in 1347, when Edward III celebrated his triumphal march into Calais, kettledrums helped make the music. Chaucer often speaks of the "nakers" in his Canterbury Tales, and nakers is an Arabic word meaning "kettledrums." In a carving in Worcester Cathedral, believed to have been done in 1396, a pair of kettledrums is shown strapped to the waist of a player, one on each side. These were small kettledrums, similar to those brought by the Moors into Spain and carried by the Crusaders from Arabia, but larger-size kettles were developed by the Germans, which are practically like our modern tympani. Henry VIII introduced these larger kettledrums into England in the first half of the sixteenth century. The German historian of music, Virdung, writing in 1511, describes the kettledrums of his day. He even draws some pictures of them which look much like the modern kettledrums. About a hundred years later, Praetorius, another German historian of music, talks about the kettledrums; and so does the Frenchman Mersennus, writing in 1627. These ancient kettledrums were hemispherical and had skin heads stretched across the top by hoops which were held in place and tightened by adjusting screws around the rim.

Kettledrums graduated from the army and the military band into the orchestra during the time of Lully and were used commonly by him and other French composers of the seventeenth century. As early as 1713 kettledrums had become popular in Germany, for Johann Mattheson, of Hamburg, composer and musical authority, writing of the musical instruments of his day, says that kettledrums were often used in both church and opera. These he says were used in pairs and were tuned a fourth apart, a practice which existed for many years. Handel knew about kettledrums, using them in his "Water Music." Bach also used them, as did Haydn and Mozart and all the other great masters who came later.

These early kettledrums, or tympani, as they are now called, were hand tuned and were pitched in C and G, the tonic and dominant of the key in which the music was written. The large kettle was tuned to the G below the C, while the small kettle was tuned to the C, making them a fourth apart. The reason for this inversion was the limitations of the instruments. If the tonic had been given to the large kettle and the dominant to the small kettle, the dominant would generally have been higher than the small kettle's compass. Therefore, the tonic was given to the small kettle, and the dominant an octave below was given to the large kettle. Kettledrums were treated mostly as military instruments, for they were hardly ever allowed to play except with the trumpets, in marches, overtures and other such music. This is only another example of following custom. Trumpeters and kettledrummers used to accompany royalty wherever it went and were used to signify rank, much as rank is signified today by cannons, a certain number for each rank. Later, when trumpets were admitted to the orchestra, the kettledrums naturally followed; also, when

[*255*]

the trumpets played, the early composers thought it appropriate that the kettledrums play, too.

It was Beethoven who freed the tympani from these shackles, not only those imposed by the custom of pairing the kettledrums with the trumpets, but also the universal tuning to G and C, a fourth apart. In his First Symphony in 1800, Beethoven startled the tympani player and the audience by having the tympani play a sort of bass part to a melody of violins and flutes. Seven years later, in his Fourth Symphony, he elects the tympani to the great honor of stating a theme of two notes which was repeated by the other instruments. The following year, in his great Fifth Symphony, the same symphony in which the piccolo, trombone and contrabassoon all make their debut in the symphony, Beethoven causes the tympani to make their debut as a solo instrument, creating for the tympani a solo effect in the scherzo movement. In 1814, in his Eighth Symphony, he tries still another innovation by having the tympani play in unison with the bassoons. By this time the fatal tie between the Siamese twins had been broken and the tympani was no longer restricted to duets with the trumpet.

In tuning, also, Beethoven experimented with the tympani. He first dared to tune the kettles in fifths, giving the large kettle the tonic C and the small kettle the dominant G above. This is common today, but in Beethoven's time it was a daring change. Encouraged by this success, in his Seventh Symphony, composed in 1813, he tuned the two kettles in sixths. In his Ninth Symphony, composed eleven years later, he positively went berserk by tuning the tympani in octave F's and introducing the unheard-of practice of playing two notes of a chord simultaneously on two kettles!

Not only did he make innovations in tuning and in ways of using the tympani, but he demonstrated their resources in musical effects. He showed that the tympani could be used not only for brilliant and military effects, but also to express mystery, solemnity and awe. He established them as versatile and useful instruments for many roles.

The composer Meyerbeer was at one time tympanist under Beethoven, and he appreciated more fully than anyone else how Beethoven had liberated the tympani, and when he began composing he carried with him the open mind of Beethoven. He excelled his master in this respect by writing for four tympani instead of the conventional two, tuned in G, C, D and E. This novel bit of tympani writing occurs in Meyerbeer's "Robert le Diable," written in 1831.

A countryman of Meyerbeer, Hector Berlioz, went even further; in fact he went to extremes. In his "Requiem Mass" he startled the musical world by writing for eight pairs of tympani tuned as follows: minor third, minor sixth, major third, fourth and diminished fifth. These sixteen tympani were played by ten players, some of them playing on pairs and others booming away on a single tympano. In this effort he was attempting to portray the crack of doom on the great resurrection day, and the effect was appalling.

In reviewing the practice of his day, Berlioz writes, in his great book on instrumentation and orchestration, that it was customary to tune the tympani in a great variety of ways: minor third, major third, second, perfect fourth, augmented fourth, fifth, sixth, seventh and octave. He also recites how he introduced the practice of having one player use three tympani instead of two. He says this occurred while he was directing an orchestra in the Paris opera house. He points out that it required seventy years of tympani playing in the orchestra to develop the simple idea that one tympanist could easily play three tympani instead of two. In this he was in error, however, for Weber in 1807 had used three tympani in his overture to "Peter Schmoll," and three tympani had also been used by Mendelssohn and by Schumann.

Wagner was partial to the tympano and raised tympano writing to new heights. Not only did he write some beautiful solos for the tympani, as in the introduction to "Siegfried," but he made of the tympano a great dramatic instrument. He prolonged the suspense before some tragic happening, by using the soft, foreboding strokes of the tympani. Or, when the whole orchestra was hushed in some tense moment, he called for a soft note on the tympani to magnify the stillness. Classical examples of this dramatic casting of the tympani are in "Lohengrin," where Talramund drops dead at the sight of the holy word of the Grail Knight whom he had wished to kill, and also in "Götterdämmerung" after Siegfried is stabbed by Hagen.

With this greater taste in writing for the tympani, the job of the tympanist became less difficult in one way and more difficult in another. He used to have to play whenever the trumpets played. He might be called on to boom his way through an overture or other brilliant music from the opening beat until the final crash. But after the new style of writing he might be called on to play a couple of short strokes, and then he'd have to wait through many measures for another couple of notes. In Rossini's "Semiramide" the tympani have a tremolo in the first measure, and then follow seventy-eight measures of rest. Schubert's Seventh Symphony is noted also for its many measures of rest. Some tympanists

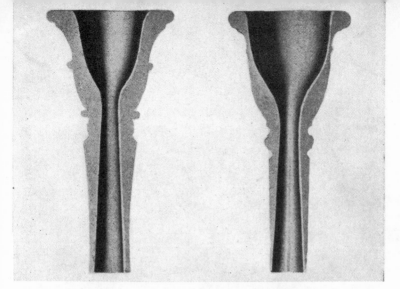

(*Left to right, cross sections*): Mouthpiece of saxhorn and mouthpiece of modern tuba. Note that the saxhorn mouthpiece is deep and funnel-shaped, while the tuba mouthpiece is more bowl-shaped. This difference in shape in the mouthpiece has much to do with the difference between the tone quality of these two types of instruments. The saxhorn is more mellow while the tuba is more brilliant in tone quality.

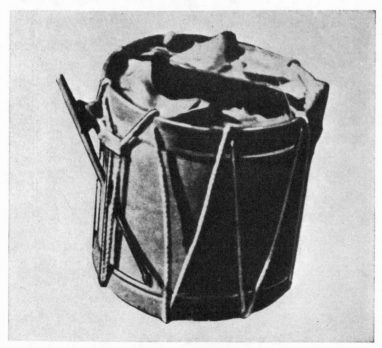

AMERICAN REVOLUTIONARY WAR DRUM

Carried by Timothy Church of Connecticut in the famous battle of Saratoga. Still has original snares and heads. Now property of Joseph W. Church, direct descendant of Timothy Church.

It was such drums as these which the Moors carried into Spain in 711 A.D. and which, five hundred years later, the Crusaders brought back with them from the Holy Land, suspended on either side of the neck of their horses.

depend on a cue from the conductor, but many count the measures and can come in accurately on an afterbeat following dozens of measures of rest. In fact, among tympanists this is a point on which to boast. Some claim they can go out for a smoke and come in just in time to pick up the mallets and play their note or roll.

An amusing story on this point is told about Pfund, the famous tympanist under Mendelssohn. He was a wizard on counting the silent measures and never failed to come in on the right beat. Once he loaned a bass viol player a thaler. Soon after, he began dunning the viol player to pay it back. The viol player was so pestered by Pfund that he decided he would pay it back and at the same time get revenge on Pfund for his illiberal attitude. One day when Pfund was out for a smoke during many measures of rest for the tympani, the viol player laid pfennigs equal to one thaler around the edge of one of the tympani. As usual Pfund came in just in time to take up the mallets and strike a resounding boom on the instrument. This blow on the tympano caused the pfennigs to jump into the air and come down in the head again, dancing, jingling and rolling to the floor, much to the consternation of Pfund, Mendelssohn, the rest of the orchestra and the audience.

This prank may or may not have been the beginning of novel effects on the tympani made by laying keys or metal plates on the head, but these effects are now written legitimately for the tympani. Certain it is that Pfund taught future generations of tympano players to play with artistry. He is regarded as the first great artist on these instruments. Mendelssohn took advantage of his artistry to write many difficult passages for the instruments, and succeeding tympanists had to be artists to play the music written especially for Pfund. Mendelssohn called for many tunings of the tympani which were queer at the time, among them C♯ and A, D and E, G and F, B♭ and D♭.

But the manufacturers of tympani have made it possible for modern composers to write music for the tympani which even Pfund could not play. Pfund's tympani were hand tuned, and to change the tuning of the instruments required a certain interval of time and a most accurately trained ear, especially when the tuning had to be changed during a number. Pfund apparently was distressed with this shortcoming, for he made the first attempt to construct tympani which could be tuned by a foot pedal. The first set he built is still in the museum of the Civic Opera House in Leipzig, Germany. They are crude, iron forgings and were clumsy to operate. Now, however, through the use of the pedal or machine tympani, the tuning can be quickly changed by a lever worked with the foot. Merely by working the pedal up or down, the pitch of the separate kettles can be changed to any pitch within the range of a fifth or sixth. The large kettle usually has a range of from F to C, and the small kettle has a range of from B to E or F, giving an overall range of a full octave. So quickly can the tuning be changed on these modern tympani that it is possible to play a tune of somewhat complicated melody on the tympani! Even Pfund would have been amazed at this.

The tendency in writing for the tympani is to make them more and more solo instruments. Some of this advanced writing is found in the works of Ravel, Strauss and Stravinsky. Ravel, in his famous "Bolero," gives to the tympani the complete bass accompaniment toward the end.

Requisites of a good tympanist are a most refined sense of rhythm and timing and a keen ear for tuning. The excellent qualities of Pfund in accurate timing are still as needful today as ever, and although tuning has been greatly facilitated through the pedal tympani, no less keenness of pitch is required. There are no stops for the pedal to indicate different notes, as there are frets on the guitar, and the tympanist must still rely on his ear to tell when the right notes are obtained. The pedal merely stretches the head tighter to obtain higher notes and loosens it for lower notes, but the tympanist's ear must tell him when the right notes are obtained.

In the old days the tympanist would throw a cloth over the heads of the tympani to muffle the sound for certain soft effects. Today the manufacturers have supplied him with an assortment of mallets with hard or very soft heads which enable him to play with brilliance or with muffled tone, as the music requires. Different qualities of tone can also be obtained, depending upon where on the head, with reference to the center, it is struck. The head is usually struck midway between the outer edge and the center. Striking the head near the center produces a tubby tone, while striking it near the edge produces a bright but thin tone.

It is the belief of some that the pitch of the kettle is determined by its shape and size. This has been disproved by filling the kettle with water. It is true that the diameter of the kettle affects the pitch. The lowest note on the standard twenty-eight-inch kettle is F or possibly E, and for some classical compositions requiring lower notes, a special thirty-inch kettle must be used. Gustav Mahler wrote low D in his Ninth Symphony, for which a special thirty-five-inch kettle must be used. Also, the highest note for the standard twenty-five-inch kettle is F or possibly G, and to play notes higher than this, a special twenty-four-inch kettle must be used. Rimsky-Korsakov wrote high E♭ in his "Mlada," for which a special twenty-two-inch kettle must be used.

Percussion instruments are conveniently classified as to those which have definite pitch and those which do not. The tympani have definite pitch, as has been related. Other such instruments are the family of bells and chimes. The bell family comprises many instruments, which are played in a variety of ways. Some are made of bars of metal, such as the orchestra bells, glockenspiel and celesta. Some are made of bars of wood, such as the xylophone and marimba. Some are struck in the center of the bar with mallets, as the orchestra bells, glockenspiel, xylophone, marimba. Some are made of tubes of metal which are struck on the end, as the chimes. The celesta is played by pressing down a key mechanism, the same as the piano.

If it weren't for the fact that bars of wood or metal were used in musical instruments a long time before the Crusades, the interesting story about Saladin might be used to explain the creation of the resonating bar. The story is a romantic one, however, and it is really too bad that it is in disagreement with the facts. When Saladin, Emperor of Turkey, conquered Jerusalem in the latter part of the twelfth century, he commanded that all bells be broken up and destroyed so the Christians could not be called together for worship. Bars of wood and iron were made and substituted for the purpose. These took up smaller space and could be more easily secreted from the eyes of the infidel.

Economy of space and greater convenience are responsible

for the substitution of the modern tubular chimes for genuine bells. In the Middle Ages, carillons of bells were one of the important sources of music. At first these carillons were comprised of three to six bells which were struck by hammers held in the hand. Later a dozen or more bells were used, and they were struck by a system of ropes pulled from below the cathedral tower. Today these giant carillons are played from a keyboard, like an organ, the bells being struck by a mechanism actuated by the keys. Two of the largest carillons in the world are those at the University of Chicago Chapel and at Riverside Church, New York. The largest bell weighs over eighteen and a half tons, and the smallest weighs ten pounds. In 1925 the largest bell was found in the fifty-two-bell set at Ghent. This bell is ninety-eight inches in diameter and weighs 20,720 pounds. Its pitch is E below Middle C.

Composers have often wished to produce the sound of these carillon bells, but it is obvious that they could not install one or several of these actual bells, because of their tremendous size and weight. It was found that metal tubes one inch to two and a half inches in diameter and only four to six feet long would reproduce the pitch and tonal quality of all but the lowest notes of these giant carillons. It is chimes of this type which are used in the modern orchestra to create such bell effects as are heard in Tschaikowsky's "1812 Overture" and in Wagner's "Parsifal." The standard chimes are built with eighteen tubes and have a range from an octave above Middle C chromatically up to F, an octave and a fourth above.

Orchestra bells are a series of metal bars of graduated length and thickness, which give a chromatic range of two octaves or more. They are made with or without resonators, are struck with hard mallets, and give off a bright, metallic sound. They are heard in Wagner's "Die Walküre," in the magic fire scene, and also in his "Die Meistersinger," in the last act.

The xylophone is a similar instrument except it has a range of three and a half to four octaves and the bars are made of rosewood instead of metal. This wood is very hard, and when struck with hard mallets it produces a brilliant sound of short duration. Some composers regard the xylophone as crude, but Saint-Saëns has used it to advantage in his famous "Danse Macabre," where he depicts the rattling of bones in the death scene.

The marimba is similar to the xylophone, but the brilliant sound of the xylophone has been deepened and prolonged by the use of resonators which build up and enrich the tone. These tubes are placed beneath the rosewood bars and are of varying length in proportion to the varying length of the bars.

A more modern creation is the vibraphone, a sort of marimba with metal bars and an electrically actuated valve which rotates in the top of the resonator tube, producing a pleasing vibrato.

To Tschaikowsky goes the honor of having introduced into the symphony the celesta, a type of orchestra bells played with a keyboard. This interesting bit of music is found in his "Casse-Noisette."

In the band a transportable form of orchestra bells is used, called the glockenspiel, or bell lyra. The metal bars are made of special aluminum alloy and are mounted on a frame shaped like a lyre, while the standard for the lyre is carried in a belt like a flag or banner. In marching bands the bright, piercing notes of the bell lyra can be heard above the band. Recently these instruments have become popular in the band at football games, and when the band music is broadcast, these instruments can be distinctly heard when the rest of the band fades to a whisper.

Everyone is familiar with the bass drum, the side drum or snare drum, the cymbals and the triangle, all instruments of indefinite pitch. Although they were used in military bands for a long time previously, Gluck is credited with introducing them into the orchestra about 1760. Desiring to create some special effects in his operas, he called in these lowly musical instruments as an experiment, and they have remained ever since. Mozart used the bass drum, cymbal and triangle a few years later, to create a Turkish atmosphere in his "Die Entführung." During the last quarter of the eighteenth century these instruments were used often when the composer wished to portray the oriental or barbaric, and Haydn used them once, in his "Military Symphony." Before the middle of the next century, most large orchestras in opera, such as those in Berlin and Paris, counted the bass drum, cymbal and triangle as standard equipment. They were also usually found in ballet and light opera, but were not admitted to the more exclusive ranks of the symphony until some time later.

The old side drum became the snare drum after snares were added. In England this drum is still usually called the side drum, but in America it is more often called the snare drum. This name comes from the "snares" which are stretched across one head, inside the drum. The creation of this device is credited to a Scottish drummer. This drummer originated the use of a rawhide whip for striking one side of his bass drum, and sometimes he would hold the whip against the head on one side while he struck the drum with the drumstick on the other side. This created a sort of dry rattle. Later, catgut strings were stretched across the head, and these were called snares. It is this device which creates the snappy, rapid vibration of the snare drum when it is struck.

The tambourine is a very ancient instrument, being pictured in the ruins of the Egyptians, Assyrians and Greeks. It is now closely associated with the Spanish, due to their love for and wide use of this instrument. One of the first uses of the tambourine in the orchestra was by Weber in his overture to "Preciosa."

The name castanets seems to have been derived from "castaña," the Spanish word for chestnut, which would indicate that originally they were made of this wood. Some authorities claim the Moors introduced castanets into Spain, but their instruments were made of metal. Now castanets are made most often of vulcanized rubber, called ebonite. This is also a Spanish instrument, and it is claimed that few people not Spanish-born ever learn to use it properly. The most celebrated use of the castanet is in Bizet's opera, "Carmen."

Then there are tam-tams and tom-toms. These two instruments are often confused by the uninitiated, and it is to avoid this that the tam-tam is now more generally called the gong. It is a huge cymbal suspended in a metal ring so the instrument can vibrate freely. It is struck with a mallet, and it resounds with a prolonged reverberation. The tom-toms are merely modern revisions of the ancient and primitive tom-toms of the savages. They are small drums with thick leather heads, and they produce a sharp, brief, hollow sound similar to that of the more familiar bass drum, only more shallow and of less musical quality. They are seldom used in the orchestra but are popular in the dance band.

The bass drum, snare drum, cymbal, triangle, tambourine, castanet and gong are of indefinite pitch. Although they cannot be used for melody, they are essential in many ways to set tempo, emphasize musical dynamics and give color. Although not a pitched instrument, the bass drum is tightened so it tunes with low F for best quality of tone. There is no definite pitch to cymbals, but they should have a distinct quality of tone. The best cymbals are made in Turkey and are hand hammered from bronze by a process which no other makers have been able to duplicate. Chinese cymbals are hand hammered, and American cymbals are spun, but neither of them has the rich quality of the Turkish cymbal, although American manufacturers have made important progress in recent years, particularly in matched pairs.

Considerable variation in tone color can be made by the player in the way this group of instruments is played. The bass and snare drummers do more than beat or strike their drums. They have an elaborate and intricate technique which is appreciated only by those familiar with drumming. Cymbals, too, must be played properly to obtain the utmost from them. One of the most dramatic actions in the symphony or band is the glancing stroke of the cymbals by the good cymbal player. This looks easy, but great skill is required to make the cymbals kiss each other at the right place and with the proper touch as one hand goes up and the other goes down.

Haydn set a precedent in his "Seasons" which he probably

would regret if he were alive. He introduced "effects" such as thunder, the whistle of the quail, a gunshot, the chirp of the cricket, and today there is no end to the "effects" which are used in the symphony orchestra, not to mention the effects used in the theater orchestra! To leaf through a modern drum catalog is something like going to a carnival or visiting a freak show. No one becomes particularly upset by such inoffensive traps as temple blocks, wood blocks, slapsticks, and jingle clogs. An eyebrow might be raised at the cyclone whistle, locomotive imitation, steamboat whistle, boatswain whistle, fire bell or police gong. One might wonder a little at such old livery-stable effects as sleigh bells, horse hoofs and horse neighs. Some misgivings might be expressed when considering such Cuban gadgets as claves, maracas, bongos, and perhaps Haydn would have been amused at the cuckoo call, the bird whistle, the rooster crow, the dog bark, the crow call, and even the cow bawl. But we reach the utmost in something or other when we come to such sound effects as hen cackle, fly buzz, pig grunt, baby cry, duck quack, monkey chatter, snore imitation and nose blow!

The number of men in the percussion section varies considerably according to the composition being played. Large orchestras use from four to eight players. The concert band as a rule consists of three and sometimes four men, but occasionally a small drum corps is added for playing certain military music and the number is greatly augmented. The average theater orchestra employs two percussionists, one to play "trap drums," a foot-pedal device for beating the bass drum while at the same time he uses both hands to play the snare or side drum. This player is sometimes referred to as the double drummer. The other player, assigned to the tympani, also doubles on bells, marimba or xylophone. Only one player is used in the percussion section of the dance band, but he must be extremely versatile, for he plays practically everything in the drum catalog—snare drum, bass drum, bells, marimba, xylophone, chimes, tom-toms, wood blocks, cymbals, gong and any of a hundred other "effects."

The percussion section has long been the stepchild of the orchestra and especially of the band. It was looked upon as something which was customary to have, but was seldom understood by the composer and still less by the conductor. The drummers were turned loose on their own, and many conductors and bandmasters knew so little about the art of the percussionist that they never knew whether the player was reading the music properly or not. Now, however, great interest is being taken in this neglected section, and musical performance is greatly improving as a consequence. Drummers must play the "rudiments" strictly and not "fake." Moreover, new effects are being tried, and the value of such instruments as marimba, xylophone and vibraphone are becoming recognized. In many respects, the percussion section is a virgin field of music, and great strides in music are being made here and will continue to be made.

The greatest bandmasters are those who best understand the percussion section. John Philip Sousa knew drumming thoroughly, and much of the secret of his stirring marches is effective drum parts. Nothing in Sousa's drum scores is left to guess: every beat, tap and roll is meticulously written out, and woe to the Sousa drummer who missed a single detail. Sousa's trained ear was sure to catch the slightest deviation from the carefully worked out score. Sousa greatly valued his snare drummer Tom Mills and often said Mills was the best percussionist he ever heard. Edwin Franko Goldman, director of the famous Goldman Band, insists that the bass drummer is the most valuable player in his band. Frank Simon, director of the popular Armco Band, regards George Carey, the snare drummer and tympanist, as the life and snap of the band.

CHAPTER XIII

Plucked and Struck Strings

THE STORY OF STEEL WIRE

AT FIRST THOUGHT, two less-related creations can scarcely be thought of than the fine concert piano and the suspension bridge. And yet their developments are but two chapters in the same fascinating story of steel wire drawn through a die. Without drawn wire we could have neither the piano nor the suspension bridge, for wire is essential to both. The ancients had their psaltery, lyre, lute and harp, strung with "catgut" or vegetable fiber, as well as their suspended footbridge, but the concert piano and the Brooklyn Bridge are so far superior as to be almost different in kind.

Wire is such a common article today that it is difficult to realize that we have not always had it. But there is no record of drawn wire before the eighth or ninth century A.D. It is true that flat or cut wire is as old as history. One of the oldest references to this kind of wire is found in Exodus, Chap. 39, verse 3: "They did beat the gold into thin plates and cut it into wires." The Assyrians and Babylonians in 1700 B.C. and the inhabitants of Nineveh in 800 B.C. made wire by the same process. Most of such wire was made of gold and silver and was used as ornament. But the first record we have of round wire drawn through a drawplate is found in the writings of an ancient monk by the name of Theophilus, a German or Anglo-Saxon of the eighth or ninth century.

Theophilus' description of the process shows that it was essentially the same as that used today. He mentions two pieces of iron "three or four fingers wide" and having three or four rows of holes in them. Small bars of metal were drawn through these holes, elongating the bar into round wire. As the wire was pulled through the smaller holes, the diameter of the wire became smaller and the length became greater. Such wire was soft and not very strong, because it is obvious that the wire must be softer than the metal drawplates, and at that time the hard steel of today was unknown. One formula mentioned by Theophilus was two parts of tin and one part of lead. Such wire lacked the tensile strength suitable for the modern piano and even for the old clavichord and harpsichord. Some of it was used for making coats of mail for the knights of old, and no doubt many of the Crusaders rode to Palestine in coats of mail made from such wire as is described by Theophilus.

In 1270 we find in Paris a small guild of wire drawers. We do not know how long this little industry had been in existence, but we do know that it did not thrive or grow very rapidly, for there were only eight such craftsmen in Paris in 1292, and in 1500 there were only nine. No doubt one reason for the small number of master wire drawers was the almost prohibitory system of apprenticeship, for an apprentice was required to work ten years for nothing and had to pay a fee of twenty sous besides. The work of these apprentices was also strenuous, for they had to pull the wire through the plate by muscular strength or by the use of a spool which was turned by hand.

The date for the beginning of wire drawing which is usually given is 1350, and this is the date given in Grove's dictionary. This reference is to the wire drawers of Augsburg, Bavaria. There was also wire drawing at this time in Nuremberg, another city of Bavaria, and in Altena, in the district of Westphalia. But these German wire drawers had been preceded by about five hundred years by the craftsmen mentioned by Theophilus. It is true, however, that Germany became the principal source of wire for the builders of clavichords and harpsichords all over Europe. Industrial England did not start drawing wire until 1565 and up to as late as 1800 imported from Germany most of its piano wire. In America the wire industry was started in Lynn, Mass., in 1665, but most of this wire was made for carding textiles. It was not until 1850 that the first piano wire was made. At that time Jonas Chickering, the piano pioneer, asked the firm of Washburn & Godard of Worcester to make some piano wire to his specifications. This was the beginning of the steel piano wire division of the American Steel & Wire Company, which today supplies practically all the piano wire used in the fine American pianos.

The oldest record of the harpsichord is found in Eberhard Cersne's "Rules of the Minnesingers," published in 1404. No doubt such instruments were strung with the drawn iron wire from Germany, or possibly with softer wire, for such instruments were plucked with quills and were not struck by hammers, as were the pianos which came later. This was a little over three hundred years before Cristofori of Italy made his first pianoforte, in 1709. Then it was that drawn wire was put to some severe tests in tensile strength. The piano makers had difficulty because of breaking, for the stress on the string when struck by the hammers was so great that the strings often broke. The best modern hard-drawn wrought-iron wire can withstand only 70,000 pounds of pull per square inch, and this old German iron wire doubtless was much inferior. The modern steel wire used in today's pianos can withstand a pull up to 375,000 pounds per square inch.

When the first pianos were built, however, the strings were not subjected to such great tension as they are today, and for a very good reason. The frames in which the wires were strung were first made of wood, and the tension could not be great. The builders found that the maximum stress on a wood frame was ten tons. Between 1770 and 1820 various wood frames were designed, but the best of them were unsatisfactory and had to be abandoned. Such frames were not sufficiently rigid to keep the strings in tune. In the upper registers, where the stress was greatest, special trouble was encountered, and even in lower registers the strings could not be kept from going flat. The frames also pulled out of shape and caused the key action to bind and stick.

The first iron used in a piano frame was introduced by Joseph Smith of London in 1799, but the first all-metal frame was developed and patented by the English firm of Allen & Thom, in 1820. This consisted of brass and iron plates in combination with metal tubes. Alpheus Babcock, an American, patented a single piece iron frame in 1825, and Jonas Chickering improved upon this design in 1837. In 1859 Steinway designed a cast-iron frame and the overstrung grand piano. Early, therefore, the iron frame became characteristic of American-made pianos.

With the development of the stronger iron frame for the piano, the tension of the strings was increased. By 1862 piano frames could be subjected to a stress of sixteen tons, and today's pianos must withstand a terrific stress up to thirty tons. It is obvious that the old iron wire could not be used for such pianos, but along with the development of the metal frame, in fact the cause for the stronger metal frame, came the improvement of wire. Metallurgists developed new formulas for steel wire, and the steel mills devised new methods of drawing and tempering it. The size of the wire was reduced, and the tensile strength was increased. The brilliant, rich tone of today's pianos is due to the development of this better wire, for after all, the heart of the piano is the strings.

Music historians trace the piano to the primitive monochord, used by the Greeks. This instrument consisted of a single string which was made either of "catgut" or vegetable fiber. Its musical possibilities naturally were extremely limited; as a matter of fact, it was used not so much as a musical instrument as a scientific device for demonstrating the harmonic intervals of the musical scale. By dividing the string exactly in half, they showed how the octave was formed; by dividing it into thirds they demonstrated the octave and a fifth; by dividing it into fourths, the double octave; and so forth. But for some strange reason it never occurred to the gifted Greeks that they could make an instrument of many strings which would have the great musical resources of the clavichord or the harpsichord.

Possibly one reason for their backwardness was a certain taboo against changing the number of strings found on their ancient lyres and harps. Writing about 200 A.D., the Greek Athenaeus recites a tale about a contemporary musician named Timotheus who had the temerity to increase the number of strings on the lyre. He says:

"Whereas Timotheus the musician, coming to our city, has deformed the majesty of our ancient music, and despising the lyre of seven strings, has by the introduction of a multiplicity of notes corrupted the ears of our youth, and by the number of his strings and the strangeness of his melody has given to our music an effeminate and artificial dress instead of the plain and orderly one in which it has hitherto appeared . . . The kings and the Ephori have therefore resolved to pass censure on Timotheus for these things, and further to oblige him to cut off all the superfluous strings of his eleven, and to banish him from our domain, that men may be warned for the future not to introduce into Sparta any unbecoming customs."

If such penalties were inflicted on Timotheus for increasing the number of strings of the lyre from seven to eleven, what terrible things might have happened to anyone who dared to build a clavichord, comprising two or three octaves! Over a thousand years transpired before any builder of musical instruments had the courage to invent the many-stringed clavichord and harpsichord.

We do not know exactly when the clavichord and harpsichord were originated, but it must have been during the latter part of the fourteenth century. Jean de Muris, writing in 1323 about the musical instruments of his day, does not mention either the clavichord or the harpsichord, but when Eberhard Cersne set about writing the "Rules for Minnesingers" in 1404, he mentioned both of these ancient ancestors of the piano. The oldest specimen which has come down to us is the clavichord now on exhibit in the Metropolitan Museum, which is dated 1537.

The clavichord was played by a keyboard much like that of the modern piano, but the internal mechanism and the way the string was contacted were entirely different. When the key was pressed down, a lever beneath the string came up. On the end of the lever was a piece of brass about an inch high and about a quarter-inch wide. This brass wedge struck the string and set it vibrating. The sound was feeble and thin, however, and not much like that produced when the piano key is struck. Some instruments had two keyboards, one for playing the full length of the string, and another for playing the partial length of the string. In playing the latter keyboard, the wedge struck the string at a predetermined place in the length of the string and divided it so that the pitch of the note was not that of the entire length of the string but only that part between the wedge and the end of the string near the keyboard. This device doubled the resources of the few strings.

The clavichord was an intimate instrument, suitable for the home and for sweet melodies. At first it had but few strings. Praetorius, writing of musical instruments about 1619, describes a clavichord with only twenty-two strings. Later the clavichord had a compass of three to four octaves. The great J. S. Bach was very fond of the clavichord and spent many hours at this instrument playing his own exquisite music and the compositions of others. His son Emmanuel expressed a definite preference for the clavichord over the harpsichord. Later Mozart learned to love the clavichord, and it is said he composed on this quaint instrument the music for his "Magic Flute." When he became acquainted with the piano, however, he dropped the clavichord in favor of the more resourceful piano. Beethoven also is on record as praising the beauty of the clavichord, although he sponsored the piano and did much by his playing and composing to establish this instrument.

Although Mozart went from the clavichord to the piano, it is said he never mastered the latter instrument. He was unquestionably a great artist on the clavichord, for it seemed to suit his delicate touch and adapt itself to his delicate musical ideas. But playing the piano was different, and Mozart was never quite able to change over to the technique necessary for playing it. It was the custom in playing the clavichord to use only the three long fingers of each hand, the little finger and the thumb never touching the keys. The touch on the keys must be light and delicate, for the clavichord could not be struck vigorously as can the piano. The strings were not pulled tightly as on the piano, and they were set in vibration with the light touch of the brass wedge. Dynamics were not used, for the string could sound only one way, and that was softly and sweetly. Notes could be sustained only for a moment, each touch of the key producing its own sweet, brief, delicate tone. Music written expressly for the clavichord must have sounded exquisitely beautiful on this instrument. Much of its beauty unquestionably is lost when played on the piano, for the piano is not suited to the moods and colorings of clavichord music. It remained for Beethoven to recognize this fact, and he wrote a different kind of music expressly for the piano. And if clavichord music loses much of its charm when played on the piano, it is also true that today's piano music could not have been played at all on the clavichord.

Another multiple-stringed instrument of the time was the harpsichord. It also had a keyboard like that of the piano, but otherwise the internal mechanism and the way the string was contacted were different. When the key was pressed down, a lever beneath the string was raised. On the end of the lever was a sort of wooden peg, called a jack, in which was inserted a quill pick, usually made from the wing feather of the crow. When the lever was raised, the quill was raised past the string, and as it passed it plucked the string and set it vibrating.

There were several varieties of the harpsichord. A small one, often held on the lap, was called the virginal. It is so called from its use by young girls to accompany their own songs. One of these instruments is interestingly described by the music historian Virdung, writing in 1511. A somewhat larger variety was called the spinet, from its resemblance in appearance to a spinet writing desk. We have records of such instruments dating back to 1490, although the oldest one extant is dated 1521. The spinet usually had one row of jacks and only one string for each note. Its compass was usually three to four octaves.

The musical effect of the harpsichord and its smaller varieties was much like a plucked guitar or zither. It was essentially a plucked instrument, and there were certain limitations to its performance which can be expected of a plucked instrument. It could not be played loud and soft, as can the piano, for no matter how hard the key was pressed down, all that could happen was that the quill passed by the string and plucked it. Notes could not be sustained for long, and when the musician stopped striking the keys, the music stopped abruptly. This led to a form of composition adapted to the peculiarities of the instrument. Climaxes had to be built up by a great flood of notes and not in the pressure with which the notes were struck. To fill in the gaps between certain periods in the music, cadenzas, arpeggios and other embellishments were employed in profusion. Harpsichord music, therefore, was highly ornate and intricate. For this reason it became popular with the composers of polyphonic music, in which two or three melodies could be played simultaneously against each other. Such music flowed from the harpsichord in a stream of intricately woven and closely knit harmony, without much interruption and, it must be said, without much to relieve the monotony except the interestingly worked out musical pattern.

The harpsichord has had an illustrious history, from 1400 until after 1800. This venerable instrument was present at the birth of both the opera and the oratorio. When Jacopo Peri in 1600 produced his "Euridice," the first opera ever presented in public, the harpsichord mingled its voice with the lutes and lyres and flutes, much to the pleasure of the Italians of Florence. And when Emilio del Cavaliere in 1600 produced his "Representation of the Mind and Soul," the first oratorio ever heard, the harpsichord sang along with the double-guitar and other strange instruments.

Having demonstrated its prowess in such early opera and oratorio, it became the principal instrument of the orchestra during the time of Bach and Handel. The conductor, who usually was also the composer, sat at the harpsichord and played and directed the music. The orchestra in those days was not as dependable and capable as it later became, and it often limped and faltered. The conductor was a sort of prompter, and when some instrumentalist or section got off pitch or lost the rhythm, the conductor at the harpsichord came to the rescue and carried the performance along. The various choirs were also unstable, and often certain musicians were not available. The important parts of the missing players could be played by the conductor on the harpsichord, and thus the gaps left by the missing players could be filled in.

But the instrument was not simply a "troubleshooter." It had its own important part to play, aside from "pinch hitting" for the missing or faltering players. The early composers did not know how to write for orchestra in the full and complete way they later learned to do. A kind of shorthand transcription of the music was given to the harpsichord, called the figured bass, and this consisted of chords in a more or less rhythmic beat. This was a sort of transparent music which meant "all things to all men" in the orchestra. Guided by this general idea of the music, the individual players more or less improvised whatever came to their mind. With such an uncertain type of composing, it is no wonder the composer sat at the harpsichord and nursed the players along. Even when definite parts were written for each player, the orchestration was so lacking in body and solidity that it was necessary for the harpsichord to furnish a substantial background of chords and musical embellishment to hold the complete ensemble together.

The conductors of those days had not yet learned how to stand in front of the orchestra and beat time so all the players could perform to the same tempo. They sat at the harpsichord and, by playing along and emphasizing the beat and by nodding their heads, they maintained the rhythm and beat. Sometimes they might lift one hand from the keyboard and emphasize the beat, while playing along with the other hand. Later, two harpsichords were used, one for the conductor in the center and another for the player who performed the figured-bass part. Next to the harpsichord stood the first chair violinist. The beat was given to this player, who passed it along to other members of his section and thence to the rest of the players.

This method of conducting started in Italy, and when opera entered Germany the same custom accompanied it. Handel, who studied in Italy, brought the custom with him to Germany and later introduced it in England. Haydn directed from the harpsichord, but toward the close of his career he added a time beater who stood in front of the orchestra and beat time while Haydn played at his instrument. When Beethoven definitely espoused the piano in place of the harpsichord he often sat at the piano and played while another man stood in front of the orchestra and beat time. Some of the early conductors occasionally beat time with their hands or with a roll of music. Lully is said to have beaten time by pounding on the floor with his cane. On one particularly frantic occasion, in an effort to keep the orchestra up to tempo, he accidentally hit his foot with his cane and injured it so that later his leg had to be amputated, indirectly causing his death. It was not until Mendelssohn and Berlioz that the modern custom of directing with a baton, and without either harpsichord or piano, became common.

It has been shown that neither the clavichord nor the harpsichord could play both soft and loud. This was obviously a distinct disadvantage. It was to overcome this limitation that Bartolomeo Cristofori, a harpsichord maker of Florence, invented the pianoforte, in 1709. Our word piano is a contraction of "pianoforte," which means literally "soft-loud." The word was first used in a letter from an instrument maker, Paliarino, dated June 27, 1598, and addressed to Alfonso II of Italy, but it is generally thought this instrument did not use hammers and was merely a clavichord or harpsichord with some sort of dynamic control for enabling the instrument to play both soft and loud. We know numerous attempts were made to remedy this fault in the old clavichord and harpsichord, and this probably was an instrument with one of these many devices.

Cristofori's piano incorporated two essential features which really permitted the player to perform on the instrument both loudly and softly, and his name has been made immortal because of them. These were an ingenious arrangement of hammers which permitted an instant escapement after the string was struck, and strength in the piano body which could withstand the great stress of the stretched string. When the key of the keyboard was pushed down, the hammer struck the strings a sharp blow from below and instantly dropped back away from the string, permitting it to vibrate freely. This may sound like a simple thing to accomplish, but nobody before had been able to do it successfully. The arrangement of the mechanism for doing this reminds one a lot of some of the famous cartoons of Rube Goldberg called "Useless Inventions." The key is pushed down; this acts on a lever with a pin in it; this releases another gadget which falls, tripping another device under spring tension; this in turn actuates another part; and so on. But the result is a sharp blow on the strings and instant escapement of the hammer from the string. This mechanism has been modified, simplified and improved in literally dozens of ways, but the essential idea is still that of the ingenious Cristofori.

The stress on the string from the clavichord brass wedge or from the harpsichord quill is much less than that when the string is struck sharply by a hammer. To withstand this blow, it was necessary to supply several strings for some of the notes and to strengthen the frame of the piano. This was also an ingenious bit of mechanical engineering. How the stress was increased up to ten tons, sixteen tons and finally up to thirty tons in the modern piano has already been told. The troubles with soft wire strings, the harder iron strings and finally with the modern steel wire strings have also been recited. It is all a thrilling story of the working out of the modern piano. And although many persons have shared in the glory of developing the piano to its modern perfection, this does not diminish the credit of Cristofori who first made the piano possible.

Harpsichord makers of other nations attacked the same problem, working along the line first laid down by Cristofori or along new lines. The Frenchman, Marius, in 1716 experimented with the harpsichord in an effort to save the cost of the expensive crow quills by substituting hammers. He also tried various ways of striking the string—from beneath, from above and even horizontally from the side. The first successful French piano, however, was made in 1777 by S. Erard, better known for his double-action harp. In Germany, Silbermann followed Cristofori and made some beautiful pianos, one of them being made for Frederick the Great. In 1747 Emmanuel Bach played on this instrument, and from his reports it must have been a most creditable one. In England, among the famous builders of pianos was Broadwood, who contributed an important improvement by determining the point on the string where the hammer should strike for best tonal quality. When any string is struck, the fundamental, or pitch note, sounds, but the overtones are also produced. Of these overtones the seventh and ninth are inharmonious with the tempered scale. Their presence in the complete tone causes an unpleasant dissonance. It had always been the custom to strike the string at its center, but Broadwood determined that if the string were struck at a point near where these two harmonics occurred, they would be dampened out. Ever after this important discovery the tone of the piano has been sweeter and more beautiful.

As has been the history of almost all improvements in musical instruments, the piano was not accepted immediately but had to battle the old clavichord and harpsichord for years before it gained precedence over them. Players who had mastered the technique of the clavichord and harpsichord did not want to labor to change their style of playing in order to be able to perform on the piano. There was a distinct difference in the touch and technique necessary for the piano, and those who played well on the old instruments were willing to let well enough alone. Mozart, who changed from the clavichord and harpsichord to the piano, is said never to have quite adapted himself to the new instrument. If such a genius as Mozart had difficulty adapting himself to the new technique, we can imagine that others found it most difficult.

Besides, the early pianos were full of faults. The great stress of the stretched strings pulled the frame out of shape and caused the mechanism to stick and bind. The strings themselves would not stay in tune, for the frame was not rigid enough to maintain a uniform tension. The upper register, where the stress was greatest, gave special trouble.

Many musicians thought the piano was impractical and predicted its early demise. It was not until 1768, nearly sixty years after the piano was invented, that it was first used as a solo instrument in England. On this occasion, J. C. Bach, son of the great J. S. Bach, played the piano in London. No doubt this had its effect in inducing the conservative King's Own Band to adopt the piano instead of the old harpsichord in 1795. So little recognition did the piano have that there was no piano music published until 1770, when the great piano artist Clementi published several sonatas for the piano.

It was about this time, too, that Mozart definitely adopted the piano and used it for the next twenty years until he died. The most famous of Mozart's instruments was a superb five-octave instrument made by Anton Walter of Salzburg. It had black ebony natural keys and white ivory sharp keys, the opposite of the arrangement used today. This reversal of the black and white keys was not uncommon in Mozart's day and before, this being the arrangement of keys found on many clavichords and harpsichords as well.

It is interesting to note that the fame of the piano had spread about this time to America. Thomas Jefferson, in 1771, was on the point of buying a clavichord for his new bride but changed his order to a "fortepiano." He and his fiancée had often played together, he on the violin and she on the clavichord, and he planned to present her with a fine clavichord as a wedding present. But in a letter to England, dated June 1, 1771, he says:

"I must alter one article in the invoice. I wrote therein for a clavichord. I have since seen a Fortepiano and am charmed with it. Send me this instrument instead of the clavichord: let the case be of fine mahogany, solid, not veneer, the compass from Double G to F in alt, and plenty of spare strings; and the workmanship of the whole very handsome and worthy of the acceptance of a lady for whom I intend it."

Haydn was one of the first to appreciate the peculiar advantages of the piano and to recognize the definite change in playing technique from that necessary on the clavichord and harpsichord, but it was Beethoven who established the piano in a firm position. He not only mastered the technique for playing the piano but saw that it was necessary to write a different kind of music if the piano was to be exploited fully. He realized that music written for the clavichord or harpsichord did not bring out the peculiar beauties of the piano. Just as composers came to realize that music written for the flute was not suitable for the clarinet or the trumpet, so Beethoven saw that the piano had a beauty and an eloquence which could not be given full expression when required to produce music written originally for the clavichord or harpsichord. He composed great, solid, sustained chords, shaded from diminuendo to crescendo, and wrote sparkling staccato passages which were unknown to the old school.

The delicate-touch players gave way to the piano pounders. This is reflected in the action piano builders gave to the piano mechanism. To withstand this terrific assault upon the piano, the action was increased to three or four ounces' pressure on the end of the key at Middle C. The performer retaliated, as it were, by changing his playing position—in golfing language, his stance. Instead of sitting low at the piano with the forearm level with the keyboard, as had the players of the old school, such men as Liszt sat high above the keyboard so they could pounce upon it with more fire and vigor. The school of Chopin and Rubinstein finally won out, however, and a more delicate touch was adopted. This change was again reflected in the making of the piano mechanism, for the touch on the end of the key at Middle C was brought down to about two and a half ounces, where it remains today.

The modern piano is a great instrument which rivals the orchestra itself. Its eighty-eight notes, comprising seven octaves and four semitones, match playing range with the orchestra, from the lowest note on the giant BB♭ bass tuba to the shrill top note of the piccolo. It can play both loud and soft and has a wealth of technique and effects which puts it in a class by itself.

THE HARP

Ancient Greek and Egyptian mythology has picturesque stories about the discovery or invention of the harp. One of the best is about some god of music who happened to be walking along one fine day and kicked the shell of a tortoise. Across the shell were thin strips of flesh or skin which had dried taut. The blow from the foot set these stretched strings vibrating and produced a sweet musical effect! There are other stories told by other peoples, and the most plausible of these is that the harp was originally suggested by the bow. After the arrow was dispatched, the string continued to vibrate and produced a musical note.

This latter story has much more to support it than the

former. Pictures of Egyptian and other ancient harps which have come down to us closely resemble the bow, for they do not have the post of the more modern harp. They consist of a framework of wood, curved or shaped like two sides of a triangle and having strings from one side to the other. The conventional post of today's harp, parallel with the strings, is missing on all ancient harps. It was left for the Irish and Saxons of the ninth century A.D. to add this important feature. Its superiority has recommended it to harp builders ever since and is a prominent feature of the modern harp.

All ancient harps were diatonic, and semitones were obtained by pressing the string with the finger. The Tyrolese improved somewhat on this method by screwing little crooks of metal into the neck, which could be turned against the string to shorten it. In 1720 the Bavarian Hochbrucker invented a harp with five foot pedals which instantaneously shortened the C, D, F, G and A strings a semitone. Although this invention pointed the way for future development of the harp, it was not successful because the stopped notes were not of good quality and the construction of the pedal mechanism was so flimsy and frail that it gave much trouble to the player. M. Simon, a harp maker of Brussels, was so sure that foot pedals were impractical that about 1758 he built a harp which was made chromatic by seventy-eight strings. This is only ten less than the modern piano has, and it must have required a tremendous reach to play all these strings, to say nothing of being able to find the notes in this thicket of catgut.

Cousineau, a Frenchman, decided he would outdo Hochbrucker and built a harp with fourteen pedals. This doubtless simplified matters for the hands but greatly complicated matters for the feet! It was a countryman of Cousineau who finally solved the riddle in 1810. S. Erard began experimenting with harps in 1786, and after working at the problem for nearly a quarter of a century he brought out his famous double-action harp which forms the basis for today's harp and did for the harp what Cristofori did for the piano.

His harp was equipped with seven foot pedals, and the range was increased to six and a half octaves. These seven pedals acted on the following strings: Gb, Db, Ab, Eb, Bb, F and C. The clever part of the invention was that when the pedal was pushed part way down, the strings were raised a semitone, but when pushed down all the way, the strings were raised a whole tone. Instead of the fourteen pedals of Cousineau, Erard secured the same results with half that number. This made the harp chromatic in all keys and brought about a great impetus to harp playing.

The harp has the honor of sitting in with a lot of other strange instruments in the earliest ensembles out of which eventually grew the orchestra. When Balthasarini produced his "Ballet Comique de la Reine" in Paris in 1581, the harp was selected as one of the instruments. Eight years later the Italian Caccini employed the harp, along with viols, lutes and lyres, to play the music for his "Intermezzo." Among the instruments used by Monteverde in his "Orfeo," produced in 1608, was a "double harp" with two rows of strings.

It seems the Germans did not take to the harp readily, for Bach did not use it, and Handel, although he experimented with the harp in "Julius Caesar" in 1713 and in the "Esther" oratorio in 1720, seldom, if ever, used it afterward. Haydn omits the harp from his classical orchestra, and Beethoven's lack of interest in the harp is evidenced by the fact that he uses it only once, in "Prometheus." The Germans before Beethoven can scarcely be criticized for not using the harp, for it was not fully developed in their day, but Beethoven wrote after Erard had brought the harp to a high state of perfection. Spohr, a somewhat later German composer, wrote much for the harp, but his wife was a harpist! Later Germans, such as Wagner, learned to use the harp effectively, but usually in some historical role to represent the ancient lyre, as in "Tannhäuser."

If the Germans disliked the harp, the French composers seemed partial to it. Berlioz uses the harp often, and in "Faust" he runs true to form in going to extremes in anything he likes, by writing for ten harps. Meyerbeer wrote separate parts for two harps in "Le Prophète." Boïeldieu, in his opera "La Dame Blanche," given in 1825, was the first to use harmonics on the harp; and Debussy, writing much later, in "La Mer," uses harp harmonics with great artistry.

Today's harp is a beautiful and resourceful instrument of forty-seven "catgut" strings, which, with the help of seven foot pedals, give it a chromatic range of six octaves and eight semitones, from C♭ two octaves below the bass clef to G three octaves above the treble. The pedals, from left to right, act upon the following strings: D♭, C♭, B♭, E♭, F♭, G♭ and A♭. When the pedals are not in use, the instrument is in the key of C♭, and the flat signatures are best for the harp, since the strings are open and have better quality than the stopped strings. The pedals work substantially as did those which Erard invented. The movement of the pedal to the first notch lowers the strings a semitone, and the movement to the second notch lowers the strings a whole tone. The strings are plucked by the thumb and first three fingers, the little finger being too short to be of use. Normally the strings are plucked a little above the middle, but when plucked near the end a brighter tone, resembling the tone of the guitar, is produced.

The harp has a wealth of technique and effects. Arpeggios, glissandi and chords are peculiarly suited to the harp. Staccato, tremolo and harmonics on the middle strings are employed—in fact practically everything is playable on the harp except rapid chromatic passages, due to the necessity of changing many pedals. It is to overcome this shortcoming of the regular harp used in this country that the chromatic harp of Pleyel & Co. of Paris was patented in 1894. This harp is not used in America but is popular in Europe. It does not have pedals, but secures a chromatic scale by the use of two sets of strings, one set of white strings on the left for the natural notes and one set of black strings on the right for the sharps and flats.

THE GUITAR

The old Greek kithara and the troubadour gittern became the Spanish guitar toward the end of the sixteenth century when some musicians of Spain changed it from a four-string to a five-string instrument.

Music terms are used so carelessly in ancient literature that we are not at all sure what instruments are referred to. The old troubadours and minnesingers played lutes and lyres and harps and gitterns, but just how much any of these were like what we have come to call the guitar is shrouded in ambiguity. The first trustworthy evidence of the existence of the guitar as we know it today is a representation on the Gate of Glory of the church of Santiago de Compostella, in Spain. This gate was erected in 1188 A.D. and definitely establishes the existence of the guitar for nearly a thousand years. Whether it was native to Spain or whether it was imported into Spain is not known, although there is a widely accepted belief that the Moors brought the instrument to Spain a century or so earlier than 1188. There are records of a guitar-like instrument in Spain from the thirteenth to the sixteenth centuries. This was variously called a Spanish lute or vihuela. Instruction books and music were published for the vihuela by Luis Milan in 1535.

The early Italian opera composers wrote for the guitar in the latter part of the sixteenth and in the seventeenth centuries. At least we can fairly assume this, for they called for a variety of "lutes," and among them must have been some guitars, for the guitar had for several hundreds of years been a popular instrument. Cavaliere, writing the music for his first oratorio, in 1600, definitely names a "double guitar" among the miscellaneous instruments of the "orchestra." Monteverde calls for two "large guitars" in his "Orfeo," performed in 1608.

Ferdinand Sor, a guitar virtuoso, brought the guitar from Spain to England, and it became so popular as to put the old English guitar, or zither, out of business. The story is also told that this wave of popularity almost swept several other instruments out of existence, too. The endangered instruments are variously said to have been the harp and the harpsichord. The fact that one story says the harp was endangered and the other says it was the harpsichord casts suspicion on the whole story. Anyway, the story goes that about 1750 the guitar became so popular as to stop the sales of the harp (or harpsichord). The harp (or harpsichord). manufacturers killed the craze by a clever move. They secured a large number of guitars and put them into the hands of people of the lower classes—servant girls, stableboys and the like. This stamped them as instruments not worthy of persons of culture, and the guitar craze quickly died out.

This stigma did not by any means cling to the guitar, for we find Rossini writing for the guitar in his "Barber of Seville," and Weber calls for it in his "Oberon." Berlioz, the great French composer and conductor, was a guitar player; in fact, this was the only instrument he could play at all, and we can see the influence of the guitar in the chord arrangements of his compositions. Paganini, the celebrated violinist, also was a proficient performer on the guitar. The most famous guitar virtuoso today is the Spaniard musician, Andres Segovia.

Those who think of the guitar as an instrument fit only for strumming chords as an accompaniment to love songs should hear such guitar artists as Segovia play the guitar. In their hands it becomes an instrument of rich beauty and great musical resources. There are two ways of playing the guitar. The familiar chording is called "rasqueado." The great artists, however, use the "punteado" style of playing. This is a melodic style, and the possibilities of this kind of playing are limited only by the ability of the musician.

Today's guitar has six strings: E, A, D, G, B and E—from E below the bass clef to E above. Its sides and back are made of maple, ash, cherry or mahogany, while the top is made of deal or spruce. The neck, fingerboard and bridge are of rosewood or ebony. The old-style guitar is known for its round hole in the top, under the strings, but many of today's finest guitars are made with the *ff* holes of the violin. The tuning formerly was done with wooden pegs, such as are still found on the violin, but in 1790 the Germans introduced the metal screws, which are easier to operate.

THE BANJO

The banjo is native to America, being a creation of the American Negro. It is a four-string instrument incorporating the unique feature of a soundboard made by stretching skin over a hoop. The bridge rests on this taut skin, and the strings are stretched over this bridge. No doubt the rough idea was brought with the Negro from Africa, where it was picked up from Arabian traders who played the Arabian rebab or other similar string instrument. In slave days it was the most popular instrument in the South. Thomas Jefferson, writing in 1784, says it was known to Negroes as the "banger." Up to 1830 it was commonly known as the "bonja." Today this word has changed into "banjo." There are two types of banjo: the tenor and plectrum, the latter being less common. The former is strung as follows, in ascending order: Middle C, G, D and A. The latter is strung Middle C, G, B and D.

CHAPTER XIV

How Music Is Made

THE RAW MATERIAL

THE NEXT TIME you hear a band or orchestra play, ask yourself what the stuff is that you call music. WHAT is it when the band is playing? WHERE is it when the band stops? Because of its elusiveness we have got into the habit of regarding it as something unlike the ordinary physical things the world is full of. This is wrong. A little thought will show you that the stuff of which music is made is everywhere around you.

A man who had an automobile without a speedometer used to speak of "turning the corner at thirty miles an hour," "riding pleasantly along at twenty miles an hour," "opening her up until she was doing forty miles." When asked how he could tell the speed at which he was traveling when he had no speedometer, he said, "Well, when she gets to going twenty miles an hour the right fender begins to rattle. When she gets to going thirty an hour a little bolt in the dash begins to jingle. When she hits forty the glass in the windshield chatters terribly."

Rates of vibration! Not music, of course, but the stuff of

which it is composed; the only difference is that music is more orderly and better controlled.

An engineer once was called in to investigate a large centrifugal fan which was rapidly destroying a brick air stack. The fan ran just like an ordinary electric fan and was used to ventilate a certain factory, pulling the foul air from the rooms and sending it up this ventilating stack. When the fan was going full speed the brick stack would quiver and tremble and vibrate, so that the bricks began falling out. The fan was mounted on reinforced concrete, and seemingly all the vibration from the motor was eliminated, but this didn't remedy the vibration of the stack one bit. Finally this engineer, who had a knowledge of the laws of sound, was called in, and he solved the problem in a few minutes.

Every time the fan went around, each of the blades in the fan boosted a column of air up the stack. When going at full speed these puffs of air went up the stack at regular intervals, causing a kind of "beat." It just happened that this stack was the right length to vibrate or "beat" in sympathy with the blades of the fan. This caused a sympathetic pulsating in the stack that became stronger and stronger until the stack was ready to fly to pieces.

There were two things that could be done to correct this evil. Either one of them would destroy this "beating together" of the fan and the stack, and everything would then run smoothly. One was to shorten or lengthen the stack so the length of the air column would be out of sympathy with the speed of the fan. The other was to gear the fan either up or down so its vibration would be thrown out of sympathy with the length of the stack. It was decided to shorten the stack just a trifle. Presto! The riddle was solved.

Music? Not exactly, but some of the stuff of which music is made.

A man who is now a prominent acoustical expert was once employed as a consulting engineer in one of the largest automobile factories in the country. He had a hobby of experimenting with sound, and his knowledge of the laws of sound once enabled him to solve a great engineering puzzle in a new model car that was being produced at the time.

This particular car had a bad hum in it when traveling at a certain speed. As is usual in such circumstances, the gears were suspected, but days and days of experimenting failed to locate the trouble. This particular engineer stood out against the gear theory, but his associates would not listen to him.

He discovered that at the rate at which the hum occurred, the rear wheels were making two revolutions a second. He also discovered that the hum had a definite pitch, closely in tune with F♯ below Middle C. That meant that this hum was being produced by a vibration of about 180 a second. Checking the teeth in all the gears suspected, he saw that none of them could produce this rate of vibration.

This much proved, he began looking for the real trouble. He found it when he counted the knobs on the tire tread. There were 90 of these, and the wheels were making two revolutions a second. Somewhere in the car was a resonator, which reinforced this vibration of 180 per second and made it a strong hum. Simple enough! Rib-tread tires were substituted, and the hum vanished.

Hardly music such as the symphony orchestra turns out, anyone will admit, but you can recognize the relation.

Some musicians playing a dance job at a summer resort

used to relate how they tuned their instruments with an electric fan. Near the stand an ordinary electric fan was running, and its hum was recognized as a distinct note. These musicians finally determined that this note was pitched exactly an octave below the "pitch" note of their B♭ trumpets and exactly with that of the B♭ trombones. By playing their trumpets an octave higher and their trombones in unison, they were able to obtain the correct pitch for their instruments. It just happened that the blades of this fan struck the air at the rate of 116.5 times per second, the vibration rate of the B♭ in the second octave below Middle C.

Not exactly what would be called dance music, but made up of the same raw material.

The reality of the stuff of which music is made is strikingly illustrated by the Illinois School for the Deaf Boys' Band of Jacksonville, Illinois. These boys cannot hear themselves play, and yet they play in unison and with a feeling and appreciation that are the envy of many bands that can hear.

Their first music lesson was through the use of a baseball bat. The bat was used to count out rhythm on the floor. The vibration was transmitted through the floor to their feet, and they learned to march to the music of the ball bat, first in their bare feet, later with their shoes on. Drums were then secured, and they were able to sense a more refined music. After some training they could rest their hands on a piano that was being played and "hear" the music through their fingertips. Band instruments were finally purchased, and now their sense of "hearing" through the nerves of their bodies is so acute and so well trained that they are recognized as a first-class band, able to hold their own with other bands that have normal sense of hearing.

The sound wave which seems so beneficent and beautiful can also become a terror when it gets out of control, because of the tremendous forces wrapped up in it. This is illustrated in the ventilating stack. It is also illustrated in incorrectly designed auditoriums where the echo or reverberation becomes so violent as to cause the auditorium to tremble from top to bottom.

The story is told of a violinist who wagered he could destroy a wagon bridge merely by playing his violin. He was laughed at and told to go as far as he liked. He chose a note on his violin that he found vibrated in unison with the bridge, and began to play. It is said that the bridge began to vibrate, and the longer the same note was sounded on the violin, the more violently the bridge rocked. The authorities of the town at last became so alarmed that they compelled him to cease, for fear the bridge would break to pieces.

There is a basis of fact in this story. It is well known that soldiers are required to break step when marching across a bridge, because the rhythmical step of marching men sets up a pulsation in a bridge which becomes stronger and stronger and threatens to rock it to pieces. A small dog trotting rhythmically across a bridge will shake a bridge to a greater extent than a horse which walks across with broken step.

RATE OF VIBRATION DETERMINES PITCH

Now that you've been introduced to the raw material of which music is made, you'll want to become more intimately acquainted with the vibrating sound wave.

Just like a zoologist when he finds a bug, we'll take the sound wave into the laboratory, dissect it and see what it is like. Of course, we can't see the sound wave, but we can learn something about it from observing the effects its activity brings about.

Extremely delicate and sensitive machines have been invented which have shown us what the sound wave is like. In the first place it is known that a sound of any pitch has a fixed number of vibrations per second. Middle C on the piano vibrates 261.6 times in a second. The C which is three octaves below it vibrates only 32.7 times per second, while the C three octaves above vibrates 2,093 times per second.

There is nothing particularly mysterious about vibration or the rate of vibration. Did you ever catch a weed or a stick in your bicycle which played a tattoo on the spokes of the wheel? The faster you rode, the higher the pitch of the note would rise. There you have in a crude illustration what rate of vibration is.

Men who study sound waves sometimes fasten a piece of cardboard so it will rest against the pegs of a revolving wheel, such as the wheels of fortune you see at carnivals and recreation parks. As the wheel turns, the pegs "tick" the cardboard. A note is produced in this way, and its pitch is determined by the number of pegs that "tick" the cardboard in one second.

In studying anything it is helpful to look at a cross section of it, and it is easy to get a cross-section view of a tone wave. The following illustration is not entirely satisfactory, but it will help a lot in understanding what a tone wave is like: The next time you ride a train, listen particularly to the sound of the bells that warn people at the crossing of the train's approach. As you zip past you will notice that the pitch of the bell starts high and takes a decided dip downward. Sound travels in dry air 1,132 feet per second at 70 degrees Fahrenheit, and when you are close, the sound waves have only a few feet to travel to reach you. Consequently they reach your ear with approximately the same rapidity as they occur in the bell. As a matter of fact, when approaching the bell, the sound waves strike the ear more rapidly than they occur in the bell, and the pitch of the bell actually rises as you approach. But as you draw rapidly away from the bell they must travel farther, each vibration farther than the one preceding it. Therefore each one reaches the ear a little farther apart. The effect is that of having the vibrations start out rapidly and gradually become slower and slower. The result is a cross section of the sound which illustrates that the rapidity of vibration determines the pitch of a note. You notice the same thing when automobiles honk while passing each other at a high speed.

There are rates of vibration below and above a certain number per second that we cannot hear. It is difficult to hear, as a continuous sound, vibrations of less than 16 per second, just as it is difficult to see, as a continuous moving picture, less than 16 exposures per second of a moving-picture film. The average silent moving-picture camera is run so 16 exposures are shown per second, and when less than that are shown per second the picture "flickers." So it is with low rates of vibration. Instead of the vibrations sounding as one tone, they separate into 16 separate pulsations.

Some persons can distinguish sounds with a vibration rate as high as 20,000 per second, but the extreme for most people is less than that. The piano has a range between 27.5 and 4,186 per second, while the pipe organ goes as low as 16, and some organs have a pipe which vibrates 8 times in a second, but this can hardly be called a musical note. In the orchestra, the lowest B♭ of the contrabass tuba has a frequency of 29.2 vibrations per second, while the top note on the piccolo is C, four octaves above Middle C, and has a frequency of 4,186. A good Turkish cymbal has a high frequency of 12,000 to 13,000 vibrations, and there are overtones in the orchestra which are heard up to 12,000 or 15,000 frequencies, but the musical scale is generally considered to lie between 16 and 4,186 vibrations per second.

Music heard over the radio, from sound films, and on phonograph records is limited to a more restricted range. Few radio stations are equipped to transmit frequencies over 10,000, and most are limited to 5,000. The lower range seldom goes below 100. Radio speakers generally are incapable of picking up even these limits, most music on the radio speaker lying between 100 and 3,500 frequencies. It is obvious that the fundamental of the low-voiced instruments and most of the high harmonics are not heard at all. The same limits apply generally to music reproduced from sound film and heard in the moving-picture theater. Phonograph-record recordings pick up a greater range of frequencies, the best of them from 30 to around 10,000, but much of this is sacrificed on poor reproducing machines. "Canned" music, therefore, still has serious limitations.

It may seem like an impossible job to count so many vibrations per second. It isn't done exactly that way. The counter of vibrations starts at the other end. He invents a machine that is geared up so he can produce an exact number of vibrations per second, and then he compares the note to be determined with the note of known vibrations made by the machine. When they coincide, he knows the vibration rate of the note in question.

These machines are capable of setting up vibrations as rapid as 500,000 per second, but those above 20,000 are not heard. The reason for this is that the human ear is not sensitive enough to pick these up and transmit them to the brain. Hearing results when an object outside the ear sets up a vibration whose pulsating is transmitted through the air to the ear and on to the brain. These pulsating air waves strike the eardrum, and this sets the eardrum vibrating. The nerves of the ear transmit this sensation to the brain, and hearing is said to result.

It is easy to understand that vibrations can become so rapid that the eardrum membrane cannot vibrate as rapidly. When this point is reached we cease to hear. Some insects have an "ear" which is more sensitive than the human ear, and science has discovered that they use as calls and "language" certain sounds which are above the limits of sound for the human sense of hearing.

LENGTH OF SOUND WAVES DETERMINES PITCH

Prize fighters know that they can get in many light licks while they are placing one heavy blow. They depend more on the quick jab than on the blow which must start a distance back and gain the momentum necessary to give a heavier jolt. While the long drive is on its way the other fellow may get in a couple of short, vicious jabs, and the "haymaker" may never land. Many short blows may be struck with greater effect than a few long ones.

Likewise the rapidly vibrating sound wave is not as long as the one that vibrates more slowly. We can, therefore, speak of the note of low pitch as being of longer wave length than the note of high pitch. When a string is stretched and plucked, the notes become higher as the length of the string is shortened. The high notes on the piano and Italian harp are made on the strings that are short, and the low notes on the long strings.

Yes, you say, but why is it that the G string and the E string on the violin are the same length while the notes they produce are widely separated in pitch? And why is it that some wires on the piano are the same length, yet they play notes of different pitch?

There is a point involved here that many do not understand and that has caused a great deal of confusion. To avoid this confusion you need only make the distinction clearly between the length of the string and the length of the vibrating sound wave the string generates. The low bass strings on the piano are the same length, it is true, but those that generate the lower notes are wound with wire and weighted down so they cannot vibrate so fast. The same is true on the violin: the E string is small while the G string is either gut of large size or wound with fine wire to weight it down. The length of the sound wave must be distinguished from the length of the string or whatever it is that creates the sound wave. It is the length of the sound wave that determines the pitch, and the shorter the wave, the higher is the pitch.

The tone waves of the musical scale, which we have already learned vary in frequency between 16 and 4,186 vibrations per second, vary also in length from about 70 feet to 3 inches. Middle C is over 52 inches long.

The longest pipe of most pipe organs is over 32 feet long although there are a few organs with a pipe over 64 feet long. The 32-foot pipe produces a note which vibrates 16 times per second, and the tone wave is about 70 feet long. A tiny pipe has been made which is only a quarter-inch long and which has a vibration rate of about 16,000 per second, while the wave length is about a half-inch long.

The cornet in B♭ sounds the B♭ in the second octave below Middle C as its fundamental note and the total length of its tubing is about 53 inches, while the tone wave is about twice this length. The trombone sounds as its fundamental note the B♭ an octave lower and since this tone wave is twice as long as that of the octave above, we find the trombone just about twice as long as the cornet, or about 107 inches. The BB♭ bass plays an octave below the trombone, and we find it about twice as long as the trombone and four times the length of the cornet, or about 216 inches. The wave length of its lowest note is about twice this.

C Piccolo ——————	
About 12″ long	Tone wave about 26″ long
C Flute ————————	
About 24″ long	Tone wave about 52″ long
B♭ Cornet ————————————	
About 53″ long	Tone wave about 117″ long or nearly 10 feet
B♭ Trombone ————————————————	
About 107″ long	Tone wave about 235″ long or nearly 20 feet
BB♭ Sousaphone ————————————————————	
About 216″ long	Tone wave about 469″ long or nearly 40 feet

Fig 1.

Above are shown lengths of various instruments and the lengths of their tone waves. Octaves are exact multiples of each other, and the instruments are nearly so.

HOW MUSIC IS MADE

Possibly you have noticed that the large G string on a violin plays a lower pitch note than the E string, that it seems to vibrate farther from side to side than the E string and sounds louder. You also will notice that, as the length of the G string is shortened by pressing the string down against the fingerboard, the note is raised in pitch, the string vibrates a shorter distance from side to side and loses some of its loudness.

If you have observed this you have observed another factor in how music is made. Not only does the number of vibrations enter into the making of music, but the width of the vibration as it travels from one side to the other also has something to do with it. "Loudness" is the chief quality due to the width of sound waves.

However, it is not wholly responsible for loudness, for loudness is made up of both rate of vibration and width of vibrating wave. A high note can be made to sound softly and a low note loudly. It is possible to play a low note loudly enough to be heard as far away as a high note played softly.

It is similar to shooting a pea with great velocity and tossing a larger pebble easily. When they strike a scale the beam flies up equally high in each case. Rate of speed in the pea makes up for lack of weight, just as rate of vibration in the tone wave makes up for lack of width. Weight in the pebble can also make up for lack of speed, just as width of tone wave can make up for lack of rapidity of vibration.

The boom of a tympano and the boom of a cannon may sound the same pitch note, but the boom of the cannon will carry farther because the width of the vibration is larger. The African signal drums used by the natives are made from large logs and sound a deep bass note. Signals from these drums carry for miles. Foghorns on ships are pitched low because the sound will carry farther than a high-pitched note. On the other hand, in the band the oboe, which is a high-pitched instrument, can be heard from a distance, standing out above all the lower instruments. The bell lyra or glockenspiel used in outdoor bands can be heard distinctly above the rest of the band. When bands are broadcast over the radio, as at football games, the bright "ping" of the bell lyra can be heard more distinctly than any other instrument in the band. This instrument is made up of short bars of steel which are struck with a mallet. It is high in pitch and seems to have some of the "loudness" qualities of the high-pitched oboe.

The explanation of this "loudness" of the low-pitched drum or foghorn on the one hand and the high-pitched oboe or bell lyra on the other is a factor known as intensity. The width or amplitude of the wave of the low note may be great, but the number of vibrations per second may be small. The total intensity of the note depends upon the amplitude of the wave as well as the number of vibrations per second. Likewise, the amplitude of the wave of the high note may be small, but the number of vibrations may be large. The intensity of the note, generally referred to as "loudness," depends upon amplitude of the wave and the number of vibrations. Thus, the intensity of both the low and the high notes may be the same.

"Loudness" is a psychological reaction to sound and is inaccurate in measuring intensity because such reaction is purely subjective. The acoustical engineer talks objectively of intensity, but to the layman this means merely "loudness."

STRUCTURE OF TONE WAVE

We have taken some measurements of the tone wave, having learned about its rates of vibration, its lengths and its widths. It is somewhat more difficult to understand just what the structure of the tone wave is like.

One character of the tone wave can be illustrated by a train of cars. We'll say the train has a hundred cars and has stopped on a sidetrack. The brakeman waves the engineer to back up, the engineer throws the reverse lever, and the engine backs. The engine hits the coal tender, the tender hits the first car, the first car bumps the second, and so on until this force is passed to every car and the whole train is in motion backward. In the same manner a vibrating object sets the molecules of air nearest to it in motion and each bumps into its neighbor. The vibration is passed on and on at the rate of 1,132 feet a second, the rate at which sound travels at 70 degrees Fahrenheit.

It is misleading to say that the molecules move on and on: they do not move far, although the wave of energy may travel many feet or even miles. Each molecule moves with the wave until it strikes a neighboring molecule, when it stops and returns finally to its original position. The neighboring molecule passes the energy to its neighbor, and so on. It is something like a relay race in which each runner stops when he tags the next man.

If we cover the surface of a quiet pool with specks of powder and drop a rock into the water, a circular wave will spread over the pool, traveling outward from where the rock hits. The wave travels on and on, but the specks of powder do not move with it. They take the shape of the wave. In fact, it is only the shape of the wave that does travel.

The manner in which a tone wave travels is also illustrated by a wheat field when a breeze passes over it. The heads of wheat are affected by the wave, bunching up and swaying forward as the wave passes over them; but they remain rooted in the ground, while the wave may travel miles across the field.

It is also important to distinguish between movement of the molecules in the air and such movement of air as we have when the wind blows. As already mentioned, sound travels 1,132 feet per second at 70 degrees Fahrenheit. This speed is at the rate of a mile in 4.7 seconds, or about the speed of a rifle bullet. It is also nearly 800 miles per hour. The most violent hurricane travels less than one tenth as fast, so we can see that it is not the air as a whole which travels, but that the impulse is passed along from molecule to molecule at this rate of speed. It is the flexibility or resiliency of air which makes this possible. Water is more resilient than air, sound in water traveling at the rate of about 4,800 feet per second. Steel is still more resilient, sound traveling in steel at the rate of 16,500 feet per second.

Stick a pin into some soft wood, pull the end over (C, Fig. 2) and let it flip back. You get a musical note, and you can see the pin vibrate rapidly back and forth. When you pull the pin back and release the top, it springs forward just about twice the distance you had it drawn back. It rushes past its upright position (B, Fig. 2) and goes over to the other extreme, where it comes to a position of momentary rest (A, Fig. 2) and then comes back again (C, Fig. 2). This performance is a complete vibration, or cycle, and is the unit which goes to make up the tone wave.

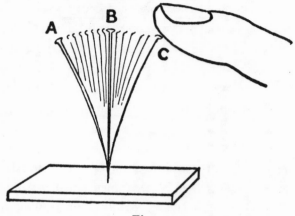

Fig. 2

As it makes its first trip across, it compresses the tiny molecules of air together. The nearer they are to the pin, the more they are compressed. Out a distance in the air they are not so compressed, and still farther out they have not felt the movement of the pin and are their natural distance apart. But they will feel it when this area of compression reaches them.

When the pin reaches the end of its first sweep (A, Fig. 3) it springs back to approximately its original position (C, Fig. 3). There is immediately a rushing backward of the molecules. They have been tightly pressed together, but when the pin reverses its motion it leaves an open space in its wake.

Immediately next to the pin there are very few molecules, and they are far apart (C, Fig. 3). This area where the molecules are far apart is called a rarefaction. Between the pin and the area of compression the molecules are distributed with various distances between them. The farthest apart are

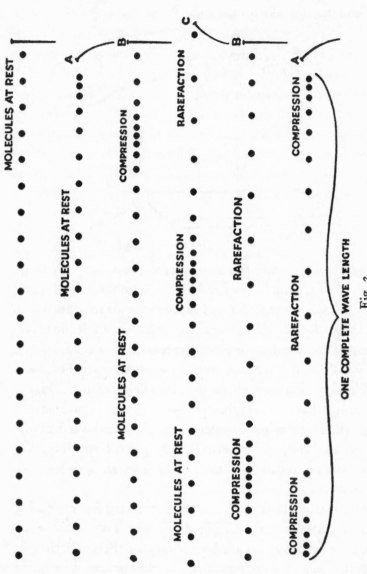

Fig. 3

near the pin, and the closest together are those in the area of compression. When the pin has sprung back on its return trip as far as it can go (C, Fig. 3) and starts forward on its second trip, the molecules begin to pile up against the pin again, and another area of compression is started (A, Fig. 3).

In the complete tone wave we have the following: First, an area in which the molecules are compressed together, or a compression. Second, an area in which the molecules are their natural distance apart. Third, an area in which the molecules are widely separated, or a rarefaction. Fourth, an area in which the molecules are their natural distance apart.

We may measure the length of a wave from any point to the corresponding point farther on, but it is more customary to measure it from compression to compression.

As the pin continues to vibrate, these complete tone waves are sent out. Each wave travels at the rate of 1,132 feet a second at 70 degrees Fahrenheit, and at the end of a second the first wave will be 1,132 feet from the pin. Between this wave and the pin will be quite a number of other waves coming along, the number depending on the rate of vibration. If the pin vibrates 261 times a second, it will sound like Middle C on the piano, and there will be 261 waves distributed along the 1,132 feet, and each wave will be equal to 1,132 divided by 261, or a little longer than 52 inches. Figure it out—it's plain arithmetic.

If a longer pin of the same thickness were used, it would not, of course, vibrate as rapidly. If it made only 32.7 complete vibrations per second, there would be only 32.7 tone waves along the 1,132 feet at the end of one second, and each would be nearly 35 feet long. Figure it out: 1,132 divided by 32.7 equals nearly 35. This is the length of the C which is three octaves below Middle C.

These computations are made at a temperature of 70 degrees Fahrenheit. If the temperature is warmer, sound travels faster, and if the temperature is colder, sound travels slower, than 1,132 feet per second. When sound travels faster than 1,132 feet per second the pitch of the note becomes sharp, for in one second there are more waves distributed along the 1,132 feet, and the more waves there are, the higher the pitch. Conversely, when sound travels slower than 1,132 feet per second, the pitch of the note becomes flat, for in one second there are fewer waves distributed along the 1,132 feet, and the fewer waves there are, the lower the pitch. That is why bands outdoors on a cold day sometimes sound flat, and why on a very hot day they sometimes sound sharp.

This fact should not be confused with changes of string instruments under changes of temperature. The strings of the piano contract and become shorter, or rather tighter, when they become cold, and hence the pitch is raised. Conversely, in hot weather they expand and become longer, or rather looser, and the pitch is lowered. This is exactly the opposite of the effect of temperature on wind instruments. That is why wind instruments and piano, when played together, are so difficult to put in pitch when the weather varies. In cold weather the wind instruments go flat while the piano goes sharp; and in hot weather the wind instruments go sharp and the piano goes flat. In the finest radio and recording studios the temperature is held constant to avoid these difficulties.

RESONANCE, OR WHY IS A HORN?

Our illustration of the train and its cars may be misleading on one point, and now is the time to correct this. Sound waves do not progress in a straight line only, but they radiate in all directions. This bumping of one molecule into its neighbor goes outward in all directions, like the radii in a sphere.

When the vibrating object is the lips of a player and his lips are pressed against the mouthpiece of a horn, this sound radiates in all directions, but that part of the total wave that comprises the air column of the horn is made to sound louder through resonance. This principle of resonance is fundamental in the horn, and it is necessary to understand what resonance is before one can understand how a horn makes music.

This principle of resonance can be illustrated by a tube with one end in water and a vibrating pin held near the open end. By moving the tube up and down in the water, a spot will be found where the note sounded by the pin will become louder. When the tube is lowered or raised beyond this point, the sound will die away, but as long as it is held at this point the note will be heard louder.

If the tube is held at this point, and another pin that sounds another note is held at the open end, the note of the pin will not sound louder. In order to make the note of the new pin sound louder, it will be necessary to move the tube up or down until another point is located. If the note of the new pin is lower than the first, the tube must be drawn up so more of it is out of the water. If the note of the new pin is higher than the first, the tube must be lowered so less of it extends out of the water.

It is clear that a certain length of tubing is necessary to reinforce each note. This principle is illustrated on the marimba. The horizontal bars give comparatively little

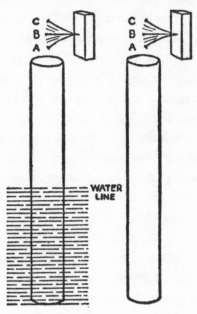

Fig. 4

volume of sound, but when tubes of various lengths are placed below the bars, this small volume of sound is built up in the tubes, making each note sound loudly when its corresponding bar is struck. On a marimba these tubes, or resonators, are long for the low notes and gradually decrease in length as the notes become higher.

What happens when a tone is reinforced and built up? We have already seen that as the pin vibrates it sends out waves one after another, one complete wave to each complete vibration. When the vibrating pin is held over a tube and moves from C to B (Fig. 4) a compression is started down the tube. As the pin moves from C to B, it gains momentum, for the pin swings like a pendulum, and a pendulum swings with greatest speed in the center of its arc. The faster the pin swings, the more compactly the molecules are pressed together; therefore the molecules are closer together at B than near C. As the pin nears position A, it slows up and finally comes to momentary rest at A before beginning its return trip. As the pin swings in this manner from C to A it sends a compression down the tube. If we could see this compression we would see its center packed closely with molecules and its head and tail less closely packed, the degree of closeness diminishing from center to either head or tail (see Fig. 3).

By the time the pin comes to momentary rest at A, the head of the compression has traveled to the bottom of the tube, is reflected to the open end and is ready to escape into the air on its way to our ear. But as it escapes, so many of the molecules leave the tube that a scarcity of molecules is found in the tube and a rarefaction is created at the open end. This rarefaction begins just at the time the pin begins its return swing from A to B, which movement of the pin also starts a rarefaction. Two rarefactions, therefore, are created simultaneously, one by the escaping compression and another by the movement of the pin away from the open end of the tube. These two rarefactions join forces and become a larger rarefaction than either alone.

It would be interesting to see what this rarefaction looks like. If our eyes were capable of seeing the movement of the molecules we would see exactly a reverse of the compression. The center would be comprised of only a few molecules widely separated, while the head and tail would be comprised of molecules less widely separated (see Fig. 3).

It would also be interesting to see the working together of the two rarefactions. As the head of the compression starts to emerge from the open end of the tube, the head of a rarefaction starts to form and descend into the tube. As mentioned above, the density of the molecules increases from the head of the compression to its center and decreases from the center to the tail. Therefore, as the head and middle of the compression emerge, an increasing number of molecules escape, thereby creating a correspondingly greater scarcity of molecules in the tube. By the time the center of the compression has emerged from the tube, the center of the rarefaction has been created. At the same time, the pin has moved from A to B, away from the tube. At B the pin is traveling at its greatest speed and is thereby creating a maximum of rarefaction.

The next half of the performance is the reverse of the foregoing. As the pin moves from B to C, it gradually decreases its speed, and the degree of rarefaction gradually decreases until the pin comes to momentary rest at C. During this same interval, the second half of the compression escapes. Both the swing of the pin from B to C and the escape of the second half of the compression create the second half of the rarefaction. The escaping compression and the movement of the pin from A to C each creates its own rarefaction, and these two rarefactions reinforce each other.

If you have followed the foregoing rather involved and detailed explanation, you can anticipate what happens next. By the time the pin has traveled on its return trip from A to C, the rarefaction has traveled to the bottom of the tube and has been reflected to the open end. An instant later the head of the rarefaction begins to emerge from the tube. This scarcity of molecules at the open end sucks in molecules from the still air outside the tube, and thereby the head of a compression starts down the tube. By the time the complete rarefaction has emerged, a complete compression has been formed, and this compression travels through the tube as the first compression did. Concurrently the pin rushes from C, past B, and comes to momentary rest at A, forming its own compression. Therefore the escaping rarefaction forms a compression, and the movement of the pin toward the mouth of the tube also forms a compression. These two compressions occur concurrently and reinforce each other.

It is this working together of the vibrating source with the reflected wave which creates resonance in a wind instrument. This process has been described in detail because it is the cardinal principle of the wind instrument. It is easy to understand, from such a recital of what takes place, how the length of the tube and the vibrating source must work together. The tube must be of such a length that the reflected wave returns on time to meet the next impulse from the vibrating source. If the tube is too short or too long, the reflected wave returns too soon or too late to meet the next impulse coming from the vibrating source. When the reflected wave returns in phase with the vibrating source, it gives the vibrator a boost, because they are both pulling in the same direction. This boost, in turn, creates a stronger impulse in the vibrating source, which is reflected with great energy to give a still bigger boost to the vibrator.

This working together is something like two persons pushing a stalled automobile. If one pushes and then the other, the car does not move far, if at all. But when both persons throw their weight against the car at the same instant, the combined force moves the car.

When the pin moves from C to A, a compression is formed. When the pin moves from A to C, a rarefaction is formed. Since one wave consists of a compression and a rarefaction, the movement of the pin from C to A and back to C produces one complete wave. We have noted that during the time it takes the pin to travel forward and back, the compression travels twice the length of the tube (down and up), and also the rarefaction travels twice the length of the tube. One complete wave therefore travels four times the length of the tube during a single vibration. This is an important principle of a tube closed at one end.

A tube open at both ends behaves like two closed tubes with their closed ends butted together. An impulse which enters an open tube does not travel the length of the tube and emerge out into the air from the opposite end. For some strange reason an impulse which enters an open tube always emerges from the same end by which it enters. Apparently the impulse entering one end does not have sufficient strength to emerge into the still air at the opposite end. The impulse travels down the tube, is reflected at the opposite end by the still air and starts back up the tube toward the end by which it entered. When the tube is of a proper length to give resonance to a certain rate of vibration, the wave is reflected up the tube where, at the very center, it meets a second wave coming from the top end. The two waves are repelled by each other at the center, and the second wave is reflected out the top end by which it entered. This meeting place in the center serves as a sort of booster station which gives the waves the needed energy to emerge into the still air at each end of the tube. The impulse entering the top end emerges from the top end, and the impulse coming from the bottom end emerges from the bottom end.

In the closed tube at any one instant there is only one quarter of a wave length. At the open end is an antinode, where the molecules are in violent movement but where the pressure is slight. At the closed end is a node. Here the molecules cannot move, because the end is closed; but the pressure here is intense.

In the open tube at any one instant there is only a half of a wave length. At the top end is an antinode, where the

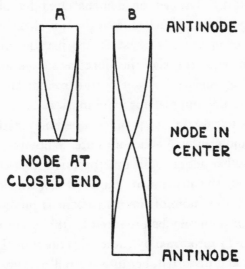

Fig. 5

Drawing to represent difference between (A) closed pipe and (B) open pipe, sounding same fundamental note. Note closed pipe is just half as long as open pipe. Both pipes are open at top, and at open end of each is an antinode. The closed pipe is closed at bottom end, and here lies a node. The open pipe is open at both ends. In the center lies a node, and at the bottom end lies an antinode.

molecules are in violent movement but where the pressure is slight. In the center is a node, where the movement of the molecules is at a minimum, but where the pressure is the greatest. At the bottom end is another antinode.

This difference is sometimes represented diagrammatically, as in Fig. 5.

In our illustration of vibration we used a pin because of its simplicity. In wind instruments the vibration is set up by the lips of the player, as in trumpet or trombone; by reeds, as in clarinet or oboe; or by eddy currents of air, as in flute or piccolo.

In all cases, the vibration itself is weak and not particularly musical. This can be demonstrated by blowing the mouthpieces alone, detached from the rest of the instrument. The tube comprising the rest of the instrument serves to build up the weak sound of the vibrating source, and not only to build it up and reinforce it until it sounds louder, but to refine the sound and make it more musical.

Every wind instrument is made a certain length so it can build up and reinforce a certain note. When the lips of the player or other vibrating source produces this certain rate of vibration, the instrument builds it up, and the fundamental or lowest note of the instrument is produced. Other rates of vibration may be produced by the lips of the player, but no sound is produced by these vibrations, or else they are very weak and distorted, because the reflected waves do not arrive on the exact instant to meet the new wave coming from the player's lips. The length of the instrument is such that *only one wave is capable of making the round trip on time.*

This is what we mean when we say a cornet is built in B♭ or a French horn is built in F or a flute is built in C. The instrument is built of such a length that it reinforces the wave length of this particular fundamental note. When the lips of the player are caused to vibrate against the mouthpiece of the horn, there may be other waves going out of the horn, because the lips do not have very accurate or exact control over these vibrations, but these other waves do not "fit" the horn. They may be reflected at the bell of the instrument so that they come back with their compression point coinciding with the point of rarefaction of the next wave. In this case, both are neutralized and no sound takes place. Or the points of compression and rarefaction may be just a little behind or a little in front of each other; in which case the tone is weak, stuffy and unpleasant.

It is this even, periodical pulsation of certain frequency which produces a musical note. If notes of other frequencies were given resonance along with the note which "fits" the instrument, not music but noise would be the result. In the physics class, this point is often illustrated by a revolving disc pierced with two concentric rows of holes over which jets of air are placed. In one circle the holes are pierced equidistant apart, and when the air jet is placed over this row of holes as the disc revolves, a clear musical note sounds. In the other circle the holes are pierced irregularly, with varying distances between holes. When the air jet is placed over this row of holes as the disc revolves, the result is an unpleasant noise. This jumble of vibrations of various frequencies produces noise and not music. The same is true in a musical instrument. But the tube of a wind instrument picks out and amplifies only one wave whose length "fits" it, and kills off all the others.

Here is a strange provision in nature which leads the

poetical or philosophical mind to believe that sweet sound is "preferred" in nature. In a wind instrument there operates a physical law which stands guard over the sound and sorts out and obliterates those vibrations which are unmusical, amplifying only those which are pleasing. In the vibrating source, whether it be the lips of the player, the single reed, the double reed or the eddy currents of air, only those vibrations are allowed to be amplified which are desirable for the pitch note. The tubing is a sort of resonance filter which lets only the proper vibrations pass. The others are dampened out. In this way a clear and beautiful note is produced out of the mixture of vibrations which originates at the vibrating source.

There is a brief instant, a small part of a second, between the time when the vibration is started at the vibrating source and the time when the full, clear note is sounded. During this brief instant, the sorting or filtering process is going on. The mixture of vibrations starts down the tube of the instrument, is reflected at the bell and comes back to dampen or reinforce the vibrations which are being poured forth from the mouthpiece. Since there is only one wave which "fits" the length of tubing, the rate of vibration having this length is reinforced by the reflected wave and becomes louder. At the same time the waves which do not "fit" are undergoing a dampening-out process. They become weaker and weaker because when they are reflected at the bell they come back "out of step" with the waves which are issuing from the mouthpiece. The tendency, therefore, is to stop at the mouthpiece those vibrations whose waves do not "fit" the length of tubing in the instrument. Soon the vibration whose wave "fits" the length of tubing is dominating, and as it becomes louder, the other vibrations become weaker and are stopped. The wave which "fits" the tubing is pulsating violently, so much so that it reacts on the vibrating source and actually causes the lips, reeds or eddy currents to vibrate more vigorously than they did in the beginning. The wave even becomes master of the vibrating source and confines its vibrations to the rate of the wave. The note then speaks out clearly and in full voice.

This filtering process takes place in a small part of a second. If the tubing is short and the rate of vibration is high, this interval is shorter than if the tubing is long and the rate of vibration is slow. For instance, in a two-foot flute sounding a fundamental of C = 261.6 vibrations per second, the interval would be short, for a rarefaction of a wave which does not "fit" doesn't have to meet a compression more than a few times until this wave is silenced. The reflected wave tries to come back out of phase once, twice or three times, and it becomes so weak that it dies. It not only does not sound, but it ceases to issue forth at the mouthpiece. At a vibration rate of 261.6 times per second, even ten attempts would require only that part of a second represented by dividing ten into 261, or about $\frac{1}{26}$ of a second. In long horns with low fundamental notes of slow vibration, sometimes the interval is so long as to be noticeable. In defective instruments in which the resonating tube is not of exactly the proper proportions, sometimes there is heard a sort of crack or noise which indicates a struggle of the note to gain ascendancy over the others. Instead of a smooth sorting out of the various waves, there is a struggle between two or more, and finally the winning note cracks out.

The diameter and taper of the bore of an instrument affect

the length of the tone wave the tubing is çapable of reinforcing. It has been found that for tubing two thirds cylindrical,
with the lowest third of conical shape ending in a bell, a tube
½ inch in diameter must be 40¼ inches long to sound A♮, but
that a similar tube only $\frac{7}{16}$ of an inch in diameter must be
41¾ inches long to sound the same note. One sixteenth of an
inch in bore makes a difference of 1½ inches in length. The
trombone and the euphonium are built in the same pitch,
but owing to the fact that the euphonium is of larger bore,
it is not quite as long as the trombone. In a flute, with
cylindrical tubing, this fact is not so pronounced. Here a 10
per cent increase in the diameter of the tubing shortens the
tubing only one per cent.

The size of the bell is an important factor in determining
the length of tubing which will produce a certain note.
Acoustical engineers call it "end correction." It has been
found that there is a certain cubic content of air outside the
instrument which operates as an effective part of the column
of air in the instrument. The amount of this air is determined
by the diameter of the bell. In a cylindrical tube without a
bell, this amount is about six tenths of the radius of the
tubing. In other words, six tenths of the radius of the opening
can be added to the actual length of the instrument tubing.
For instance, if a tube is found to be 105 inches long and is
4 inches in radius, the effective length of the tubing will be
105 inches plus six tenths of 4 inches or 2.4 inches, giving
a total length of 105 inches plus 2.4 inches, or 107.4 inches.
In tapered tubing ending in a bell, the end correction is much
more difficult to computate, but the principle still obtains.

It should be said here that although the lowest note on the
instrument is that which has a wave length twice its length

(the clarinet excepted), it is not easy to play this low note in some instances. The horn may be capable, but the performer's lips may not be equal to the task. The upper octave of the fundamental is more easily played, and the fundamental itself is less often used. In the case of the French horn, the first two octaves above the fundamental are difficult to play, and the usual playing range begins at the third octave.

Resonance in a violin or other string instruments is different in principle from that in a wind instrument. Both types of instruments have this in common: the vibrating source is weak, and this weak sound requires reinforcing. The manner of obtaining this reinforcement is directly opposite in these types of instruments, however. In the wind instrument the resonating chamber, which is the tube, determines what note shall be given resonance and through the selecting process brings about this resonance. In the violin the note to be reinforced is given to the violin by the length of string, and the sound chest merely reinforces this note. The sound chest has nothing to do with what note is given resonance: it only amplifies whatever note is given it by the string. An exception to this is the case of a "wolf" note, where the periodic vibration of the sound chest itself forces a note to sound.

In the string instrument it is easy to control the pitch of the notes. The string is pressed down against the fingerboard, and when its length is thus determined there is only one note which can result. The weak vibration of the string does not sound very loud, nor does it have much musical quality. The string cuts through the air without setting much of it into vibration. But when this weak impulse is transmitted down through the bridge to the belly or top of the violin, the whole top is set in vibration. When the top vibrates, it in turn sets into vibration the large cubic content of air in the sound chest. The back also vibrates in unison with the top, the impulse not only being transmitted through the air in the sound chest but through the sound post which touches both top and back. This greatly amplified sound, which originated weakly in the string, passes out through the *ff* holes and is many times greater in volume than the weak vibration of the string.

The main point to bear in mind in comparing these two types of instruments is that the sound chest of the violin is simply a magnifying agent, a sort of megaphone or soundboard. It takes the pitch of the string and amplifies it. The wind-instrument tube, on the other hand, actually determines the pitch of the note through the very process of amplification. In the wind instrument the source of the vibration is not easily controlled, hence the mechanism that reinforces the note must be under exact control. In the string instrument it is the source of the vibration that is under exact control, and hence the mechanism which reinforces the note does not have to be under such exact control. That is why making the tube of the wind instrument is such an exacting job, while the violin body need not be made with such precision.

MAKING ONE LENGTH OF TUBING PRODUCE MANY NOTES

We have been talking about one wave "fitting" an instrument. Perhaps you are wondering how the bugler manages to make several notes "fit" his bugle. He uses several notes to play his calls. If only one wave length will fit a given length of tubing, how can he play several notes on the same instrument? That's a fair question, and we'll see if we can find the answer.

Everyone knows that if a person takes hold of a rope at one end, with the other end tied to a tree, and shakes the end up and down, waves will form in the rope. When the rope is shaken very slowly, there will be but one long, complete wave. If shaken twice as fast, two waves will form in the rope. The faster the rope is shaken, the more waves there will be in the length of the rope.

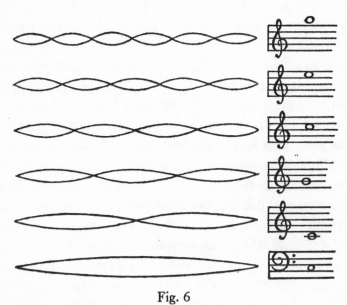

Fig. 6

Showing how the tone wave divides and produces the open tones of the natural harmonic scale.

This illustrates what happens in a wind instrument. When the lowest note is sounded, one complete wave twice the length of the instrument results, which is C on the instrument. When the lips are tightened and the instrument is blown harder, the vibration rate is increased until the one complete wave divides up into two waves, each just half as long. The resulting note is an octave higher than the former. By holding the lips tighter and blowing still harder, three waves result, each one third as long as the first, and the note produced is G. When the lips are tightened still more and the instrument is blown still harder, there are four waves, each one fourth as long as the first, and the note sounded is C. When five waves are produced, E is sounded, and when six are produced, G above the staff is sounded. These are the notes the bugler has at his command, but he doesn't use the fundamental.

If the performer were equal to the task he could go on and on, compelling the wave to divide into seven, eight and up to twenty or more separate waves. (See Fig. 7.) These notes would all be the harmonics of the fundamental, and the resulting scale would be the natural, or harmonic, scale. The notes in this harmonic scale are called partials, the lowest being the first partial, the octave being the second partial, the next one (G) being the third partial, and so on. These notes are also spoken of as the "open" notes, no slides, valves or keys being necessary to play them. It is easy to see (Fig. 7) that there are wide gaps in the lower parts of the scale, but that as the higher partials are reached the notes are close together until, when the thirteenth partial is reached, the notes are a half-step apart. In this upper range we have all the notes we need, but in the lower range there are some wide gaps that must be bridged over in some way.

The lowest note any tube can give resonance to has the lowest frequency for that tube. If we *gradually* increase the frequency, the note will fade out until the tube has no

Fig. 7

A.	1	2	3	4	5	6	7	8	9	10	11	12	13	14	15	16	17	18	19	20
B.	130.8	261.6	392.0	523.2	659.2	784.0	932.3	1046.5	1174.7	1318.5	1480.0	1568.0	1760.0	1864.7	1975.5	2093.0	2217.5	2349.3	2489.3	2637.0
C.	C_1	C	G	C^1	E^1	G^1	$B\flat^1$	C^2	D^2	E^2	$F\sharp^2$	G^2	A^2	$B\flat^2$	B^2	C^3	$C\sharp^3$	D^3	$D\sharp^3$	E^3

The natural harmonic scale, produced when the tone wave of a horn divides into smaller sections. The line of figures marked "A" shows the number of the partial in the natural harmonic scale. Line "B" shows the vibration rate of each, while line "C" shows their relation to Middle C. C_1 means first octave below Middle C; C, G, mean in the same octave with Middle C; C^1, E^1 mean in the first octave above Middle C; and so on. These are the notes that we call partials, har-monics or overtones. The fundamental, or lowest partial, usually predominates over all the other partials and determines the pitch of the note, while certain other partials sound with the fundamental in lesser volume, giving richness of tone quality. Frequencies as shown are not exactly as would be found in a harmonic scale based on $C_1 = 130.8$ but are what would be found on a well-tuned piano.

resonance. If the frequency is gradually increased until it is doubled, a rate of vibration will be reached which will be built up by an open tube. What happens is this: The waves cannot quite make the round trip on time as the frequency is increased. Their efforts, as they are reflected, become more and more futile because they become farther and farther "out of step." Finally resonance stops. Then, as the frequency increases still further, the waves are able to set up substations, as it were. Although they cannot make the complete round trip on time, they shorten their travel, cutting the distance in half. Two waves, then, each half as long as formerly, span the length of the tube. These two halves, each traveling concurrently, make the shorter trip on time. The pulsations do not travel faster—their speed is constant—but they cut the trip in half. There are two waves now, each half as long as at first. The frequency is twice what it was formerly, the waves are just half as long, and the pitch is raised an octave.

This is true of open pipes only. On the closed pipe the first note above the fundamental is reached when the frequency is three times that of the fundamental. Instead of one wave there are now three, and each wave is one third as long as that of the fundamental. The note sounded is a twelfth above the fundamental. This third partial is sounded, both on the open as well as on the closed pipe, although of course the open pipe is twice the length of the closed pipe for this note.

When the frequency becomes four times that of the fundamental, the length of the open pipe is spanned by four waves, each one fourth as long as that of the fundamental, and the note sounded is two octaves above the fundamental. This even partial cannot be reproduced on the closed pipe. The

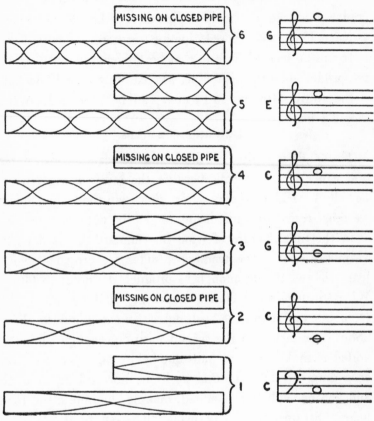

Fig. 8

Diagram showing how waves break up into smaller waves to form various notes of the harmonic scale. Observe that the length of the wave for the second partial is half that of the first, or fundamental; that the length of the wave of the third is one third that of the fundamental; that the length of the wave of the fourth is one fourth that of the fundamental; etc. Also observe that the even-numbered partials are missing on the closed pipe.

next partial for the closed pipe is reached when the frequency is five times that of the fundamental. The wave is one fifth that of the fundamental, and the note sounded is two octaves and a third above the fundamental. This fifth partial is of course produced on the open pipe also, although the pipe is twice as long as the closed pipe for this note.

It will be seen, therefore, that both even and odd partials are produced on the open pipe, whereas only the odd partials —the third, fifth, seventh, etc., can be produced on the closed pipe.

BRIDGING THE GAPS

The bugle is limited to the harmonic scale of open notes and can execute its calls because the music is written especially for it; but to play notes other than these open notes, we must resort to some means to get the notes in between.

In the manufacture of wind instruments this is done in various ways. In the trombone, slides are provided which lengthen the tubing enough to produce the notes to fill in. When the slides are closed, or are in "first" position, the trombone can sound the open notes. By extending the slides about four inches to the second position, enough tubing is added to make the next half-tone below this open note. By extending the slides another position, more tubing is added and another half-step is added, making the note a full tone below the open tone. By using all seven positions, it is theoretically possible to play six steps below the open notes.

The author is well aware that the trombone is not treated in music as a transposing instrument, but the method of treatment here has been chosen to eliminate confusion in comparing it with the harmonic scale of open notes used as illustration for all instruments (Fig. 7).

From the fundamental, or lowest open note, to the second partial, which is the octave of the fundamental, there is a gap of twelve half-tones which are partially bridged by the use of the slides. The second partial is sounded and sufficient length of tubing is added by extending the slides to secure a total length of tubing capable of producing the desired notes. However, the seven positions of the slides are able to take us down only six half-steps, or down to F♯ (sounds E♮), leaving a gap of notes between F♯ and the lower C which cannot be produced. Composers who write music for the trombone bear this in mind and do not call upon it to play these notes, giving them to other instruments that can.

The bass trombone is called upon to play these notes, but it has an extra length of tubing which can be added by operating a valve with the left thumb. This lowers the pitch of the trombone five, and sometimes six, half-tones. By lowering the pitch of the trombone five half-tones the six slide positions then can be added, making it possible to play down to D♭ (sounds B). Then the thumb valve is closed by releasing the lever, and the open C (sounds B♭) can be played, completing the chromatic range of twelve half-tones.

In the second octave above the fundamental we have one open note which we can play without the use of the slides. This note is G and is the third partial in the natural scale. It is produced when the fundamental wave breaks up into three parts. This makes the following open notes available: C, G and the octave C, all of which are notes of the natural harmonic scale. To play C♯, D, D♯, E and F, which lie between the open tones C and G, it is necessary to use the slides, descending from the G and adding lengths of tubing necessary to make each corresponding and lower note. Between G and C above, the G♯, A, A♯ and B are lacking from the natural scale and must be played by adding necessary lengths of tubing to the upper C, or fourth partial.

In the third octave above the fundamental we have more

notes that lie in the natural scale, and it is not necessary to make so many of them by using the slides. In this octave we have E, G and B♭ (quite flat), besides the upper and lower Cs. The fourth octave above the fundamental is out of the range of the trombone, but we know how these notes would have to be played if it were possible for the player to produce them in this octave. Here we have a more complete natural scale comprised of C, D, E, F♯, G, A, B♭, B and C. In this octave the slides would need to be used to make only some half-steps. To produce C♯, for instance, it would be necessary to play the open D of the natural scale and drop the slides to the second position, thereby adding a length of tubing necessary to produce the lower note.

As stated before, the scale becomes almost complete as the upper part of the harmonic scale is reached, but it is impossible to produce these notes on some instruments.

The same natural scale as on the trombone exists on the cornet or trumpet or any other wind instrument, except the clarinet, but the C of each scale must be the C of the instrument, depending upon the key in which it is built. If the instrument is built in F, C of the natural scale for this instrument will sound F. If built in B♭, C will sound B♭; and so on. The relation between the notes of the natural scale is the same, however.

HOW VALVE INSTRUMENTS DO IT

On valve instruments the valves take the place of the slides on the trombone. The gaps of the natural scale are bridged by adding various lengths of tubing to the open notes. The first valve on the cornet or trumpet opens up a length of tubing which enables the performer to play a whole tone lower than the open note. The second valve opens up a half-tone, and the third opens up three half-tones or a tone and a half.

By combining the various valves, more than one and a half tones may be added. By combining the second and third valves, a length of tubing is added equal to two full tones; by combining the first and third, two and a half tones are added; by combining all three, three tones are added. These combined lengths of tubing enable the performer to go six half-tones below any open note and are sufficient to bridge all the gaps in the natural scale except in the first octave above the fundamental, in which only six of the twelve half-tones are available.

These six half-tones are sufficient in smaller-bore instruments such as cornets, trumpets, alto horns and baritones, because the fundamental is seldom used. The lowest partial called for in music for these instruments is the second, or C, an octave above the fundamental. With the valves it is possible to play six half-tones below this second partial or down to F♯. But the fundamental is playable on larger-bore instruments such as the euphonium, bass tuba and sousaphone. Therefore, on some of these a fourth valve is added which controls an extra length of tubing capable of lowering any open tone five or six half-steps. The four valves have a combined range of twelve half-steps, which are sufficient to lower the second open note a full octave, thereby bridging the gap chromatically from the fundamental upward.

HOW THE KEY INSTRUMENTS DO IT

On flutes, oboes, bassoons and saxophones, the same gaps in the scale are found, but these gaps are bridged in a different manner—by a system of keys. When all holes are closed and the lowest note is sounded, one wave lies in the instrument, one half of the wave extending from the mouthpiece to the bell, the other half being a reflected wave extending from the bell to the mouthpiece. As each lowest hole is opened, the wave is successively shortened. In this way it is possible to play chromatically from the lowest note a full octave upward. Then the instrument is "overblown," changing from the fundamental, or first partial, to the second partial, an octave above. To assist the player to obtain this second partial, an octave-key hole is opened. With all keys closed and with the octave key open, it is possible to sound this second partial. Then, successively opening each lowest hole, it is possible to play chromatically up the second octave. The same fingering is used in the second octave as in the first, the fingered notes sounding an octave above because they are based on the second partial. This is theoretically the principle of all such "open pipe" keyed instruments. Actually there is a slight deviation from this principle in the second octave. In the saxophone, for example, from D to G♯ in the second octave is played with the first octave key open, but beginning with A, a second register key higher up is opened.

HOW THE CLARINETS DO IT

The clarinet is peculiar in that its natural scale comprises only the odd partials. The length of its fundamental tone wave breaks up into three parts but will not break up into two or four; it breaks up into five parts but will not break up into six. That leaves gaps in the natural scale which are not found on other instruments that have both the even and odd partials. Between its fundamental note and the first occurring partial is a gap of nine and a half whole tones, or a twelfth, which must be bridged. This is the third partial in the natural scale, the second, or octave, being absent.

The second, fourth, sixth—all the even partials are missing from the natural scale of the clarinet, leaving wider gaps than on all other wind instruments that must be bridged. Since there are wide gaps in the natural scale of the clarinet, a great number of keys are necessary.

As in the saxophone or flute, when all keys are closed, the lowest note, or first partial, is sounded. Then, successively opening each lowest key, the player can ascend chromatically. Since the second partial is missing on the clarinet, it is necessary to bridge the gap from the first to the third partial, a gap of a twelfth. Then a register key is opened to assist the player in sounding the third partial. The ascending notes from here are then based on the third partial, and each lowest hole can then be opened in ascending chromatically upward.

TONE QUALITY AND WHAT MAKES IT

There are apple pies—and apple pies. People go through life eating apple pies, and they are never a bit uncertain that each apple pie is an apple pie. There is a difference, however, among them. Some are good, some are fair, and some are bad. What makes the difference is the quality and proportion of the ingredients. Some may lack butter, some nutmeg, some sugar. But they are all apple pies.

That is just the way with some musical instruments. They may blow a certain note in pitch, but the quality is gone. The note is dead, it lacks richness, beauty, flavor. The skeleton of the tone is there, but the sweetness is gone.

We shall now try to find out what it is that accounts for this tone quality in an instrument.

Do you know why telephone operators are instructed to trill their *r* when repeating the number three? It may seem strange, but the reason for this lies at the basis of tone quality in horns.

It has been found that "two" and "three" often sound the same over the telephone. The vowel sound in "two" is like the vowel sound in "moo," and the vowel sound in "three" is like the vowel sound in "bee." These two vowel sounds do not ordinarily seem similar, but the telephone mechanism sometimes dampens out the distinguishing characteristic of the vowel in "bee" until it cannot be distinguished from the vowel sound in "moo."

It has been determined that the common characteristic is a group of overtones which lie on either side of 300 vibrations per second, but the vowel in "bee" has an additional group which lies near 3,000 vibrations. This high group is lacking in the vowel in "moo."

In other words, take the vowel in "moo" and add the high overtones and the result is the vowel in "bee." The telephone mechanism is sometimes incapable of reproducing the high overtones, and consequently the vowel sounds as in "moo" instead of as in "bee."

It may seem strange to think of vowel sounds as being composed of combinations of notes of various rates of vibration, but scientists have been able to produce all the vowel sounds accurately by machines capable of sounding variously pitched notes with the various intensities at the same time. By using these machines it is possible to set various vibrators going together, and by selecting the proper vibrators and by regulating the intensity of each these machines can be made to "talk."

It is a common observation that it is difficult, if not impossible, to sing distinctly such vowel sounds as in "moo" and in "mow" at a very high pitch. It is equally difficult to sing distinctly such vowel sounds as in "bee" and in

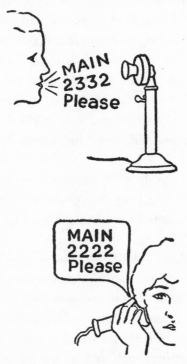

Fig. 9

Illustrating that the characteristic in the vowel sound in "three" is often filtered out when transmitted over the telephone and comes out at the receiver sounding like "two." This characteristic that is lost has been found to be a high overtone whose vibration rate is about 3,000. The rest of the vowel sound in "three" is the vowel sound "two," which is a group of overtones around 300 vibrations a second. It is such overtones as these which regulate tone quality in the horn.

[*341*]

"bate" at low pitch. To get the characteristic overtones of the former, the pitch at which they are uttered must be low, so that the low overtones will be produced. To get the characteristic overtones of the latter, the pitch must be high, so that the high overtones will be produced.

This is the basis of all the discussion about "opera in English." When the opera is translated from the foreign tongue into the English, the vowel sounds which the music indicates must be sung at high pitch may be such that their distinguishing characteristic is a low overtone. On the other hand, vowel sounds that must be sung at low pitch may happen, through translation, to be those whose distinguishing characteristic is a high overtone. It is physically impossible to sing such notes and utter the vowel distinctly at the same time.

What has this to do with quality of tone in musical instruments? Just this: It is the presence or absence of these overtones that determines what the quality of tone of the instrument shall be. Just as the presence or absence of the high overtone makes the difference between the vowel sounds in "moo" and in "bee," so the presence or absence of the proper overtones in the instrument makes the difference between a sweet, rich tone and a flat, ugly tone.

The presence of overtones can be graphically illustrated on a stretched string, such as a violin string. When bowed in a certain place and manner the string can be made to vibrate as a whole. This tone is dull; such a tone is that produced by the beginner. The more skillful player can make the string break up into smaller sections while vibrating as a whole. The pitch is that of the longest tone wave because it predominates over all the others, but the other smaller sections are vibrating as units and producing overtones of less energy. These overtones blend in with the fundamental tone, producing a richness of tone quality. The more of these overtones that can be produced in the proper relation to the fundamental, the richer the tone quality is.

The same is true of the wind instrument. Some players haven't the trained lip control, or embouchure, which enables them to play a note so that the tone wave vibrates as a whole and in many smaller sections at the same time. Often the inferior instrument is defective, certain spots in it serving to kill the overtones where they should appear. It is very important that the instrument be built to accommodate these overtones, as their presence determines the tone quality.

Although the baritone and euphonium are approximately the same length as the trombone, difference in bore makes a difference in tone quality. The euphonium is the broadest and fullest in tone, the baritone is brighter in tone, and the trombone is the most brilliant of the three. The difference in bore regulates what overtones are possible on the instrument, and we recognize this fact by listening to the characteristics of each. Each instrument may possess the same number of overtones, but in the large-bore horns it is the low overtones that are produced while the high overtones are dropped out, and in the small-bore instruments it is the high overtones that are favored. This results in difference of tone quality of the euphonium, baritone and trombone.

Not only the width of bore influences the tone quality, but the taper in the bore is equally influential. In general, the wider or more tapered the bore, the fewer overtones there are. Conversely, the more nearly cylindrical the bore, the more overtones there will be. But while we say it is the width of bore and the taper which affect the tone, it would be more accurate to say that the bore and taper regulate the production of overtones, which determine the tone quality.

A beautiful illustration of the fact that overtones govern tone quality in instruments is given in comparing the mellophone and the French horn. The French horn is about twice the length of the mellophone and should play an octave lower. As a matter of fact, the playing range is about the same. The tone quality, however, is different, the French horn having an unusually beautiful and rich tone. The fundamental tone of the French horn is an octave below that of the mellophone, but the French horn player doesn't use the lower range of his instrument, confining his playing to the upper range. The playing range on the mellophone being the same as that on the French horn, and its fundamental or lowest note being an octave higher, it is evident that the mellophone uses a lower part of its range than does the French horn.

Now we have seen that, as we ascend from the fundamental note of a horn, the overtones become closer together until in the upper ranges the scale is almost complete. Since the French horn uses its upper range to play the same notes the mellophone plays in its lower range, we can readily see that there are many more overtones present in the French horn's tone than in that of the mellophone.

That overtones account for quality of tone has been demonstrated in various ways. A German scientist by the name of Helmholtz invented a rather complete set of resonators which looked like a lot of Christmas-tree ornaments.

They were so made that each would vibrate in sympathy with a certain pitched tone, shutting out all others. When one end was inserted in the ear, the resonator would pick out its particular note from a complex and rich tone and would vibrate violently, causing its note to sound loudly in the ear. By the use of these resonators, rich tones were analyzed into the fundamental and all the overtones that were present.

Now if you are good at fractions you can look at this subject of overtones in a little different way. If fractions and ratios and other arithmetical calculations bother you, just skip the next few paragraphs. But after all, music and harmony are all tied up in such considerations as fractions and ratios and can hardly be understood without a little figuring. A little effort expended in wading through the following few paragraphs will pay handsomely in the understanding of this fascinating subject of the harmonic scale and the overtones.

Quality of tone is not due entirely to the number of overtones: they must be the overtones of the harmonic scale. When an overtone occurs which is not in the harmonic scale of the fundamental, an inharmonious sound results. What we call "noise" is a combination of notes of various rates of vibration that are in an inharmonious relation to each other. That means that the lowest note in the combination is combined with other notes whose wave lengths are NOT ½, ⅓, ¼, ⅕, etc., of its wave length. These other notes may be ⅔ or 5/7 of the wave length of the lowest note. The result of sounding such a group is a harsh, unpleasant noise, especially if sounded loudly.

A professor of physics once used an ingenious illustration to show this harmonious relation of the partials of a musical instrument. He fashioned some blocks of wood, each so cut to size that it had a definite pitch. He dropped the blocks successively on a table and thereby played an ascending harmonic scale of C, G, C, E, G, C. Then he showed that when he dropped all the blocks together the sound was a sort of musical chord. He also had other blocks whose pitch stood in odd ratios to each other, not of ½, ⅓, ¼, ⅕, etc., but of ⅔, ⅗, 5/7, etc. When these were dropped together on the table, the result was not a musical sound, but only a dissonant sound which we call noise.

This same principle can be illustrated on a revolving disc in which concentric circles of holes are bored and which can be "played" by air jets, one jet to each circle of holes. Let the circle nearest the center have 16 holes, the next ones 18, 20, 22, 24, 27, 32. If the circles having 16, 20, 24 and 32 holes be played together, a pleasing chord is sounded:

A little arithmetic will readily show these numbers to stand in relation to 4 as 4, 5, 6 and 8 respectively. These notes therefore are the fourth, fifth, sixth and eighth partials of 4, which can be considered as the fundamental. If the disc revolves 10 times per second, the fundamental would have a frequency of 40 and the partials up to the eighth would have a frequency of 40, 80, 120, 160, 200, 240 and 320 respectively. Now, taking 40 vibrations as a fundamental, all of these partials are related as 1 (fundamental), 2, 3, 4, 5, 6 and 8. Also, taking the note with a frequency of 40 as the fundamental wave, the wave lengths of these partials are related

as 1 (fundamental), $\frac{1}{2}$, $\frac{1}{3}$, $\frac{1}{4}$, $\frac{1}{5}$, $\frac{1}{6}$ and $\frac{1}{8}$. For our purpose we will deal only with the fourth, fifth, sixth and
eighth. When these are sounded together a pleasant chord
results, as related above. But if the other circles of holes are
sounded together, that is, those circles having 18, 22 and 27
holes, only noise is produced; and if they are sounded with
the others, the pleasant chord is turned into noise. Applying
our simple arithmetic, we readily see that the circles having
18, 22 and 27 holes do not stand in simple relation to 4 as
$\frac{1}{2}$, $\frac{1}{3}$, $\frac{1}{4}$, $\frac{1}{5}$, and so on, but as $\frac{4}{18}$, $\frac{4}{22}$ and $\frac{4}{27}$. These odd
fractions of 4 produce noise and not harmony.

Since the tube of a wind instrument, as shown previously,
gives resonance only to those partials which are $\frac{1}{2}$, $\frac{1}{3}$, $\frac{1}{4}$,
etc., of the fundamental, these odd and irregular partials,
such as $\frac{4}{18}$, $\frac{4}{22}$ and $\frac{4}{27}$ in our illustration, cannot sound, and
therefore only the musical overtones can occur. Here is an-
other amazing provision of nature which gives us harmony
in wind instruments and dampens out all inharmonious
overtones which would produce noise.

Some marvelous machines have been invented which reveal
in an even more interesting way the presence of overtones.
These machines are called oscillographs, and they picture
sound by means of lines which look something like a sales
curve or the fluctuations of the stock market when drawn
on a graphing chart. For instance, the note of the tuning
fork for A$_2$-110 may look like the top curve marked A in
Fig. 10, while the note from the tuning fork for A$_1$-220, an
octave higher, would look like the curve marked B. The note
from the tuning fork for E-330 would look like the curve
marked C.

You will observe that the first curve has but one "hump,"

while the curve marked B has two complete "humps." This you would expect, since the second note is an octave higher than the first and has twice as many vibrations per second. The distance from left to right in our illustration represents

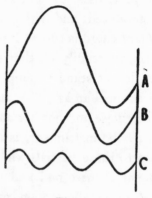

Fig. 10

a certain interval of time, in this instance $\frac{1}{110}$ of a second, since only one "hump," representing a complete vibration, is shown for a note which has 110 vibrations per second. To show what the oscillograph records in a second would require a drawing 110 times as long as the illustration in Fig. 10, and there would be 110 "humps." Since the second note is an octave above the first and therefore has twice the frequency, in a second the oscillograph would show 220 "humps." Since our illustration records what happens in $\frac{1}{110}$ of a second, there are two "humps" in our illustration. The third curve, marked C, has three "humps" and therefore is a recording of a note which has three times the frequency of the first note, or a twelfth above the first note.

With this elementary understanding of how the oscillograph functions, we can now look at some more complicated curves as they are recorded when notes are sounded which have overtones in them. The three curves in Fig. 10 are of pure notes without overtones, such as come from the tuning

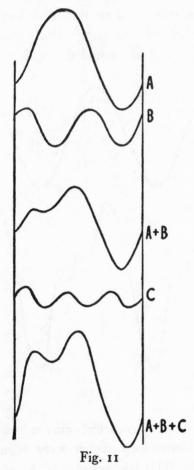

Fig. 11

fork. Such notes are soft and definite to the ear, but are rather colorless. It is the presence of overtones which gives color, or timbre, or quality to notes.

In Fig. 11 we show the recordings of A_2-110 and A_1-220, first separately and then when combined. When the two notes are blended together by being sounded simultaneously, the oscillograph curve looks like the curve shown marked A + B. Below this we show the curve for the pure note E-330, and below this the curve which records the sound when all three notes are sounded together. This curve is

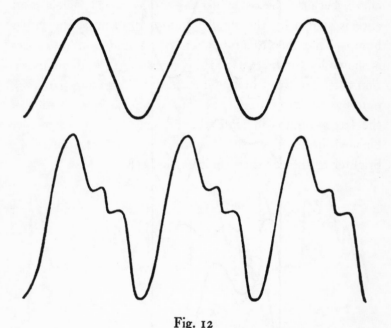

Fig. 12

marked A + B + C. This curve begins to look like the notes from musical instruments which have several overtones sounded together. This synthesizing of the pure tones from the tuning fork will help us understand the meaning of the curves for notes from musical instruments.

In the top curve in Fig. 12 we see the oscillograph of a note from the flute when played softly. Here only the fundamental of the note sounds, the overtones or harmonics not being emitted, at least not strongly enough to be recorded by the oscillograph. Such a curve is much like that of the tuning fork, and the soft flute note sounds to the ear much like the note from a tuning fork. But when the flute is blown loudly, the curve changes character, as seen in the bottom curve, because the overtones are strengthened. Their presence is shown by the smaller humps in each of the larger humps. That the same pitched note is sounded in both cases is shown by the fact that in the given length in our illustration there are three humps in each curve, proving that each note has the same frequency. The smaller humps in each of the larger humps indicate the presence of the harmonics blended in to give color, or timbre. Such a note seems brighter to the ear than the soft flute note.

Fig. 13

In Fig. 13 three cycles of a note from the oboe are shown as recorded by the oscillograph. Since this illustration is drawn on the same scale as that in Fig. 12, the three cycles in each show that both instruments are sounding the same pitch note. The curves differ only in characteristic shape. Observe that the oboe curve is considerably more complicated than the curve of the flute note sounded loudly. This intricacy of pattern indicates the presence of many harmonics. Scientists who have analyzed oboe notes find they may have six, eight, or even more harmonics. Usually the fourth and fifth harmonics are stronger than the fundamental, with the sixth harmonic next in strength. Any two notes may have the same harmonics present, but their relative strengths, if different, will make the notes sound different in timbre, or quality.

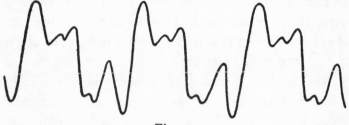

Fig. 14

In Fig. 14 three cycles of a note from a clarinet are shown as recorded by the oscillograph. Since the graph in Fig. 14 is on the same scale as the graphs in Fig. 12 and in Fig. 13, these three notes are of the same pitch. Their only difference is in the number and strength of their harmonics, which account for their characteristic difference in tone color. Acousticians would also add another factor—their phase— but we'll skip that, for it makes the explanation much more complicated and much less easy to understand. Observe the erratic ups and downs of this curve pattern, but notice that each cycle is practically the same in shape. Analysis of the clarinet tone reveals that the first and third harmonics are usually prominent and of about equal strengths. The eighth, ninth and tenth partials are also fairly strong. Other harmonics may be present besides these, but they are weaker and sometimes do not show up.

A note from the French horn records as shown in the curve in Fig. 15. Three cycles are shown, and since this illustration is on the same scale as those for the flute, oboe and clarinet, the note sounded is of the same pitch. The curve, however, differs in character from that of the flute, oboe or clarinet. This difference is of course due to the number and strength of the harmonics reproduced by the French horn, which give it its characteristic tonal coloring. When the tone is analyzed,

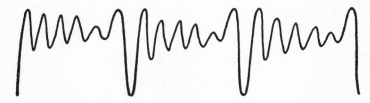

Fig. 15

the fundamental, the second and the third harmonics are usually prominent, their strength varying in descending order, from 1 to 3. But these are not the only harmonics present. In fact, it is the presence of many harmonics which makes the tone of the French horn so peculiar in tonal quality.

Since the curve of the note from the bass tuba, shown in Fig. 16, is drawn on a different scale from the curves of notes from the flute, oboe, clarinet and French horn, we cannot make a comparison as to pitch but can only notice its characteristic shape. This curve is comparatively simple, showing that it is made up of but few harmonics. Only one hump, or cycle, is shown, the smaller humps indicating the harmonics.

As illustrated in the flute curves, the loudness with which an instrument is sounded has something to do with the harmonic mixture for any note. The curves in these oscillograph records are shown as being fairly characteristic of each instrument. Loudness may change any of them in varying degree. The notes in different parts of the scale on any one instrument differ in pattern also. The ear detects this difference in some instruments more than in others, and the curves

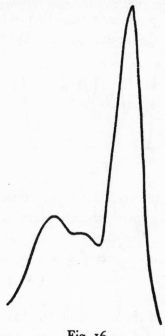

Fig. 16

in different registers vary more in some instruments than in others. The middle register of the clarinet, for instance, is of different tonal coloring than the top register. But while there are these variations, each instrument has its characteristic curve pattern. Two Irish setters may not look exactly alike, but nobody would have any difficulty in telling them from two collie shepherd dogs. There is also a general family resemblance in curves from different instruments. Some of them are very similar to others, but experts who study these characteristic curve patterns can tell them apart.

Looking at the question of tonal quality from the opposite angle, we would hardly expect the same sound to come from a bassoon and a French horn, but sometimes it is difficult to distinguish them. If these notes are recorded on an oscillograph, we find a definite similarity in the two curves, for it is the presence in both instruments of the same harmonics in the same relative strengths which makes this similarity in tone quality. When the French horn is blown vigorously it often sounds much like a trombone. This blasting of the French horn accentuates certain harmonics, which makes the oscillograph curve look something like that of the trombone.

Tone quality is simply the result of mixing different harmonics in different proportions. Some instruments are built so they reproduce or give resonance to certain harmonics rather than to others and give greater power to some of these than to others. Just as a painter selects different pigments in varying proportions and mixes them together, producing a distinctive blend of coloring, so the different instruments select the various harmonics and temper them in degree of loudness, producing a distinctive tonal quality. It is this difference in the selective process which makes each instrument sound different from another.

MOUTHPIECES AND WHAT THEY DO TO INSTRUMENTS

An apple bud grafted on a peach tree produces apples and not peaches.

Musicians should take this tip from the horticulturist in choosing their mouthpieces, because the mouthpiece stands at the head of the instrument and is an important factor in determining how the instrument performs.

This point is strikingly illustrated in the following experiment. The embouchure was removed from a flute, and an alto-clarinet mouthpiece was substituted. The flute immediately took on all the characteristics of the clarinet. It was no longer a flute. It was capable of producing only the odd partials of the natural scale, possessed the same gaps in the natural scale, no longer played in octaves as does the flute, and acted up in general like an incomplete clarinet.

This is just like grafting a clarinet bud on a flute tree! The result is clarinet fruit hanging from a flute limb.

This illustration brings up one of the most interesting questions in wind instruments, a question which is now being heatedly debated and which is a long way from being satisfactorily answered. Why does the addition of a single-beating reed to a cylindrical pipe make the resulting instrument perform like a closed pipe? The body of the flute is practically cylindrical. With the flute embouchure, or mouthpiece, the instrument behaves like an open pipe. When a single-beating reed mouthpiece is substituted, the instrument changes to a closed pipe. Does the reed close the end, making it a closed pipe such as a closed organ pipe? The reed, however, is open half the time and closed half the time.

As a matter of fact, although the wave of the fundamental is four times the length of the instrument, and although the second and fourth partials cannot be utilized in the scale, the instrument still preserves some of the characteristics of the open pipe.

The clarinet is substantially like our hybrid instrument described above, having a cylindrical body and a single-beating reed. Delicate analyses of the clarinet tone reveal that the second and fourth partials are present, although they are usually very weak and cannot be used in the scale. The eighth and tenth partials are quite strong—as strong, in fact, as the ninth. These, however, are so high in the harmonic scale that they cannot be used.

That the single-beating reed is not the only factor is shown by the fact that a cup mouthpiece actuated by the buzz of the lips also makes a cylindrical tube behave like a closed pipe. The slides of a trombone are cylindrical, and if a cup mouthpiece be fitted to them the resulting instrument behaves like a closed pipe. Analysis of the tone of the instrument, however, reveals the presence of the even partials, although they are very weak, as on the clarinet. The buzzing lips also close the pipe, just as does the reed, although the opening is open half the time and closed half the time. The blowhole of the flute, however, is open always, and the cylindrical tube alone, on the flute, is not sufficient to produce a closed pipe. The closed pipe, therefore, seems to require a coupled system of cylindrical tubing and a device for closing the end. The fact that the reed on the saxophone and the cup mouthpiece on the cornet do not produce a closed pipe can be laid to the fact that in these instruments the cylindrical tubing is lacking, the tubing of both being conical in general shape.

The layman has an idea that wind instruments are "blown." The usual practice of the layman in picking up a wind instrument is to blow a blast through the mouthpiece. No sound results, for such instruments are not "blown." The sound is produced by creating a vibration in the mouthpiece, this vibration being given resonance by the tube of the instrument.

The flute comes nearest to being "blown" of all wind instruments, but this blowing is of a distinct kind. A thin stream of air is directed by the lips against the edge of the blowhole. How this produces a vibration is illustrated by a flexible stick in a stream of water. Everyone has seen such a stick vibrate or has felt the vibration when the stick is held in the hand. The water pushes the stick to one side. When displaced to one side the water rushes past, and the pressure against the stick on this side is relieved. But when this occurs, the pressure becomes great on the other side, and the stick is pushed back. So the stick is made to oscillate back and forth with regular periodicity. In the flute, the edge of the blowhole is stationary. The air rushes by the edge, outside the flute. This rush of air raises the pressure outside and lessens the pressure inside. The stream of air, therefore, changes its course to the low-pressure area of the inside and is deflected inside. But, again, pressure is built up inside while the outside becomes rarefied. The air then reverses its course and escapes outside the flute. In this way pulsations of air are sent down the flute and a vibration is set up.

In the cup-mouthpiece instruments the lips are stretched across the cup and intermittent puffs of air are permitted to escape between the opening of the lips. These pulsations of air set up a vibration in the instrument. The same sort of pulsations are created in reed instruments. In the single-reed instruments, intermittent puffs of air are permitted to pass into the instrument as the reed opens and shuts on the table of the mouthpiece. In double-reed instruments, the same sort of vibration is created by producing puffs of air as the two reeds open and close against each other.

Index